America Eats!

BY THE SAME AUTHOR

Pie Every Day
A Soothing Broth
Secrets of Saffron

America Eats!

ON THE ROAD WITH THE WPA

*The Fish Fries, Box Supper Socials,
and Chitlin Feasts That Define
Real American Food*

PAT WILLARD

BLOOMSBURY

Recipe for chicken pilau is from *The Historical Cookbook of the American Negro*, by The National Council of Negro Women. Copyright © 2000 by The National Council of Negro Women. Reprinted by permission of Beacon Press, Boston. Recipe for root beer using extract is reprinted by permission of David Fankhauser, University of Cincinnati Clermont College, http://biology.clc.uc.edu/Fankhauser/. Recipe for root beer using herbs is reprinted by permission of Root Beer World, http://root-beer.org.

Published by Bloomsbury USA, New York
Distributed to the trade by Macmillan

All papers used by Bloomsbury USA are natural, recyclable products made from wood grown in well-managed forests. The manufacturing processes conform to the environmental regulations of the country of origin.

LIBRARY OF CONGRESS CATALOGING-IN-PUBLICATION DATA

Willard, Pat.
    America eats! : on the road with the W.P.A. : the fish fries, box supper socials, and chitlin feasts that define real American food / by Pat Willard.—1st U.S. ed.
        p.   cm.
    ISBN-13: 978-1-59691-362-2 (hardcover)
    ISBN-10: 1-59691-362-2 (hardcover)
    1. Cookery, American—History—20th century.   2. Food habits—United States—History—20th century.   I. Writers' Program (U.S.)   II. Title.

    TX715.W71125   2008
    394.1'20973—dc22

                                                                2008015815

First U.S. Edition 2008

1   3   5   7   9   10   8   6   4   2

Designed by Rachel Reiss

Typeset by Westchester Book Group
Printed in the United States of America by Quebecor World Fairfield

For my sons, Sam and Al

Contents

A Note on the Manuscript

The *America Eats!* papers reprinted in this book have not been altered in any way. All idiosyncrasies in spelling, grammar, punctuation, and dialect—except for where there are obvious typing mistakes in the original—along with racial and social attitudes expressed in the original papers remain intact as a reflection of 1930s America.

★ 1 ★

The American Cauldron

If each of all the races which have been subsisted in the vast Middle West could contribute one dish to one great midwestern cauldron, it is certain that we'd have therein a most foreign and most gigantic stew: the grains that the French took over from the Indians, and the breads that the English brought later, hotly spiced Italian dishes and subtly seasoned Spanish ones, the sweet Swedish soups and the sour Polish ones, and all the Old World arts brought to the preparing of American beefsteak and hot mince pie.

Such a cauldron would contain more than many foods: it would be at once, a symbol of many lands and a melting pot for many people.

Many peoples, yet one people; many lands, one land.

— Nelson Algren, Illinois Office

America's culinary history is enough to make anyone scream. By which I mean the accepted line of thinking held mostly by the folks who write about food and who reside in the populated cities along our coastlines. You know the line I mean, the great lament concerning our national cuisine and the poverty of its heritage. It is not a pretty tale they tell at all. I have a feeling that at the heart of these hard appraisals lies a self-conscious regret that the food we think of as truly American—think pies and barbecues, thick stews, a good roasted chicken, a tender slab of steak—did not romantically develop over hundreds of years from the rustic charms of peasant fare through to the haughty demands of imperial refinements. Instead, our cuisine, like much of American life, developed on the fly, in a rush from one place to another, in a great confluence of necessities, contrasting agendas, and, most important, unprecedentedly varied cultural influences. Our dishes were bound by the imperative to survive. The strange things that were discovered growing along the way, tramping in the woods, or swimming in the streams could perhaps be made tasty, or at the very least palatable, with the addition of some dried herbs and spices, which by forethought or fortune had been tucked in a calico pocket or leather pouch for the long journey out from a distant home to this unfamiliar new land where another, possibly better, life could be made.

What else but a mess could develop in such a haphazard fashion? And a mess is what many have taken American food to be when compared to the glories of other countries' cuisines. Let me just clarify that I am not excusing the corporate adulteration of our national food supply and the resulting mess this has engendered to our health and palate. Nor am I forgetting any of our truly lamebrained cooking stumbles (white sauce—and its horrid sister, French dressing—as an accompaniment to everything; the entire health craze of the 1870s; and anything with potato chips or canned fruit in the recipe, to name some of my favorites). Instead, what I am trying to untangle from these knots are the roots of American cooking and the unique traditions that went along with sitting down at a table among our fellow countrymen.

The bad press that our national cuisine has received at times is partly due to timing. You can't tell me every other country in the world has not had its share of bad kitchen days. But, in comparison to others, ours is a decidedly young cuisine. Think about it—compared to our four hundred years of cooking, nearly every cuisine that is considered great has been developing for at least a thousand years. On top of this, our cooking has had the misfortune to develop just when mass media was beginning to flourish, which subsequently allowed our most egregious sins to be so widely broadcast. Yet, in its continuing development over the last few decades, a new reverence for some of our culinary treasures has taken hold. This, in turn, has spurred the increasing growth of fresh, well-grown fruits, vegetables, grains, and meats that are now being offered in most markets—from high-price chichi organic outposts to inner-city chain groceries. Greenmarkets chock full of local farm produce now take over many city streets and town squares, and a long overdue scrutiny of our food supply is increasingly being demanded. And yet, despite all this,

Forks and spoons laid out for the Junior Chamber of Commerce buffet,
Eufaula, Oklahoma, February 1940. (Russell Lee)

there remains a stubborn conviction about the history of American cooking that it amounts to nothing more than a lowly inheritance of indi-
gestible sauces, unhealthy lard-laced dough, and everything fried in killer
fats to a flirtatiously golden fare-thee-well.

Thank God, then, for *America Eats!*, the manuscript written for the
Works Progress Administration (WPA) by out-of-work writers during
the Great Depression. The WPA, which grew out of the 1934 Civil Works
Emergency Relief Act, employed nearly 9 million people who completed
more than a million projects across the country, including the construction of roads, bridges, parks, and public buildings. Several art-related programs for the relief of writers, artists, and theater professionals were also
set up. The Federal Writers' Project, alone, involved thousands of laid-off
reporters, fledgling novelists and poets (some of whom would go on to
greatness), country librarians, housewives, and recent college graduates.
After a somewhat lengthy, and what many considered to be a personally
invasive, financial screening process to certify they were poor enough, the

writers employed by the project were paid—depending on the cost of living in their state or city—anywhere from $50 to $103 a week. For this,
they produced such works as histories of local institutions and communities, nature guides, and, most famously, state travelogues and oral histories of former slaves and general laborers—from stonecutters to circus
dancers.

In the later years of the program, one more assignment was added to
the docket: writers, sometimes with photographers from the Federal
Artists' Project in tow, were asked to find out how America ate. Specifically, they were told to produce "an account of group eating as an important American social institution; its part in development of American
cookery as an authentic art and in the preservation of that art in the face
of mass production of foodstuff and partly cooked foods and introduction
of numerous technological devices that lessen labor of preparation but
lower quality of the product." It was to be called *America Eats!*—that final exclamation point a critical cue for the exuberance the subject was intended to arouse.

It was not to be a cookbook—the editor and chief motivator behind
the book, Katharine Amend Kellock, was adamant about this point. In
fact, she forbade any former cookbook writers or cooking teachers from
submitting material for the book. What she envisioned, instead, were
stories about local events where food was to be served: political, church,
and community fund-raisers; religious revivals; possum dinners at Elks
Lodges; ladies' tea socials; family reunions; rodeos; state fairs; harvest
festivals; cemetery-cleaning parties; and hobo encampments. The great
theme of *America Eats!* had little to do with food—very few recipes
were to be included—as it was to celebrate the "importance of social
gatherings that glorify the non-professional cook and keep traditional
cookery alive."

The timing of the project was particularly fortunate. In the 1930s,
people were still alive who, as pioneers and immigrants, crossed the
Great Plains in wagons or worked their way as miners, loggers, and saloon keepers. There were old Native Americans whose memories held
faint traces of daily lives and rituals before their tribes were shattered.
There were cowboys and chuck wagon cooks who once roamed along the
cattle trails. In the 1930s, the family farm was still producing much of
what the country ate and, although grocery shelves held some processed
and engineered foodstuff, it was hardly what it would be even five years

later. In the window of time the federal writers were out gathering material for *America Eats!*, the dishes set on many of the nation's tables could be traced back in ingredients and structure to our forebears. No matter how humble the circumstances, a delicious meal could still be gathered from the land—hunted or foraged, grown in garden patches or out in fields that were tended the way they had always been tended for generations.

In the course of several months, and sometimes expanding on research conducted for other projects, such as the slave narratives and travel guides, the writers filed hundreds of evocative stories that captured as never before the role food played in forming America's society. These stories—often less about particular dishes than about what swirled around them—showed how singularly important it was to our traditions to congregate around a table with one another and enjoy the meal at hand. This practice is stronger in our country than anywhere else because, in a nation inhabited by strangers, sharing a meal lessened the loneliness of wandering across unfamiliar landscapes and enabled us to quickly form alliances and governments where none had existed before. The stories written by the federal writers displayed all our peculiarities, devotions, and inclinations; the social, racial, and ethnic prejudices of the period; our inventive natures honed from our frontier-age experience that led to some glorious creations, but also the growing threat posed by that very ingenuity, which was increasingly leading us astray in a new age of technology. When strung together, these stories formed a picture of a lively people still uneasily coming together as a nation—and yet coming together indeed with the help of an ever-evolving and intriguing cuisine.

"If the book has a basic purpose, it is to make people appreciate a much-neglected aspect of our culture, the American table, as much as a few expatriates do the French," wrote a supervisor in a memo to the state offices. "If we can make Americans realize that they have the best table in the world, we shall have helped to deepen national patriotism."

And yet *America Eats!* never saw the light of day. The Federal Writers' Project (as was true of all the WPA's arts programs) was always a contentious program that was continually attacked by Congress as both frivolity and a haven for communist reprobates. The *South Bend Tribune* in Indiana singled out the *America Eats!* project in October 1941 for particular scorn, calling it a "foolish boondoggle." With World War II looming on

Women cutting cakes and pies at barbecue dinner, Pie Town,
New Mexico, October 1940. (Russell Lee)

the horizon, funding for the project was gradually withdrawn and, in 1943, cut altogether. State offices were told to box up whatever WPA papers they had on hand—including all of *America Eats!*, which had been in the final editing stages—and to send the material to the Library of Congress. A few states ignored Washington's directives and kept the material in their own archives. In other regions—as in Rhode Island, where the great New England hurricane of 1938 flooded coastal offices—material was completely lost.

Every now and then, though, parts of *America Eats!* have surfaced. Culinary historians and social scientists have long combed through the papers to use as source materials and to add color to their own theses. A wonderful cookbook, *A Gracious Plenty*, by John T. Edge, incorporated snippets of text, recipes, and photographs. A number of years ago, the University of Iowa published the Midwest region manuscript of *America Eats!* reputed to be written by Nelson Algren, who worked as the supervisor of the Illinois office, but it was more likely the work of many hands—including Richard Wright and Saul Bellow.

But the general public has not had the pleasure of sinking deep into the best of *America Eats!* with its cheerful, colorful writing, so filled with tasty tidbits and lore (ever wonder who stirred the first American cocktail? Or how the Plains Indians made jerk meat?), strange recipes (anyone for that entrails-and-cow-heart-laden cowboy favorite "son-of-a-bitch" stew?), and affecting songs and chants ("See dese gread big sweet pertaters/Right chere by dis chicken's side,/Ah'm de one what bakes dese taters/Makes dem fit to suit yo' pride"). The FWP was the first professional writing job for many of the people employed by the project, and the Washington editors' main directive to avoid "effusive style and the clichés adopted by some writers on food" and to have "a keen interest in sensory perception and in their fellow-men, their customs and crotchets," was hard for many of them to follow. Frankly, a lot of the notes and stories in the *America Eats!* archives, apart from those submitted from the big cities (New York City, especially) and pockets in the South where there was a glut of professional writers employed by the project, can be pretty flat. The editors in the Washington office were always chiding the local state offices to produce better copy—make the stories more enticing and to the point, more grammatical and better spelled. Yet even the most pedestrian entries for *America Eats!* manage to capture a spark of found knowledge, a bit of whimsy lent by distinct characters or a chance line of dialogue that brings the subject and the times alive.

The difficulty of bringing *America Eats!* to full life in an accessible way has dampened what the surviving papers came to celebrate so clearly: a lively cuisine that is always evolving with the continual influence of a changing populace. One of the most contentious yet most important themes rumbling through the papers was how a region's cooking manners were influenced by different people, especially foreigners, moving into a territory and gradually rubbing one method of doing something against another until it became incorporated as a local tradition. What immigrants shared with the people who had settled before them was the hard experience of leaving behind their homelands and being faced with the prospects of a vast wilderness filled with unfamiliar plants and animals that forced them to be imaginative about the ingredients they used. Drawn together out of necessity and loneliness, out of the need to create something beyond themselves simply to survive, all these strangers—the constant flow of newcomers weaving among the people who preceded them—slowly inched toward conceiving a common table and helped to give birth to an inimitable national identity.

I found *America Eats!* the way most people do—seeing it first mentioned in a book I was reading for research and becoming intrigued enough by the passage to get on a train and take myself to the manuscript room at the Library of Congress. Three days later, I emerged wanting nothing more than to tuck a sheaf of the *America Eats!* stories under my arm and take off in pursuit of our national cuisine. I was certainly hungry enough after reading about Aunt Orianna's heap of spicy chitlins, which she made to help her niece put on a rent party down in North Carolina. I wanted to taste raw sugarcane juice bubbling in tubs in Barbour County, Alabama, and have a say in who should be crowned the next Sauerkraut Queen at the harvest fair in Forreston, Illinois. I knew a good political season was shaping up and, as someone in the Oklahoma office wrote, "Politics and barbeques go so naturally together because it takes the same amount of time to cook the meat as it does to stroke the voters," so I figured there was bound to be a richly sauced, slowly smoked pig somewhere. There were salmon roasts to savor in the state of Washington, fish fries to attend in Louisiana, clambakes on Long Island, and pancake breakfasts in Vermont. And I imagined that would just be the start of a really great drive.

In my enthusiasm, there was a lot I was conveniently forgetting about the Federal Writers' Project and the experience of its writers. Take, for instance, the fact that, except for the Library of Congress holdings, the *America Eats!* papers are spread across the nation and in varying degrees of preservation, most typed on fading, fragile onionskin paper. Of the original five sections (Northeast, South, Middle West, Far West, and Southwest) only the South's was fully completed when the project was suspended. At first glance, this isn't at all surprising, considering that the South is thought of to this day as the heart of American cooking. It was and still is naturally blessed with a vivid agricultural and social heritage, its people rooted to their communities unlike anywhere else in the country. This formed deep veins of traditions the staff writers could readily draw from. However, the section's completion had more to do with Lyle Saxon, the South's editor who was also put in charge of the entire project, and who finished his work in record time so the other regions would have a working example of the content and style he expected from them.

The other regions were—and remain—a little harder to complete because of a more mobile, and in some places (especially parts of the West) sparse, population. The Great Depression forced people to leave their homes—sometimes out of necessity with the Dust Bowl or foreclosures or unemployment; sometimes because of our inherited belief there is always someplace, anyplace, better than where we find ourselves. People roamed about the country, lost contact with where they had been, wished to put the past behind them. And yet the past was still alive in old memories and a wistfulness for the seeming stability and bravery of years gone by.

The writers in many of the state offices had a time hunting people down and, when they found them and succeeded in getting them to sit still for a talk, found it difficult to sort out truth from fables. The writers were handed imprecise recipes and unreliable sources as if they were written on stone tablets. So, too, when push came to a deadline shove, the writers (as practitioners to this day are wont to occasionally do) weren't above making up whole stories and characters. So while my arms were filled with a pile of stories from the library, I soon realized I would have to search out other holdings to fill in the gaps, and spend considerable time distinguishing truth from myth and sorting out the differences between a pinch and a dab.

The bigger challenge I faced, though, was to try to stay true to the original spirit, as well as the guidelines, that were set out by the Washington editors for the project. Delving into the correspondence, it soon became clear that, strictly from a structural point of view, *America Eats!* was wobbly from the start. There was a fairly deep divide between the editors and writers about what exactly constituted American food. The editors, sitting in their offices, had strong (and sometimes contradicting) opinions about what food and traditions to include, while the writers, in their travels about the countryside, were simply recording what they were finding or personally knew about specific regions and their dishes, and which many times ran counter to what the editors dictated.

Kellock, herself a strong and directive personality, had her own ideas about how the book was to be put together. But she was less than effective in making her wishes and desires understood by her editors and writers, and the correspondence reveals much to-ing and fro-ing between an increasingly hassled Kellock to her fraying staff about what she wanted and what she was not getting. If there had been time to bring the book to fruition, she would most likely have rewritten the final copy herself. Most times, this would have meant treating the writers' stories merely as notes, extracting lines of information, using snips of dialogue for color, but leaving much of the original writers' styles and substances on the cutting-room floor.

For my purposes, then, I would have to find a way to bring the narrative together that would explore the original ideas behind the project, but would honor what the writers eventually uncovered. I tried to stay within Kellock's directive to discover "the part [American cookery] has played in the national life, as exemplified in the group meals that preserve not only traditional dishes but also traditional attitudes and customs." I decided the best way to do this was to follow the papers, to go to the places the original writers went to, and to find the group meals they recorded. If the events or gatherings no longer occurred, I would attempt to find a modern equivalent.

What this also meant was that I would have to forgo any meaningful discussion about ideas and trends in American cooking that have emanated from sections of the country the FWP editors considered at the time to be unnecessary for their purposes. I would not, for instance, be able to explore much of California, even though it has contributed so much to our culinary table in the last forty years. The state is woefully underrepresented in the original papers because the editors considered it (particularly the Los Angeles region) to be a culinary wasteland. One editor fumed: "What these contributions exemplify is the mongrel character of Southern California today—its eagerness to have traditions, the commercial character of its attempts to make such traditions."

Cities would be hard to cover, as well. There are few, if any, papers specifically on Chicago, San Francisco, or Miami—places we take for granted today as having a robust culinary style. The federal writers' New York City office was the only one asked to produce material about eating in a city because it was, at the time, considered the epicenter of urban life in a way the editors considered other American cities were not. Even the unrivaled culinary traditions of New Orleans—long established and honored—are told in the papers not as a product of city life but as part of a unique ethnic culture.

What, exactly, to do about immigrant dishes was another contentious area between the writers, Kellock, and her editors that I would have to

Chitterlings, fish, and sugarcane on a street in the Negro Section in the Delta, Clarksdale, Mississippi, November 1939. (Marion Post Wolcott)

accommodate. The raw reporting notes and manuscripts from the writers reveal that, from the start, our dishes—deriving from the traditions of the original settlers and conquerors (British in the North; French in the northern Midwest and Louisiana; Spanish in Florida, the West, and Southwest)—were always being tweaked, and at times wholly transformed, by the arrival of other traditions. Yet, the heavily edited final manuscript (or what is left of it) clings pretty much to the standard British image except, that is, when the editors felt otherwise. Much of the correspondence between Washington and state offices about *America Eats!* suggests that, in most cases not settled on an editor's personal caprice, a dish's national identity—whether it was sufficiently distinct to our country or remained foreign—depended on the region and how the editors felt about the particular immigrant group or the length of time the group had been settled in America. For instance, the editors allowed the Wisconsin office to write about Norwegian lutefisk dinners in November but not German sauerkraut festivals during the cabbage harvest, although they did ask for the inclusion of German booya suppers (which, when the arguments start, are generally decided to be more French than German) as a great example of traditional American eating. Another editor insisted the writers find what he called a "German New Year's Dinner" that he had once read about in a memoir. For years, the writers hunted for such a dinner but never found that one even took place. Unconvinced, the editor continued to demand an account of the dinner up until the end of the project.

Finally, I came up against the hard fact that I wouldn't be able to count on an army of fellow workers who would help me scout the countryside for good modern-day stories. Many of the people on the FWP payroll lived in the communities they wrote about. They knew the people they interviewed—or had enough local experience to know exactly who to turn to when they needed information. If they didn't know the communities, the writers traveled in teams, with one of them going in first to scope out the territory and get names and addresses of people to talk to. (In an interview on NPR's *The Kitchen Sisters*, Stetson Kennedy, one of the few remaining FWP writers, talked about having to use Zora Neale Hurston as a front runner because, as a black woman traveling through rural Florida, she'd be safer if she wasn't seen in the company of the white writers.) The best I could come up with was a thin membrane of friends stretched across the country who had friends of their own to send my inquiries to. The Internet, of course, became a huge help—as was calling up local newspapers, chambers of commerce, and government offices and needling them for information and contacts.

Eventually, though, I just decided I was ready to go out there and let the story find itself.

"You're going to do what?" was the common response when I revealed my plan—to follow in the federal writers' footsteps—contemplating as I was a land of pulled pork sandwiches, coconut layer cakes, roasted corn, Brunswick stews, pecan pies! My friends' disbelief reflected their acceptance of the belief that "our food sucks," augmented by a widespread (and, let's admit it, snobbish) belief that nothing remains of regional food anymore—let alone good food—west of the Hudson River and east of California's Interstate 5. It'd be strip malls and fast food as far as the eye could see out there, I was warned.

I'm not a bubble-headed fool: I knew I'd encounter mountains of fried foodstuff and streams of rehydrated, reconstituted, and carbonized concentrated something or other, but I was also dead certain I'd find plenty of goodness, too. So I'd pull out the federal writers' stories and explain how I would use them as guideposts, traveling to the same towns and communities, many of them down unmapped country roads, some even off the grid. I'd tell them I would be attending the same fairs and dinners the 1930s writers went to, all the while trying my best to discover similar local blue-ribbon dishes and cooks. After I'd get through my explanation, I'd invariably invite my listeners to come along on the ride with me, especially if they promised to help me eat whatever we came across. As often as not, my generous offer was met with a dubious look and a polite refusal.

Well, fine then, I said and went out and bought a lot of maps. In lieu of payment from any farsighted federal arts program, the home-equity loan on the house was increased to supplement my way, and then I stopped at the drugstore and stocked up on Tums and Pepto-Bismol and a host of other stomach remedies (just in case). I arranged piles of *America Eats!* stories and an equal pile of Internet searches and newspaper clippings on the car's front seat, and at least a dozen different maps on the dashboard. And then, on a hot day in May, filled with an optimist's giddy spirit, I took off across America, looking for good things to eat.

★ ★ ★ ★ ★ ★ ★ ★ ★ ★

Traditional Polyglot
by George Natanson, Oregon Office

There was a controversy going on in Prineville Church circles. Mrs. Cyrus Montcalm had scoffed at the idea that Oregon had produced anything in the way of traditional foods. The argument waxed hot among the members, especially the ladies, who prided themselves on being of pioneer stock. They were certain that many present day dishes must have been originated by the old settlers who came to Oregon in the great migration period.

Mrs. Cyrus Montcalm was adamant. She insisted that there were no dishes that could be called distinctly Oregonian. The upshot was, that the indignant members decided to show Mrs. Cyrus Montcalm that she didn't know what she was talking about. They decided the best means of settling the argument was to give a church supper featuring what they considered traditional Oregon cookery.

*Tables set up for St. Thomas Church picnic supper, Bardstown,
Kentucky, August 1940. (Marion Post Wolcott)*

At the appointed day and hour in the church basement on rows of tables, a gastronomic display lay spread before eager eyes. Mrs. Showem
exhibited what she termed was Oregon Baked Beans, despite the fact that
Boston was credited with the recipe.

"Beans are beans," said the determined Mrs. Showem, "whether they
are baked in Boston or Prineville. There wasn't any Prineville when my
grandmother landed on this sage brush plain and cooked the first mess of
beans in this part of the country. If that ain't tradition, what is? And
don't forget, Mrs. Cyrus Montcalm," said the lady with great emphasis,
"Oregon can make just as much noise about it as Massachusetts can!"

Mrs. Peckem displayed what she termed Oregon Johnny Cakes. She
had come prepared to serve them piping hot right off a griddle especially
prepared for her. Her grandmother brought the recipe from Rhode Island. Mrs. Pettycomb displayed Oregon Hash. Her grandfather boasted
of that dish. But, she admitted, he had remembered it from a New England boyhood.

Down the line they went. Dishes from the south, east, and north. Each woman insisting that her contribution should be considered a traditional Oregon dish. Mrs. Cyrus Montcalm scoffed at them all.

"Ridiculous!," she cried. "Every one of these dishes is a copy of an original brought from another state. It's remarkable how biased you Oregonians can be! If we are to abide by the word tradition, I fear, ladies, you are all doomed to disappointment. But if you insist upon being traditional, let us compromise by calling this tempting display, polyglot tradition. That is what it can be aptly termed and you must accept it as such."

"Well!" piped up Mrs. Snaily. "I wouldn't insult my parrot with that kind of a name."

"However," retorted Mrs. Cyrus Montcalm, "parrots come under the same category."

"Hm," whispered Mrs. Snickers to her neighbor. "Maybe parrots belong to that—that poly business—but I'll bet theys [sic] more cat in her than in a catamount."

"Ladies!" The sonorous voice of the Reverend Heavenly boomed forth. "I'm sure we can console ourselves with being polyglot. I dare say that puts us in a class by ourselves. Let us consider for a moment how very fortunate we are. Here in Oregon we have collected the best dishes from all over America. From those pioneer families we hail from our southland we have the best of southern cooking. From the east comes the traditional dishes that are so widely known. From the north the hearty foods of the woodsman and the trapper. Now let us put all these together and see what we have. We have the best that our sister states have boasted. We have a wealth of ideas that will in time become traditional with us. With this blend of gastronomic ideas, think of the opportunities for hospitality that lie before us. Yes indeed! Polyglot tradition will lead us to greater things! You ladies, by blending a delicious sauce of the south with a meat recipe of the east, will, in time, bring our state into epicurean glory." He bowed.

The ladies applauded heartily. He raised his hand in dramatic signal that he was not yet through. Smiling broadly, he reached over and lifted a tempting looking dish from the table. Slowly and lovingly he pushed his spoon into the smooth and purplish substance. Lifting the spoon, he placed it in his mouth, drawing it out slowly with a delighted, "Ah-h!" He turned to Mrs. Surprise, who was watching him with apprehension, and bowed. The Reverend Heavenly then turned to the ladies. "Ladies, I am convinced that we may lay claim to a tradition. I have just tasted what

Mrs. Surprise calls Summer Pudding. In Oregon we claim that our wild berries have an exceptional flavor found nowhere else in America. Mrs. Surprise," he turned toward her and held out his plate, "While I indulge in another plate of Oregon's traditional pudding, will you tell the ladies how it is made?"

Mrs. Surprise happily helped his reverence to another plate, and said, "First you pick the berries."

"Do tell!" piped up a sarcastic retort from somewhere in the room.

Mrs. Surprise realized she was not in favor. With her chin in the air and eyebrows arched, she continued. "Stew them with sugar to taste. Butter slices of white bread and cut the crusts off. Arrange alternate layers of bread and stewed berries in serving dish. Press a plate firmly on top of serving dish and drain off juice. Set the pudding aside for half a day, and serve cold with heavy cream."

"Ah," sighed the Doctor of Divinity, rolling the last mouthful of pudding reverently in his mouth as though he were loath to part with it. "We have tradition with us. This is indeed Oregon short cake."

2

The Big-Hearted Feast

Fund-Raising Dinners

Bad Advice Ruins Brunswick Stew
from the North Carolina Office

"Brunswick Stew ain't fit for hound dogs 'less you got squirrel meat." Addie Mae Spicer, of Caswell County, North Carolina made that statement, and the native of Brunswick County, Virginia would agree. There they say all that is stew is not Brunswick, and they ought to know, for of course that is where the genuine article was born. And—as always—there is a story about it.

Men, it is said, accustomed to bringing a variety of foods for hunting trips, left one of their number to do the cooking while they pursued game in nearby territory, and this lazy fellow, whose talents were not culinary, dumped all the provisions, including the squirrels that had just been killed, into the pot. That is how the miracle was accidentally wrought.

Residents of Brunswick County say you must cook nine pounds of squirrels in two gallons of water until the meat is tender, throw in six pounds of tomatoes, two large onions, two pounds of cabbage, five large potatoes, one pound of butter beans, six slices of bacon, a pod of red peppers, and salt. After this cooks for six hours, add eight ears of corn sliced off the cob. Stir constantly for a few minutes and serve. That they contend is real Brunswick stew. Accept no substitutes.

However, some twenty years ago, John G. Saunders, City Sergeant of

Richmond, inaugurated his "Sergeant Saunders' Brunswick Stews" for the benefit of the American Legion, and since they have become legend in Virginia. On the first occasion, selling at fifty cents a quart, enough stew was sold to net the Legion five hundred dollars. But Sergeant Saunders' recipe is heretical, for, instead of squirrel, he uses beef and veal and chicken. It is a colossal feat of cooking, too. In a stew given for the benefit of a Richmond policeman killed in the line of duty in 1930, Sergeant Saunders directed the cooking of 600 gallons of stew.

Addie Mae Spicer follows the North Carolina tradition of giving a stew for all the neighboring farmers who have assisted her husband at the climax of his thirteen months of toil with the tobacco crop. On that last day Zeb will at last turn his back on the dry, man-high stalks that once were orderly rows of leafy plants, and, forgetting himself, enter Addie Mae's kitchen.

"Why don't you come set a spell on the porch," he'll ask her.

"Set!" exclaims Addie Mae, wiping wisps of graying hair out of her face. "Who in the name of Satan can set with enough things to do to keep heaven's angels away from their prayers? My nerves are rilified now, so keep out of my way. Getting ready is the hardest part of stew-doings. Me and Pearline and Daisy has worked right faithful since yesterday. Got our hens picked, our potatoes diced, and our mixings together best we knowed against party day."

"When the fellows give me a helpful hand, it's only right I have them over for a little repayment. Lots of times they stewed me, and it's only right I stew 'em back," Zeb will grumble.

Addie Mae gives him an exasperated stare at that pont. "Time you was putting up the big iron pot in the yard," she says, "and getting the dry oak piled under it. Fore you know it folks'll be arriving."

Last year Zeb had just lighted the fire when the neighboring farmers and their wives and children began drifting into the yard, the men all in clean overalls, the women in spotless housedresses and low-heeled shoes—simple country people with lean, large-boned, suntanned faces. They gathered around while Addie Mae poured a bucket of water into the pot, then dropped in a six-pound smoke-cured ham with a heavy plop, added the contents of a paper bag.

"What you putting in now, Addie?"

"This here's the tasty seasoning—red peppers, black pepper and a little salt. Ain't nothing goin' to happen for an hour now. This ham's got to have it all for itself."

The hour up, Addie Mae directed, "Pearline, you go get the chickens, while I glimpse the ham. Booker, you're the firewatcher. You other men get the eatin' tables out of the barn."

The Negro named Booker grinned. "Miss Addie, ain't a man in this country more able to keep him a slow fire than I is."

Pearline returned, and two women lowered the six dressed hens into the boiling water. As the lid was lifted and rich ham odors filled the nostrils of the bystanders, Pearline glanced with approval at Addie Mae. "Pays to feed hogs peanuts," she said. "They pays it back in the end."

"These hens have an hour to cook," said Addie Mae. "Let us set."

Old Hooker Taylor appeared from around one end of the barn, where he had been enjoying a couple of swigs of corn liquor. He had long, unkempt white hair and a white beard, and a banjo was strung over one shoulder with a fraying bit of rope. He was trailed by two ancient cronies, one carrying a second banjo, the other a violin and bow.

"I know one thing," said Old Hooker, "there ain't nary a bit of beef goin' in that pot."

"Ain't," said Addie Mae, flushing slightly. "Wish this were squirrel season. Brunswick Stew ain't really fit even for hound dogs, 'less you got squirrel meat."

"Go 'head, Addie Mae," said Zeb. "This is going to be the best stew ever tasted in this county."

"Hush your mouth, Zeb," she protested, modestly, though blushing with pleasure. "You know my stews ain't hardly fit to eat."

"Sure can tell a body what not to put in a stew," said Old Hooker. "Don't never put in no mutton, don't never put in no coon, nor 'possum, lessen you want to spoil your Brunswick entire. 'Courses to me the best part of a stew feast is the swig of corn behind the barn."

The farmers guffawed and slapped their thighs. "Ain't Old Hooker a card!"

But Addie Mae glared at Hooker. "Beef ruins a stew," she said, "rabbit ruins a stew, and bad advice ruins a stew."

When ham and chickens were done, the women lifted them from the pot to a table, allowed them to cool on the platters a few minutes, then boned the meat all carefully, chopped it fine and returned it to the pot.

"Fetch the roasting ears, Daisy," directed Addie Mae. "It's near time for me to get to the house and make corn pone and coffee."

While Zeb sliced the grains nicely from the cobs, Addie Mae and Daisy added the sliced potatoes, and, fifteen minutes later, the tomatoes and corn. Then Addie Mae returned to the house and put two large granite coffee pots in the stove to boil. After that, moving quickly, humming the refrain "That Old Time Religion," she watered her cups of cornmeal, added a tablespoon of lard, and patted the dough between her hands to a half-inch thickness, preparing four large panfuls of corn pone, and setting them to bake in the oven. A few minutes later she was calling from the door, "Somebody come help me tote, you all!"

Hooker climbed the trees and lighted the lanterns that had been hanging there since early in the morning. It wasn't dark yet, but Addie Mae said that "they always look so prettified," and everyone agreed. One last inspection of the pot and she announced momentously:

"Stew's done!"

All the guests lined up, inviting Zeb, politely to "Help yourself, afore us. This is your stew feast." Then they all accepted tin plates and cups from stacks on the table and began filling them.

Addie Mae kept asking anxious questions while they ate. "Is it got enough salt? Enough pepper? Pone brown?" Then, receiving all affirmative answers, she settled down to eat her share.

And, later, relaxing against a tree trunk, listening to Old Hooker and his cronies play a catchy tune, she was heard to sigh: "I'm plumb wore out, but it's worth it to see so many folks eat their part of wholesome vittals."

Zeb glanced about at the crowd, now settled, some of them on the benches, others on blankets and gaily patched quilts spread on the grass, then up at the lanterns, bright against the darkening sky. "You has done noble, honey," he said, picking his teeth with a twig. "I've sure had me a supper. To me there ain't nothing ever so satisfying as a Tobacco Barning Brunswick Stew."

A Booya Picnic
from the Minnesota Office

The roof of the place where the booya is held is the blue Minnesota sky. Of course, the dish is obtainable in certain restaurants at certain times. It

Brunswick stew dinner in front of the tobacco warehouse on opening day
of the auctions. Prepared by Parent Teachers Association of Prospect
Hill, to raise money for a new gymnasium for the Prospect Hill
Consolidated School, Caswell County, North Carolina, October 1940.
(Marion Post Wolcott)

is a frequently advertised treat at taverns. But real booya lovers wait for summer and the special pleasure of a picnic booya.

These outdoor feasts are particularly popular where the population is largely German. Sometimes the American Legion acts as sponsor. Sometimes the town fire department. But always it is a strictly male affair. Each community has its favorite booya cook, who takes great pride in his skill and is much in demand. However, the women folks are not excluded from a share in the cook's savory creation after the cooking is finished. They and the children join the men at the site chosen for the outdoor festival, usually a grassy lake-side spot with plenty of shade trees.

The menu is simple: booya and crackers with beer for the men and pop for the women and children. Some of the women drink beer, too, especially the older German women.

At the first hint of dawn, the preparations are under way. Oxtails, a meaty soup bone, veal, and chicken are simmering in a huge vat, almost as high as the cook is tall, and as big around as three men. Several helpers are busy paring bushels of fresh vegetables, opening cans putting allspice in a cheesecloth bag. The beans have been soaking since the previous afternoon. As soon as the meat is tender, it is removed from the bones, cut in small pieces and returned to the broth. The vegetables, cut very small, are added. When the booya is ready to be eaten, the separate ingredients have lost their identity. It is neither soup nor stew, but something of both.

Around seven o'clock, a beer truck arrives, and a couple of husky drivers set up kegs, leaving a few in reserve. Bartenders tie on big white aprons and line up rows of steins. They pile bottles of pop in pails of cracked ice. Delectable odors are rising already.

About the time the beer is well chilled, the first customers start arriving. They stay a respectful distance from the chef who is seasoning, tasting, and seasoning some more, with critical intentness. The booya won't be ready to serve until about eleven.

Nobody minds waiting. They like having their appetites edged by good outdoor smells of cold amber beer. Little girls sit around primly, conscious of their ruffles, while their brothers wade in the lake or skip stones on the beach. The women cluster in chattering groups. Children quarrel over the comic section of the Sunday papers.

The teasing odors grow stronger. Not until about a half hour before the first helping is dished out, will the servers set out bowls, spoons, and plates of crackers.

As soon as the shout, "Come and get it!" goes up, an eager crowd swarms around the table in front of the steaming kettle. There is much good-natured jostling. Some buy their tickets in advance, others pay a dime a bowl as they are served. The first bowl is considered merely as an appetizer. Occasional cars pull up all afternoon. Their occupants carry away two-quart jars and pails of booya.

★   ★   ★   ★   ★

Certain dishes in the American repertoire seem to be more enjoyable when a crowd is expected. A few of them are very specific to different regions and are rarely made, and may be unknown by anyone outside the region. Brunswick stew and booya are at the top of the list, and it is hard to prepare either recipe for less than ten people. Fifty people—okay, a hundred—seems to be the actual minimum to undertake what are really simple dishes. The number of ingredients and amount of simmering time required until either stew is deemed ready to devour pretty much demand that other things should happen at the same time. That usually means congregating, socializing, perhaps even sipping something stronger than water. And if you're going to congregate, it might as well be for a good cause, whether it's to help pay somebody's medical bills or give thanks to all the neighbors who came running to help the last time the roof fell in. There was a time when you didn't have to walk too far to hear about a pie social happening to raise money to build a new schoolhouse; a chicken dinner to put a new steeple on the church; or a beef and beer night to outfit the local Little League for the season.

It's nice to report that, when a community need arises, we're still inclined as a nation to pull out a big pot and start throwing into it a lot of ingredients, with the understanding that sharing a large batch of something delicious with neighbors and strangers alike is a fine and proper way to accomplish some good. What's more, these dishes are felt to be a significant and proud part of the heritage of the neighboring countryside. Brunswick stew and booya are old recipes and are still made the way settlers cooked—using whatever is available, boiled slowly for hours and hours in a cast-iron vat placed over an open fire. What the years have done to Brunswick stews and booya recipes is to marginally refine them with occasional newfangled ideas about flavoring. New immigrant groups trying to fit into a community by participating in neighborhood events inevitably sneak in some of their own flavors, adding vegetables and spices familiar to them but not to the recipes. The basic formula for Brunswick stew is a little more cast in stone, if only because there's been open warfare about it. Still, a cook's whim and inclination almost always lets something extra slip into the broth, which is why you can taste either of these dishes over and over again and still not have the slightest idea what a "real" Brunswick stew or booya should taste like. But this is part of their great charm as classic American dishes because, not unlike the Constitution, they are constantly accommodating new ideas, while still adhering to the founders' ideals.

In the early days—and they weren't too far back, either—squirrel meat was one of the chief ingredients thrown into Brunswick and booya pots. The main reason for this was there were so many squirrels around. In the spring and fall, when a lot of community events took place, the critters were out and about so much that they might as well just jump into the pot. Many people in quite a few sections of the country continue to consider squirrel a delicacy, no different than a rabbit to a Frenchman. A wild, bushy-tailed squirrel tastes like what it has grown up eating—nuts and berries: bag a squirrel nesting by a pear or apple orchard, and the meat will be sweetly redolent of fruit. (This is why it's not such a good idea to hunt city squirrels, even though they're easier to catch, considering their habit of sitting right down next to you on a park bench: at best, they're liable to taste just like pretzels and hot dog buns.) The meat on a young squirrel is tender and best cooked simply—pan-fried, perhaps, with a little wine sauce on the side. Grilling is good, too. Stir-fried squirrel heads is another delicacy because of the tender cheek and neck meat— and, of course, the tiny scoop of brain that goes down in one swallow just like an oyster before you have time to worry about mad squirrel disease or anything else like that. For both Brunswick stew and booya, you want an older squirrel—the long cooking will make the meat almost melt together with the vegetables and broth.

You never could find squirrel meat in the local butcher shop and it surely isn't offered in supermarkets. That's why Brunswick or booya benefits often started with a squirrel hunt. But the hunts don't happen anymore, not for community benefits at least, because government officials have a thing about unregulated wild meat (e.g., mad squirrel disease) being consumed at public events. Still, hunts before compiling a vat of either dish for friends and family are known to occur and some game and wildlife reporters claim they are on the increase, if only because squirrel hunting is reckoned to be a lot of fun. Apparently, this pursuit has all the elements that make hunting the thrill that it's supposed to be: marksmanship, woodsmanship, scouting, observing tracking signs, camouflage, sitting still, stalking, preparing game for the table, and, of course, bragging rights. A good squirrel hunter will tell you the most important and pleasurable aspect of all these is getting a chance to sit still, your back against a comfortable tree in a quiet forest, just listening to the woodsy noises around you.

Local hunters—hunters, that is, living within a thousand-mile radius of Brooklyn, New York—who were willing to take a completely gun-scared, antsy-pants novice along with them and then cook up a mess of Brunswick stew or booya did not prove easy to find. While the search was on, I tried to get over my gun-shyness at a local practice range and proved surprisingly capable (although the kickback of a hunting rifle, even a lightweight one, is not something easily gotten comfortable with). Then I heard from the instructor how squirrels were commonly hunted: scoping them out by looking for foraging mothers, then picking the hell out of all the squeaking youngsters that scurry from the nearby nest. By the time I found someone in West Virginia who was willing to do a relative a favor and take me into the woods, I couldn't get around the fact that what were good sport and a scrumptious dinner to some, were cute, defenseless families to me.

So a good old-fashioned hunt and feast was out, which was okay because, these days, the modern recipes for Brunswick stew and booya rarely mention squirrel anymore. This may be lamented by some but it sure makes it easier to cook. Newer recipes for both dishes call for chicken or turkey, plus oxtails, beef, pork, maybe a good smoky ham butt. Occasionally lamb and mutton, but then you're moving into burgoo territory, another great regional American fund-raising dish. The recipes for Brunswick stew and booya—and burgoo—are, in structure and content, strikingly similar, their differences coming down to just a few things:

> *Location*: If you're eating Brunswick stew, chances are you're points south, starting in Virginia and moving down to Georgia; booya marks the Midwest, around Minnesota and thereabouts; burgoo is Kentucky, possibly Indiana.
>
> *Order*: How the ingredients are added to the pot
>
> *The cook*: Who inevitably slips in his or her own flavors

Controversy about origins (as has been previously noted, battle lines have been drawn between Virginia and Georgia about who spawned Brunswick stew) and pedigree are common; a snobbery among cooks is mandatory (a sour opinion about everyone else's recipe is a major seasoning).

In fact, the antagonism about how the different versions of these dishes are prepared stems from everyone in their respective states claiming ownership and having strong opinions about how and where the stews were first cooked. It inevitably turns personal, since these recipes are handed down from father to son (despite the WPA's Addie Mae's Brunswick Stew, these dishes have a very strong male heritage. Burgoo cooking, for instance, is still mostly the province of Kentucky men). For generation upon generation, the recipes have apparently been divulged only on deathbeds, and never before. Antagonism breeds competition, which breeds cook-offs, which means you'll get a curious crowd happy to take sides and offer up a dollar or two to push their respective opinions forward. All of which means that some good cause is surely going to get a fine helping hand. And no one will walk away hungry.

One of the best places to see this in action is at the annual Brunswick Stew Festival in Richmond, Virginia. For one Saturday in November, the festival takes over the historic 17th Street Farmers' Market in the Shockoe Bottom neighborhood across the James River from the Capitol Building. One of the oldest continually operated markets in the country, it is a collection of stalls in a two-block area surrounded by a couple of congenial bars, bakeries, and restaurants. On festival day, the stewmasters pretty much crowd out most of the farmers' stalls, but that's okay because the dollars the cooks earn, selling small samples and quart-size containers throughout the day, support good causes, from local hospitals to disaster relief here and abroad.

As they mix and stir ingredients into their big iron pots, the contestants comport themselves with Southern grace and hospitality, betraying very little sense of rivalry between the teams. Trash talking about the different stews is done, instead, by the people who mob the event and go from stall to stall around the market square, sampling the different stews.

"You can *not* tell me this is Brunswick stew," says a woman to her friend who is all but licking the last of a fairly gooey, pale substance from the sample cup offered by the American Legion Post. While it has all the ingredients and is probably the closest recipe at the festival to the historical version, the post's concoction is extremely bland, its long-simmered chicken reduced to nothing more than filaments. Despite a rumor that inexplicably ignites in the line about the possibility of squirrel meat in the pot—and how much citified people in Richmond would not like that one bit—the post's stew has a strong fan base. (The rumor proved false, or at least denied by the cooks and the festival organizers: "If there's squirrel here, it's off the grid and I don't want to know about it," said Adam Nathanson, the market's operations manager.) In truth, though, the second pot the post offers, made from a recipe that is tinkered with each year, is much better. A good amount of pepper that has been stirred in contributes a much-needed heft to the ingredients.

Better yet is the Episcopal Church of the Creator's version. Their stew is thick with chunks of chicken fighting for space with the lima beans and corn in a spicy broth. There's a very long line in front of their stall and the nice women spooning out samples have all they can do to keep up with the demands.

"There's a shitload of people here," exclaims a man in line and then suddenly shuts his mouth tight and looks sheepishly around. "I beg your pardon, ma'am. Didn't mean to cuss out loud," he says, as I try to sneak in front of him. Assuring him that I often hear far worse up north where I come from doesn't seem to placate him much, as he bows slightly in a very gentlemanly way and insists that I proceed before him—actions that my hardened little Brooklyn soul finds to be truly shocking.

"Can't believe I cussed out loud like that," he mutters again and fingers his handful of dollar bills.

A fine example of how the basic recipe can be altered is found on the other side of the market. Bill Kisor makes a mean Cajun-inspired stew in which chunks of sausages and shrimp swim around with the chicken.

"Honey, get over here," a woman howls to her husband who is three stalls away at the Sonny and the Boys station, where two comely blonde women in pink cowboy hats are dishing out a soupy stew. It's sort of bland but there are different hot sauces on the table to heat things up.

"Jack!" the woman yells again, but her husband is talking to the cowgirls and doesn't hear her. "You go on over and tell your father I found his favorite, and if he don't get over here he's not getting any," she says to her teenage daughter. The girl's face is hidden within the deep hood of her tight sweatshirt, but the rest of her body language makes it clear that she is incredibly appalled to be at the event at all, let alone anywhere near her mother. Still, she obediently slithers through the crowd, fishing for her dad.

"I would guess that in Virginia, the majority of the Brunswick stews made are designed to raise funds for an organization or a charitable event," J. R. Bush, better known as Randy, says, as he stirs his team's stew. A cordial, charming man in his fifties, Randy has a process for everything the crew does at the competition—from chopping the vegetables to adding seasonings and stirring the pots that are always kept slightly bubbling. His team is called the Red White & Blue Stew Crew and Randy has been making the stew for one benefit or another since the early 1980s. He learned from his Brunswick stew mentor, Norman Long, who has been cooking stews for over forty years now and raising in the bargain, by one casual estimate, a few hundred thousand dollars for various charities. In turn, Randy is teaching and inspiring others to start their own crews, and raising money for good causes.

"The process of making Brunswick stew is usually very time intensive, so it naturally lends itself to making a large batch," Randy observes. His initial recipe belongs to Norman but he's fooled around with it every time he's made it and no two of his pots ever taste the same.

This year, his crew is cooking for the Children's Hospital in Virginia and, by the end of the festival, he's sold over eighty gallons. His wife, April, can't close the cash box, it's so full.

The winners are about to be announced—who made the best stew, which stew was the people's choice—but neither Randy nor anyone else in his crew, for that matter, really cares. The cowgirls in their pink hats seem to be the only participants near the stage; many of the other crews have packed up their gear and gone home, which is not surprising, considering they've all been at the market since three thirty in the morning, making their stews. Randy—although a little bleary eyed—is remarkably affable and, while it would be nice to win, that's not why he does what he does at the festival.

As he says, "The constant enjoyment of doing something like this are the relationships you develop just standing, stirring, and chatting over the stew pot with your friends, and the enjoyment in knowing that your efforts are designed to 'do good' or to give people something they enjoy. Each time you cook a stew, you hear stories from crew members and the public alike of their memories of the past and that helps build upon the tradition of Brunswick stew."

Out in Saint Paul, Minnesota, booya is such a big draw for local fundraising events that Highland Park on the southwest side of the city has a special booya shed—a fully equipped kitchen with three kettles and a sort of screened-in porch for serving. A few years ago, city officials were threatening to close the shed because there wasn't a shutoff valve for the gas lines under the kettles and the city didn't have the forty thousand dollars it thought fixing the problem would cost.

"There will be a pickle-low party," Pittsboro, North Carolina, July 1930.
(Dorothea Lange)

At the time, Tom Riddering, a building official with the city's Office of License, Inspections and Environmental Protection, told a reporter, "We all agreed it was potentially dangerous, especially if you have a person who's had a few beers."

Drinking beer while tending to the kettles is almost a part of the recipe for true booya cooks, so the danger of an explosion from built-up gas was real. Still, the hullabaloo and soul-searching that arose for months after the announcement was incredible. Newspapers proclaimed it the death of booya in Saint Paul and intimated that a part of what makes the city such a terrific place to live would be lost. Being that it was close to an election year, local officials voiced their keen support for keeping the shed open yet failed to come up with any viable solutions. But just as the spring fund-raising season was fast approaching and such groups as the St. Francis de Sales Casinos Men's Club were facing the tough dilemma of where to cook their annual pots of booya, an amateur metalworker sent the city a catalog from an industrial burner manufacturer and the city ordered the necessary parts and fixed the pipes themselves for something like three thousand dollars. Booya was once again bubbling in Highland Park and Saint Paul's soul was saved!

The people in South Saint Paul don't need the city to provide them with a booya shed; every October, they set up their own kettles in the parking lot of Grace Lutheran Church and have themselves a "World Championship" cook-off. Unlike Richmond's Brunswick Stew Festival, this is a highly competitive although fairly good-natured tournament. The championship is part of the neighborhood's annual autumn celebration and the proceeds from the hundreds of cups of booya that are sold each year pay for the awards ($200 to the first-place, $100 to the second-place, and $75 to third-place winners) and the cost of the celebration, which, in turn, does a fine job of bringing people out to support the local community. The fact that booya is cooking makes it easy for people to find the event: a meaty, spicy scent is detected at least five blocks away; at three blocks' distance, people are quickening their steps, walking with their noses tilted up in the air, only to come to a full stop by the church, where a traffic jam of eager booya eaters are struggling to find their way into the lot.

Across the street, the parking lot is slightly obscured by a ring of large campers; a tent; a small stage where a band composed of men well into their fifties are playing some good, fast hard rock; and tables and chairs quickly being claimed by hungry hordes. The iron booya kettles—about waist high and a good yard across—are bubbling away beside the campers and tents where the nine or so competitors have spent the night preparing their brew. The Vietnam Veterans of America, Chapter 639, use a recipe that's about forty years old and was handed down by an older vet, one Chuck "Catfish" Jones. But the actual genius behind their recipe is Jim Mason, who is considered the vets' booya master. He and the rest of the vets cook booya throughout the year at various venues, raising money for veterans' benefits and children's activities that aren't covered by the charitable gambling events they run out of a local bar called Bugg's Place. Mason couldn't make it to this year's competition. Instead, the proceedings are being tended to by his disciple, Dorothy Sokolowski, who has been worrying over the kettle all night. A tall woman with short hair and a cigarette dangling from the side of her mouth, she's learned everything she knows about making booya from

Mason but is adamant in the belief that she, herself, is not yet ready to take on the task single-handedly: she's just following his commands, which means being picky about the order in which the ingredients are added to the broth.

"It makes a difference," she says. "You have to add things at a particular time and you have to get the broth going at a constant roll."

Beyond these instructions, she's not willing to wander and when she thinks someone else in the crew is giving a little too much of the recipe away to me, she yells forcefully, "Shut the fuck up," and throws the culprit a look that is pure menace.

The original recipe for booya does not seem to have any German ties at all. A highly unscientific yet exhausting poll taken at the competition strongly favors that booya is America's answer to bouillabaisse, the legendary fish stew of Marseille. The story goes that some French fur traders and settlers were homesick for the stew but, since they were so far inland, they made it with the variety of meat they had on hand. It's hard to see how the legend could be true: although Minnesota was home to a lot of French settlers and traders, a quick scan of the two recipes clearly shows they share only a faint syllabic similarity. Be it French or German—and let's throw in the possible influence of the huge number of Irish in the city—booya's lineage at this stage in the game doesn't really matter except to a few sticklers. Let's leave it by stating that the dish is a mutt, which means it has been thoroughly Americanized.

"Ahhhhh! I think it's time to start drinking," Al Shipton says as he emerges from the VFW's camper a little before noon. And he doesn't even drink.

"How we doing, Dorothy?"

"I don't know," she snaps at him.

"Her and Mason get stressed out over the least little booya thing."

"Hey, let me tell you, there are some crappy-ass booyas around," Dorothy counters. "Here's the secret to a great booya: bones. How you make soup? With bones. You need bones."

Another woman in the crew slowly stirs the kettle with a big wooden paddle that is not unlike a canoe oar. The stirring brings to the surface shards of cabbage, rutabaga, onions, and lots of knobby bones.

No one knows how the other competitors make their booya, but they all spy on one another through the night. At a crucial moment, Dorothy disappears into the camper to mix up the spices that distinguish one booya recipe from another. Then, under the cover of darkness, she scatters them in the broth and stirs. Nodding across the lot toward another contestant, Dorothy whispers, "They use fucking allspice," and sounds perfectly horrified if not disgusted.

Next to the allspice offenders is a group of women who call themselves the Twisted Sisters & Co. Members of their squad actually started the competition as something fun to do at the celebration—being women and not privy to firsthand knowledge of how to cook booya, they figured they had all grown up eating enough of it at local firehouse benefits that they supposed they could do it. The Twisted Sisters have a history of taking the first-place trophy away from the Vietnam vets. Or it's the other way around, depending on who you're talking to. The Twisted Sisters' booya is distinguished—and is a consistent crowd pleaser—for the gallon of Merlot that is used to brown the meat. The women, themselves, are drinking beer and by the time their booya is ready, one of the crew is gyrating in a twist, pulling in whomever ventures by. The others are just having a marvelous time dishing out cups to the paying crowds. Terrie Davis, the ringleader for the Twisted Sisters, is a little more forthcoming than Dorothy about what is in her booya: two hundred pounds of beef, pork, and oxtails.

"You're not afraid of oxtails, are you?" she asks. "I love oxtails."

Unlike most of the other competitors, the Twisted Sisters are not subsidized and pay for everything themselves. But Terrie gets the meat cheap from the local stockyards because her husband was once a butcher and they know where to go.

Once the meat is browned in the wine and a broth starts forming from the oxtail bones, the women put in two hundred pounds of carrots, cabbage, corn, and onions that were diced the previous week in Terrie's garage. The potatoes get diced the night before and are put in last. It's a thick brew and extremely aromatic.

"You should be here around midnight," Terrie says and smiles. "The whole parking lot smells incredible with the different kettles bubbling away. We have a great time just kicking back and cooking: even when it's been snowing, we're out here stirring and laughing away."

The vets' booya is even thicker and subtly spiced; somehow the different meats retain their distinct flavors while still blending nicely together. The allspice kings, otherwise known as the D&B Boys, have a very spicy and absolutely delicious soup (although you do have to like allspice) from a recipe that was one of the team's grandfather's, who made it for years at fund-raisers throughout Saint Paul.

Everyone's booya is ready to eat at around noon and eager customers have purchased tickets. Besides the wine and barley and allspice, there are subtle differences that change the taste of each booya slightly, yet significantly enough. Maybe it's more chicken in one, or beef in another; maybe it's the thinness of one broth versus another's denseness. No two are alike and all the competitors are extremely proud of their respective concoction. The booya is served in Styrofoam cups (small and large) but some people—actually a lot of people—bring large plastic containers with lids and go from table to table, mixing the different versions together and taking it home to freeze for later (one warning about saving booya—if it has cabbage in it, you don't want it to sit out too long with a lid on before heating it up—at room temperature, the cabbage will begin fermenting the broth and put out a stench the whole house won't easily forget). Others sit with their families and friends at the long tables in the middle of the lot and finish one cup from one team, then go off to purchase another cup from another team.

The music goes on, the singing and yelling "hi" to neighbors and friends gets louder. Beer, not for sale at the competition but carried in

Mountaineers and farmers eating at a church benefit, Campton, Kentucky, September 1940. (Marion Post Wolcott)

camouflaging plastic cups from nearby houses and stores, is flowing everywhere. At three P.M., the winners are announced: This year it's the Vietnam Veterans of America, Chapter 639; second place goes to the Twisted Sisters & Co.

A Fifteen Center Pig Foot Supper
from the Virginia Office

A month ago gathered in the basement of one of our local churches, was a small band of Negro women consisting of nine in number. The president is an old lady of seventy years.

"Ladies, we's got to do somepin' to raise a little money. Les all put our heads together and think of a supper we might give."

One sister suggested pig feet.

Another protested. "Who wants ole pig feet? They give you indigestion. The last time the pig feet were cold and half done. Why can't we give a chicken supper like we did years back? We served brown fried chicken, potato salad, hot rolls, butter, hot chocolate, and every bit of the food was sold."

"But chicken is too high. Les get back to pig feet," said the president.

"I cooked the last time and you all knows I don't know how," said Sister Graham. "I had many complaints."

"Well I'se from Georgia, and everyone will want a second helpin' if you'll let me cook them," another member argued.

"All right. Two weeks from now I'll expect you sisters here at 1 p.m., and that will give us ample time to prepare our supper," said the president. "Let's divide our members and bring everything down to the knives and forks."

On September 29, 1941, the group gathered.

Sister Covington brought her pig feet—split lengthwise, put them in two huge pots filled with water. Into each pot she added a pinch of soda. Pig feet need lots of water and a tiny bit of soda. They let them boil until tender.

"Well I've collected a few chickens," said Sister Curtis. "I make a savory chicken stew in the following manner. Brown a few sliced onions and a whole stalk of celery slightly in some butter. Add the chicken for just three minutes and then cover with water—just cover. Add salt and pepper, lots of pepper and simmer for an hour or until chicken is tender. Thicken the stew a little with flour."

On one side of the church kitchen, Sister Jones was making sweet potato and apple pies. Such a good smell pervaded the atmosphere, the odors of cooking cabbage, chicken, pig feet, coffee boiling, and pies baking.

Came seven o'clock and the dining room table was laden with huge yellow brown sweet potato pies, luscious apple pies, bowls of potato salad lavishly trimmed with pimiento, green lettuce, pickles, mustard, hot chili peppers. On the stove the chicken stew, pig feet, cabbage and rice kept warm.

First customer was a fat old minister.

"Doctor said I wasn't to eat no sweets, 'cause I'm too fat—but bring me in a supper."

A beautifully arranged plate was taken consisting of a half pig foot, a generous serving of potato salad on lettuce and cabbage. Coffee and cocoa were five cents extra.

"Oh, dis sho is good food. Gimme another order," said Reverend Lee.

And so on through the evening, the pig feet disappeared. Only fifteen cents for a generous stewed chicken and rice or pig feet supper.

Some were taken out but most customers came in, sat down, and ordered a second helping.

And the small supper brought in seven dollars. Which encouraged this group of women to give another in the near future.

★   ★   ★   ★   ★

Recipes

While both of these recipes come directly from the federal writers' files (Brunswick Stew from the Virginia office; Booya from the Minnesota office), they are, at best, basic versions of the dishes, and stew cooks worth their salt will consider them as mere starting points for their own inventive flights. My clarifications about ingredients and procedures are bracketed in italics.

Brunswick Stew

10 pounds chicken, either whole and cut up or bought cut [*you may also use any combination of beef, pork, or ham, depending on your desires*]

½ cup shortening
1 cup chopped onions
4 cups skinned and seeded tomatoes
6 cups butter (lima) beans
2 cups boiling water
½ to 1 teaspoon cayenne [*much more depending on taster*]
4 cloves
6 cups corn, cut from the cob
4 tablespoons Worcestershire sauce

In a large Dutch oven, iron kettle, or soup pot, saute the chicken pieces slowly in the shortening until lightly brown. Remove the chicken to a platter.

Saute the onions in the fat until golden then place the chicken on top of the onions. Add the tomatoes, beans, water, and spices to the chicken and bring to a simmer. Let cook until the chicken is cooked and falls from the bones. [*If you are using a combination of other meats, add the chicken about an hour later than the other cuts because you'll want to let beef, pork, or ham simmer longer. Depending on the cut and toughness of the meats you're using, this could add another hour, probably two, to get all the meat cooked through. After the meats are cooked, you may want to remove them from the broth before they fall off the bones, then shred the meat by hand and return it to the broth. Or, for more flavor to the broth, let the meat fall off the bones of its own accord and fish as many of the bones as you can out of the broth later, before serving.*]

Fifteen minutes before you're ready to serve, stir the corn kernels into the broth and the remaining seasonings. Taste and correct the flavors to your personal taste.

[*This will serve about 16 people. The more you double the recipe, the longer you will have to cook the ingredients.*]

Booya

30 pounds oxtail, or 20 pounds oxtails and 15 pounds veal
10 pounds beef soup bones
4 fat hens
Water to cover

1 bushel tomatoes, peeled, or 2 gallons of canned puree[d]
    tomatoes
4 or 5 large onions, peeled and chopped
2 pounds carrots, peeled and chopped
2 pounds of celery, chopped
10 large potatoes, peeled and cut
2 bunch[es] of kohlrabi, peeled and chopped
2 bunches of rutabagas, peeled and chopped
6 heads of cabbage, cored and chopped
4 (24-ounce) cans of corn, drained
2 (12-ounce) cans of peas
2 pounds of dry navy beans, soaked 12 hours
1 pound fresh string beans, remove strings and chop
2 tablespoons allspice [*more or less according to personal taste*]
1 tablespoon paprika
salt and pepper to taste

Place all the meats in a very large soup pot or booya kettle. Cover with enough water to cover the meat. Bring to a boil then lower to a gentle rolling simmer, stirring occasionally. Cook the meat until it is done. [*You may remove the meat from the bones, which at this phase is a messy proposition, or you can do what a lot of booya cooks do, and let the meat fall by itself from the bones so the bones can continue to add flavor to the broth— through the continuing cooking, the meat will shred into fairly good serving pieces of its own accord. As you stir, try to crush the hen carcasses with your spoon or paddle so the bones add further flavor, then try to remove the bones with your spoon as much as possible, since they are small and may pose a risk of choking.*]

Add the vegetables, one at a time and stir until thoroughly incorporated before adding the next vegetables. Add more hot water if needed to keep ingredients covered.

Now add the seasoning. Taste and add more if necessary.

Continue to cook until you think it's done—no more than 12 hours and always better the next day after a rest.

Makes 60 gallons, which serves about 120 people, with a serving size of about 2 cups.

Recipe for Kentucky Burgoo
*Submitted by the Kentucky Office and taken from
an article in the* Courier-Journal, *May 15, 1932*

Burgoo, Burgou or Burgout, is defined as a thick gruel or porridge used by French seamen in the eighteenth century. In Kentucky it is an entirely different dish that traces its development from the War between the States. According to tradition the command of General John Hunt Morgan included a Frenchman who had a reputation with Morgan's men for being able to prepare a palatable meal from most incongruous articles. During the latter months of the war, when food was almost unobtainable, a foraging party was detailed to bring in anything that would appease hunger. In due time the detachment returned with potatoes, tomatoes, onions, some cabbage, twenty-nine blackbirds, three crows, a goose, several hens and a shoat. The entire booty was cooked in a giant powder kettle under the Frenchman's supervision.

Ravenous appetites brought shouts of applause and commendation when the men tasted the contents of the kettle. Meanwhile the Frenchman, half-apologetically, recounted the ingredients he should have had to be able to prepare a really good burgoo. One of Morgan's men made a memorandum of the formula, and brought it back home after the war. In time various versions of the recipe were used in the Bluegrass country, and the burgoo party slowly encroached on the barbecue as a popular mass-feeding commodity. However, it was not until a decade after the World War that Kentucky Burgoo forged to the front to gain nation-wide publicity.

In November, 1929, at the second of Colonel E. R. Bradley's one-day charity race meetings at Idle Hour Farm, the Colonel, well-nigh frozen, as everyone else was, walked over to the burgoo booth.

"Is this stuff hot?" he asked.

"Yes sir," said James T. Looney, a grocery man of Lexington, who had prepared it.

The Colonel ate.

"This is fine," he said. "To whom am I indebted?"

"To me," Mr. Looney answered.

"Glad to meet you, Mr. Looney," said the Colonel as he shook hands. "This burgoo hits the spot. You, I think, are the burgoo king. I'll name a horse after you. Maybe he'll win the Derby."

The fame of Looney's burgoo grew. At each of the succeeding Idle Hour race meetings he was on hand to serve his steaming burgoo, for usually the weather was damp and cold. In 1931 forty coke-burning stoves were located over the grounds and each of these was hugged by its quota of the Colonel's guests. At this "chumming party," as it was called, Mr. Looney served 900 gallons of burgoo to "a never diminishing line of customers."

Colonel Bradley kept his promise to name a colt for Mr. Looney. He chose the bay son of Bubbling Over, dam Minnawand, foaled in 1930, to bear the name Burgoo King. Mr. Looney was fortunate enough to have $50 on him in the winter book at 40 to 1 to win the Kentucky Derby in 1932 and a week after he cashed that bet he won another on his namesake when Burgoo King won the Preakness.

Mr. Looney has made public his recipe, showing quantities sufficient for 5,000 people. He withheld the identities and amounts of certain condiments he uses as seasoning:

> 800 pounds of soup meat
> 4 dozen squirrels, if in season
> 24 gallons of canned corn
> 4 bushels of onions
> 240 pounds of fat hens or roosters
> 15 bushels of Irish potatoes
> 60 gallons of canned tomatoes
> 6 gallons of tomato puree
> 200 pounds of cabbage
> 4 gallons of canned carrots or 2 bushels of raw carrots
> Burgoo seasoning, consisting of salt and red pepper pods

★   ★   ★   ★   ★   ★   ★   ★   ★   ★

Chittlin Strut
by Katherine Palmer, North Carolina Office

These struts are held in the homes of the Negro for the purpose of making money to be used for anything from paying church to buying a winter coat. The meal is served on a long table reaching across the room. Wash tubs of cider sit on each end of the table where it is served with tin dippers. The pickle, slaw and potato custards are placed at intervals along the white cloth, but the chitterlings and corn pone are served hot from the kitchen.

The Negroes begin to gather by sundown. The host walks around barking:

> *"Good fried hot chittlin's, crisp and brown,*
> *Ripe hard cider to wash dem down,*
> *Cold slaw, cold pickle, sweet tater pie,*
> *And hot corn pone to clap your eye."*

By nine o'clock the feed is over and the shoo round strut begins. The table is pushed aside. The banjo pickers take their places back under the stair steps out of the way. With the first clear note a high brown leaps to the center of the floor and cuts the buck. Couples form, then comes the steady shuffle of feet and the strut is on. [Introductory note from the North Carolina office]

Mehitable Dorsey and her man Doak butchered their hogs on the creek bank last Thursday. The chill of late fall has set in, the new moon is on the rise, so there is no danger of the meat swelling. The chittlins have been soaked in salt water for two days now and ought to be just right for frying in the pan.

By word of mouth the invite has been broadcast to the Negro population of the upper Cape Fear.

"Yall goin to Mehitable's chittlin strut?"

"Iffen we lives, we is. How's 'bout yall?"

"We's good as there this verisome minute."

Darkness is falling over the low-lying lands of the river bottom as the guests begin to arrive at the Dorsey cabin.

Doak stands by the door while Mehitable works feverishly in the little lean-to kitchen. Large maroon eyes bulge from Doak's narrow, long skull. A bright blue serge suit hangs loosely on his spare body.

The unmistakable odor of frying chittlins fills the cabin. Some have declared this scent to be obnoxious, but not so the chittlin lovers, and most country Negroes of the South relish their chittlins.

Doak bids his guests welcome, at the same time transacting business with each comer.

"What you mean, 'how much?' Hector Shadwick, you been comin to this chittlin strut long as I can 'member, and you knows the price is two-bits, twenty-five cents."

"Evenin, Deacon Basswood. And you too, Miss Flossie. Yes suh, Deacon, you and Flossie, chittlins and cider and pickle and cabbage sallet for two, fo' bits, a half-a-dollar, fifty cents. Thank you Deacon. Come right in, and make yallselfs t'home."

Doak does not insist on money payment. He has accepted a can of sorghum molasses, bags of eggs, and canned fruit in lieu of cash. Kinfolk and a few others enter free.

The cabin fills rapidly. The Negroes are wearing their Sunday go-to-meeting clothes, mostly bright of color, inexpensive, and poorly fitting. Chittlin strut is one of the gayest events of the year.

The house is lighted by kerosene lanterns, hung from the low rafters, barely clearing the heads of the guests. They are safer than lamps, which might upset after the strutting gets under way. The cabin contains two rooms besides the kitchen. Each has a fireplace and blazing hearth fire of pine knots. A table improvised by placing planks on wooden horses has been set in the larger room almost filling the space and providing places for twelve persons. A smaller table, seating six, fits snugly into the adjoining room from which bedroom fixtures have been removed. Chairs, benches, and stools of various sizes and descriptions are set around the tables. Unframed pictures, apparently taken from magazines, are tacked on the wall. There is a broken mirror with a Kodak picture of a young Negro woman stuck between the glass and the frame. Above the fireplace in the larger room is a card with gold and blue letters: "Feed My Lambs."

Without preliminary ceremony the guests take places at the tables which have already been set with thick china dishes and wooden handled steel cutlery. There are large bowls of cole slaw and pickles, and molasses in tin cans.

The faded blue curtains separating the kitchen from the larger room part, and Mehitable appears bearing a large platter of fried chittlins in each hand. She is followed by another Negro woman with pans of corn bread. A third carries cups of steaming coffee on a tin serving tray.

Immediately there is a cacophony of talk and laughter.

"Quit yer hollerin a minute," Mehitable shouts above the din, and when the noise subsides: "Jes help youselfs from the platters. And don't be 'fraid to eat. They'd more where this come from."

"Wont take long to find how much is in the kitchen."

"Take some of them chittlins and leave some, and don't be all night."

Mehitable returns with another platter for the smaller room. Perspiration covers her coffee-colored face. Her heavy, shapeless body is encased in a grey gingham dress; her large spreading feet slide along within broken carpet slippers.

Onto each plate is taken a mound of the chittlins with helpings of the slaw and a mixture of pickled green tomatoes and cucumbers. The corn bread is broken open and eaten with molasses. Swigs of coffee follow mouthfuls of food.

Prodigious quantities of chittlins are consumed as Mehitable and her two helpers move between kitchen and the eating rooms. Several times Mehitable fries up more chittlins.

"Chittlins gettin low, Mehitable."

"More comin up, Zack."

Conversation flows without inhibition or restraint. Early efforts to shout across the room have been abandoned, and now only the strongest voiced are able to make themselves understood by their neighbor closest at hand.

For an hour the feasting continues, though a few have previously given up hope of eating any more. At last all have surrendered their plates except Moonstone Peeley, an enormous Negro with a bell-shaped head, spreading nostrils, and huge mouth.

"Put the chittlins to Moonstone."

"Don't weaken, Moonstone, else we know you gettin ol."

"Last time Moonstone done eat six plates smack clean. Betcha six bits he caint do it tonight."

"I call you. Jasper, hold the money. Moon, I's bettin on you for six plates or better."

Moonstone has but little trouble in polishing off six big helpings, not only of chittlins, but of corn bread and all the trimmings.

As the bets are being paid, Aunt Orianna, an ancient neighborhood Negress, enters the cabin. She pauses on the threshold, and leaning on her persimmon-wood cane, sniffs the air. The brown skin of her wrinkled face is like old parchment. Beady dark eyes peer from sunken sockets. Grey wooly hair is covered with a man's hat, much the worse for wear. The old woman hobbles to the fireplace, where she sits on a low stool and takes a plate of chittlins brought to her by Doak.

Mehitable joins Aunt Orianna at the fire and settles near her on an overturned orange crate. "Back's down bad. I'll res me some while Doak and others cleans up. Shuckin caw and cotton-pickin parties all put together don equal chittlin doins," she says to her old friend. Mehitable's bulky figure is outlined in the glow from the fireplace. Her black hair is longer than that of most Negroes. She works out the kinks with possum oil.

Aunt Orianna nods assent. The two survey the gay scene before them. Aunt Orianna sucks her toothless gums over her chittlins and corn bread. Shadows flicker across their black, shining faces.

The guests wander restlessly between tables and fireplace, waiting for the banjo boys to finish their supper and tune up for the strut.

Presently the two women on the hearth are joined by Clossie Jones. She is the color of old brass, with thin lips, and resplendent in purple silk and white canvas shoes.

Settling herself by the fire, she addresses her hostess: "Mehitable, I wants to know how does you get these chittlins flavored so tasty? How come they's the beatingest chittlins I ever eat?"

"No flavor to it, 'cept natcheral flavor," Mehitable replies. "It's jes in the fixin. You got to get yore chittlins clean and sweet." Going to the fireplace, she throws on more pine knots from the boxful beside the hearth. "Them chittlins been done fussed with right smart. After the hawgs is kilt and scraped and the chittlins took out, I squeeze them chittlins clean as I can with my hands. Then I washes them through two waters. Then I cut them open lengthwise and wash them two more times, then I scrapes 'em good and plenty with a dull knife. After that I washes them in two more waters and they is ready for the salt-water soakin. After soakin them two days they is boiled three hours 'fore I sets to frying."

"Does you fry 'em in deep fat, Mehitable?" asks Clossie, much interested.

"After they soaks in the salt water I rinses 'em good ag'in, and cuts 'em in fo-inch lengths, and rolls 'em in meal, and fries 'em in medium fat. Hawg lard's the bestest."

"And make sure to cook 'em crisp and brown," puts in Jordan Perdew, the undertaker from town, a bald little man with a nervous twitch to his upper lip. He stands staring into the fire.

"That's where you wrong, Jordan." Moonstone Peeley now joins the group. "You misses the good flavor by fryin you chittlins too brown. Jes so's they's cooked through makes the choicest chittlin eatin they is. I knows, because I's a real chittlin eater."

"Quit you fussin," Mehitable admonishes. "Some likes 'em brown, some likes 'em medium, and some likes 'em jes warmed through. Now the deacon there is the onliest one I knows what pours vinegar on his chittlins. Seem to me sour would spoil the taste."

Deacon Basswood, who is the shade of ginger cake, shakes his head. "I's perticular 'bout my chittlins."

Moonstone glances in the direction of Doak. "I know of some folks what would eat 'em any way a'tall, jes like they come from the hawg, even."

This brings a round of uproarious laughter that drowns out Doak's reply.

Aunt Orianna has remained silent during this argument, scratching the wart on her ear meditatively. Now the old woman takes a dip of snuff, and peeping over the brass-rimmed glasses set aslant her flat nose, she speaks in a thin treble voice: "When I come in the do, I didn't smell no collards cookin, nor turnips neither. 'Course," she glances at Mehitable politely, then grins at the empty plate on her knee, "Mehitable's chittlins is purest and best of any in this whole Cape Fear country. They is most tasty as possum gravy."

Truletta Spoon, belle of chittlin struts for the past two seasons back, sits beside Aunt Orianna. Truletta is wearing a bright yellow cotton dress, which goes well with her russet skin. A wide red belt encircles her slim waist. Red slippers are dyed with "sto-bought" colors.

"My Granny says chittlin dinner sets better iffen a mess of collards and green vinegar pepper goes long with. I likes mine seasoned with red pepper. I have eat sweet taters and biscuit served at strut suppers, but my fambly likes to refresh our hawg meat with corn pone."

"Does you cut yo chittlins afore they is cooked, Auntie?" Mehitable asks respectfully, "or does you cook 'em before you cuts 'em?"

"I cooks 'em whole, honey, and cuts 'em after. After we takes the intrils from the hawg, I rids* 'em and empties the waste in a big ol hole dug in my yawd. I gits back to where there is water aplenty, and I fills them chittlins full, and rinses 'em up and down, up and down." Aunt Orianna motions with her skinny arms, and makes a sucking noise with her lips to imitate the water washing through.

---

* Cleans

"My Granny soaks 'em in clean cold water without salt not less than four to six hour, then she soak 'em in salt water from twelve to fourteen hour. My Granny turn her chittlins on a switch."*

Truletta shuffles her feet self-consciously. "I knows hawgs is moon-killed."

"Everybody know that, honey. Hawg meat aint fitten to eat if it aint killed either three days afore or after moon turns. Grease will all fry out iffen you kills a hawg on too ol a moon. Same's a body must mind not to pity no hawg at butcherin, lessen it die hard."

The women remove the table cloths and the men pitch in, moving chairs back against the walls and taking down the tables, which are carried outside the cabin. While the house is cleared for the dancing, jugs of cider are brought out and guests are served from tin cups.

The banjo boys are tuning up, taking much time in the process, while the guests fret for the fun to begin. After a few preliminary flourishes the musicians swing into the rapid tempo of "Left Footed Shoo Round." The strut is on.

Hands clap softly, and bodies sway back and forth with the music. Men move toward the women, inviting partners. The leader, standing by the banjo boys, calls out in a sing-song tenor:

> "Ketch you partner by the arm
> Swing her round, 'twont do no harm."

Into the center of the floor jumps Carter Dunlap, a town Negro who never misses a strut. Dunlap is dressed in a tightly fitting suit of black and grey checks, padded substantially at the shoulders. His light tan shoes are well polished. Shirt and tie are checked, but of lighter tones than the suit.

With a glass of cider in each hand, and a third balanced on the top of his head, Carter begins shifting his feet on the floor. At first the tan shoes move but slightly. Then, as the banjoists swing into "Guina Walk," Carter moves with more energy. He slides one foot forward and draws up with the other. Round he spins, faster and faster, now squatting, now

---

* Negro method of turning chitterlings inside out.

leaping toward the rafters. Sometimes the glass on his head teeters precariously, but he finishes up without spilling a drop, a feat that draws a round of noisy applause.

Moonstone Peeley gives a demonstration of "cutting the buck," then turning, he takes Truletta Spoon in his arms and swings her dizzily in the middle of the room. Couples vie with each other in cutting didos. Some of the men lift their partners off their feet and whirl them rapidly around.

On goes the dance, the banjos strumming faster and faster. The hearth fires blaze brightly, and soon the dancers are perspiring freely. Men take off their coats and throw them over chairs. Sweat flows from cheek and jowl; shirts become wet through. The women mop their faces with damp handkerchiefs. The floor boards creak, the lanterns bob up and down. More tunes and more dances until past midnight, when the strut breaks up.

Mehitable and Doak stand at the door, bidding their guests goodnight.

"Sho glad everything went off good and social and no trouble."

"No use fightin like they done over to Uless Sherman's. Reckon Uless ever goin to get outten the jailhouse?"

"Caint rightly say. 'Tween chittlins, strut, and chin music,* I's ready to go to roost."

"Was sure a tasty feast, sister. Must have took a lot of cawn to fatten yall's pig-tail."

"Glad it set well. See you at meetin."

The slim crescent moon rides high behind the slender trunks of spindly pines. Bare gourd-vines on the cabin porch are dimly etched in the pale light. Across the river a hound bays. Mehitable and Doak turn to enter the cabin.

"Les let the dishes res till mornin come," sighs Mehitable.

---

* Talking

3

The Harvest Queen

AGRICULTURAL FAIRS

Rocky Ford Melon Day
from the Colorado Office

Colorado has several unique agricultural festivals, of which Melon Day, held at Rocky Ford during September each year, is the most noted as well as the oldest, dating back to 1878. The festival was originated by Senator George W. Swink, an agricultural pioneer of the Arkansas Valley, who did more for the development of that region than any other individual.

In the early history of Melon Day the entire event was handled by Swink but the celebration soon grew in popularity and attendance to a point where it became more than a one-man affair. It was Swink's idea of advertising the adaptability of the Rocky Ford section for melon growing that prompted him to announce that melons would be given away on a certain September day in 1878 at Rocky Ford.

The country then being very thinly settled, the crowd was quite small, not more than twenty-five people being present. Those people were mostly from La Junta coming in a Santa Fe caboose. Swink cut the melons on the grain door of a box-car. Only one wagon-load was required to feed the crowd and give them all they wanted to carry home.

In 1879 Mr. Swink gave the same invitation and the crowd disposed of a wagon-load of melons—in 1880 the crowd increased to 100 and consumed two wagon-loads of melons. In 1881 there was another increase.

That year a table was built, twelve feet long and the melon supply correspondingly increased.

The same growth of attendance was noted in 1882, the pile of melons steadily growing, so that all wants were supplied. During these years the feast was served in the old Swink store adjoining the Santa Fe track.

In 1883 there was another marked increase in the crowds, and the table for melons was transferred to the grove north of the town. The feast of melons was accompanied by a basket picnic, a table being built separate from the melon table. On this occasion, the ladies spread a dinner for the visitors. Adjacent to the tables was a display of plums, grapes and apples, which were given to the crowd before the day was ended. This was the beginning of the now celebrated Rock-Ford fairs of the Arkansas Valley Fair Association.

The 61st annual fair held in 1938 drew a crowd large enough to do away with 25,000 watermelons. Seven bands and delegates from many Southeastern Colorado communities saw Governor Teller Ammons cut

Entrance to the county fair, San Augustine, Texas, April 1939.
(Russell Lee)

the first melon and vie with Warden Roy Best of the Colorado State Prison in a calf roping contest. The crowd was estimated as the largest in 15 years, and 40% larger than last year.

There were stock exhibits, as well as farm produce, culinary experts and demonstrations, a carnival provided rides and entertainment of various kinds for the visitors. The day ended with a dance, in which old and young participated.

The year 1941 repeated the success of 1940. Governor Ralph L. Carr pulled a huge, juicy melon from a pile of prize watermelons, and officially launched Watermelon Day. After the governor secured his watermelon, a free-for-all dash was made by visitors, as they grabbed for the melons. No one went hungry, because thousands of melons were given away.

Melon day will always be celebrated on the first Thursday of September for the reason that Senator Swink donated 80 acres of his old timber claim to the Otero County Fair Association for use as fair grounds. There is a provision in the deed specifying that Melon Day must be observed annually on the date mentioned, otherwise the property will revert to the Swink estate.

★   ★   ★   ★   ★

It just may be possible that Senator Swink's melon celebration is more appreciated in Rocky Ford than ever before.

"It keeps our town going," a resident told a reporter for the local newspaper, the *Pueblo Chieftain*. "It's bad enough we have to shop out of town."

Rocky Ford is a very quiet little hamlet out on Highway 50, in the southeastern part of the state, where the Great Plains peters out before crashing into the Rocky Mountains. It's a town where the stores along Main Street have generally thrown in the towel against the Wal-Mart Super Center eight miles away. It's pretty, though, in that low-slung, big sky sort of way, peaceful most days because there really isn't a whole lot going on.

Except for a few days in mid-August, that is, when the streets tingle with bells and music from the fairground on Swink's old timber claim. Excitement sparks the air from morning to night, triggered by the rodeo broncos and the tractor pulls, the churn of derby cars, and the screams and shouts from amusement rides. Prized farm animals are paraded about and the hot prairie wind carries the scent of popcorn, fried dough, and char-broiled meat—a seductive, delectable perfume.

The fairground's gates open just about the time parents are near to losing their minds with the endlessly blazing midsummer days. Their kids have saved their pennies and nickels through the year and are chomping at the bit to get at all the rides and games. The one annual dark cloud on the long horizon of the Rocky Ford Fair is whether the bigger Colorado State Fair that happens around the same time in nearby Pueblo will affect attendance. But local residents are loyal—especially since the state fair is an hour west on the highway, charges a lot more, and has longer lines. There may be some work to be done around the town's fairground: A hard winter has damaged the 4-H Exhibit Hall and the adobe horse stalls built by WPA workers in 1936 are in desperate need of immediate repairs. But everything else—from the grandstands and its splendid dirt track, to the twinkling beer garden—is spiffed-up and shimmering when the gates open. Saturday is Melon Day, and a huge pile of the locally grown, luscious melons materialize early, starting a frenzy with children climbing over the green, (literally) rolling hill to find the best one they can carry down to their parents.

There's testimony far and wide that the Arkansas Valley Fair is great and I wish I could report that I was there for it. But that's one of the insurmountable problems of being a lone writer instead of part of a nationwide crop. When mid-August came around, I was actually about five hundred miles away at another watermelon festival in Rush Springs, Oklahoma. Why? Well, I got the impression from my initial research that the Arkansas Valley Fair had grown quite a bit, to the point that it no longer resembled the rural celebration the federal writers had written about. I thought it'd be more interesting, instead, if I found a festival whose spirit was more in keeping with the *America Eats!* piece, a festival that was simply about watermelons and the local farmers, and that seemed more like Rush Springs than Rocky Ford.

Granted, this was all a leap of faith, especially since the entry for the Rush Springs festival in *America Eats!* reads in its entirety, "Annual watermelon festivals are held at Lamont and Rush Springs, Okla., in August. Plenty of free watermelon is served to all. Melons furnished by raisers in the community."

Nevertheless, I drove to Rush Springs and found exactly what I had hoped. It's a little town of about thirteen hundred souls, sixty miles or so south of Oklahoma City, down a two-lane highway through prairies that refuse to lie flat. Turning into a smaller road yet and, over grassy train tracks, trucks piled high with watermelons begin to appear. According to local lore, there is a long history of growing the fruit in these parts, stemming back to the Wichita Indians. Beside the trucks are makeshift fruit stands—nothing more than a couple of sawhorses holding up a plank of wood—where the melons are sold, mostly whole but a few giant ones are cut in half to show inside the gleaming fruit as bright red as a valentine heart. Even the Rush Springs fire company has a truckload of watermelons for sale at the station house in the center of town, where the line of cars snakes slowly forward toward the fairground. Traffic is being directed by the local National Guard unit who are invariably as polite as can be but completely serious about what they are doing and what they think others should be doing. It's hot; good Lord, is it hot in Oklahoma in August! and as dry as a stripped wishbone. People don't so much walk as slowly shuffle across the open pasture toward the drooping trees of the fairground. The shade only marginally tames the heat. But found beneath the trees is cool water burbling out of a pipe into a cement trough, part of the natural springs that gave the town its name. It is sweet and free for the gulping—though perhaps not as filtered as intestines from other parts of the country are used to. The water is guarded by a small metal sign: TRUST IN THE LIVING GOD WHO GIVETH US RICHLY ALL THINGS TO ENJOY, 1 TIM. 67.

It's estimated that close to thirty thousand people will wander through the fairground during the one-day festival, with opening events occurring at nine A.M. and lasting well past seven P.M. That number may be optimistic. At close to noon, only a couple hundred people are milling about the grounds, beneath the baking metal roof of the stage and in the long hut where the prized watermelons are kept. There are a few more, if you count the kids and their parents hopping on and off the small collection of amusement rides cooking in the open field, and another hardy bunch wandering slowly between the booths of local artisans scattered along the little dirt path leading up the hill to the town's cemetery. Everyone, though, is having a good time.

The prized watermelons are presented in an open-ended hall. It has not been a great year for watermelons: too hot and dry, making the melons mature too early. This explains why only ten local farmers had entered their watermelons for judging, and the winner is just 135 pounds; the biggest ever in the festival was 146 pounds in 2004. There are Royal Sweet, Cobb Gem, Jubilee, Black Diamond, Tendersweet, and Orange Glow varieties on display and all, to the novices eyes at least, look like winners. People gravely note the watermelons' beauty as they slowly and solemnly file past as if the melons are lying in state.

Which is more than you can say about the pictures of former Watermelon Queens that hang above the melons. They draw some harsh fashion criticism from women who remember those times, and decidedly abusive opinions from teenagers who believe that they, in their own time, will never, ever, look so dopey. The young girls seem most concerned about hairstyles, favoring the '90s, by which time official beauty pageant glamour had been so perfected as to strip the individual queens of any personal style, making them indistinguishable from one another: one leg forward, torso quarter turned, wearing a strapless sequined dress, with blonde hair (they're *all* blondes) piled up and back. The boys dwell on more earthy speculations, making low-voiced jocular decisions about who would have been, in a fashion, the friendliest toward them, completely unaware of how lucky they are there were never any Watermelon Kings.

The queens stretch back to 1940, when the festival was begun by the local Lions Club on what was then the grounds of the Rush Springs Civilian Conservation Corp (CCC) camp. The CCC was another WPA project that put young men to work improving farmland and forests for thirty dollars a month—twenty-five dollars of which was sent home, while the government picked up all their living, educational, and medical expenses. (IT WOULD BE DIFFICULT FOR A YOUNG MAN NOT TO HAVE BENEFITTED FROM THIS EXPERIENCE, reads the monument at the top of the hill erected by alumni of the camp on May 2, 1987.) In 1940, there was a lot of civic pride in the town having survived the Great Depression, and the Lions Club determined that it would be a good thing to celebrate the local farmers and their crop with a festival. Four thousand people are said to have attended the first festival, whose highlights were the free watermelon served that night and choosing Ada Mae Tims to be the Watermelon Queen. She was a genuine beauty, as were most of her fellow queens in the 1940s and '50s: their formal pictures depict them as sweet and demure farm girls. By the early '60s, the queens are striking more sassy poses, long haired and showing some leg as they bite into watermelon slices with youthful abandon. Then the bad-hair decades begin—the late '70s and '80s, when clearly women lost their minds over waves upon waves of *big*, rolling, frizzy hair.

Some of these beauty queens are now at the festival with their children and at least one of them is standing with her own mother before the prized

Orange Glow watermelons over which her picture hangs. The younger woman seems absolutely lost in the contemplation of her former self—blue satin dress with puffy off-the-shoulder sleeves, huge head of brown hair sticking almost straight out from around her face. She has her hair cut short now. It's plastered in the heat into a little red scrunchy at the back of her head, and her neat white T-shirt is tucked into a short white denim skirt. Her young daughter shakes the frame of her stroller—she wants out. The woman's mother says: "We really ought to get them a new picture to hang. That one's faded." The former beauty queen responds in a flat voice, "Uh-huh," and wheels her child out of the building, to find something to eat.

The best thing to drink at the watermelon festival is "Okie Old Time Root Beer." A tubful of ice-cold brown bottles with cork stoppers are for sale and the couple who brew the root beer offer free samples, which is good because this is not your everyday store-bought-in-a-can root beer. It's slightly bitter, like the herbs used in making fresh root beer: wintergreen, sarsaparilla, ginger. A woman emerges from a trailer with more bottles in her hands. She seems whittled down to her essence, with a hard, thin face made starker by her short hair combed straight back across her head. A half-smoked cigarette clings precariously to her lips. Her husband, smaller in stature than she and a little meatier—but not by much—is behind the cash box, counting out change for a customer. She takes the box from him and begins to make order of the folded and crumpled dollar bills. Where do they make their root beer, I ask. She nods her head back toward the trailer.

"In there," she replies, keeping the cigarette between her lips. Her eyes narrow with the smoke or the heat or the impertinent nature of the question. "Why?"

Her tone of voice doesn't welcome follow-up questions but one is ventured anyway: does she use root beer extract or the fresh herbs?

"Extract?" she repeats in a disdainful spit, and her husband, appearing a little more forgiving, shrugs his shoulders and lets a smile flirt briefly across his lips as he collects another dollar from a customer.

There's catfish—locally caught and fried by the Boy Scout master; and barbecued pork sandwiches offered by a store owner in town. Some people have brought picnic bags and coolers from home and have spread blankets out on the hillside under the trees near the cemetery's fence. Plastic bowls filled with fried chicken and pasta salad, a few paper-wrapped sandwiches, and bags of chips are plentiful on the blankets. By far, though, the most popular thing to eat at the festival is a chili pie, a corn shell folded up to fashion a bowl, then filled with layers of beef chili, cheese, lettuce, and sauce that's made at a truck parked down by the amusement rides.

Come lunchtime, people sit on the hot metal benches under the aluminum roof of the stage and fork through their chili bowls as they watch the great event of the day unfold: the annual watermelon seed–spitting contest. This year's queen is an attractive, big-boned blonde, prettier in person than in her picture and dressed in a flirty watermelon-printed sundress for the occasion. She is a very good sport about everything she is asked to do, including opening the seed-spitting contest. Les Dawson, the very genial MC of the event, explains the rules: you must stand behind the starting line ("touching, crossing, or letting your false teeth fly out" are grounds for automatic disqualification); the seed must land inside the designated fairway (which includes off the backside of the stage if the judges can find it); and the judge's decisions are final. In case of a tie, Les says, a spit-off will be held.

The queen is handed three seeds. She throws her head way back and right off the bat shoots 35 feet, a pretty good distance, which is not eclipsed until the teenage boys step up. The winner in their age group goes 8 feet farther. Last year's overall champion fizzles out at 39.6 feet and the winner comes in at 63 feet—clear off the end of the stage and almost to the fence by the spring. After each spit is launched and the distance measured, the stage is swept clean with a big broom and Les imparts a few encouraging words to the contestant standing at the line. The audience keeps a steady rooting of their own going, as a sense of suspense pervades the event.

"It's over here, Les," a woman calls out as a seed spins off the stage.

"We got a runner!" one of the judges yells. Everyone cranes their necks, hands full of chili bowls and water bottles and sweaty babies, to see just where the seed landed.

"Figures it was Joe's," Les says, kidding the spitter—the town's democratic state representative, Joe Dorman. Dorman, who is in his late thirties, is dressed for the occasion in a baggy T-shirt and even baggier cargo shorts hanging somewhat capriciously from his thick waist. After his last seed, Dorman, who was raised in Rush Springs, receives some kind words from Les about all the good work he's doing for the district and Dorman actually seems to blush.

There are quite a few other politicians at the festival; the governor has promised he'll stop by later that night. For now, there's the governor's campaign manager, the state insurance commissioner, and a Republican

state representative, all of whom are competent but by no means champion spitters (the queen beat them all). The people seem to know their
elected officials enough so as to keep a familiar, slightly teasing, banter going between them that is rare in more populated areas of the country. For
the politicians' parts, Rush Springs isn't just a stop on a long day of cam-
paigning. They stay on at the watermelon festival not only to see who the
seed-spitting winner is but to participate in whatever else is happening.

That would mean listening to the music—everything from bluegrass
to gospel, all of it pretty fine. Some people, not many but some, take the
opportunity to wander up to the cemetery and visit for a while. But everyone, at one time or another—and often several times throughout the
day—takes it upon him- or herself to stand in line for a hunk of watermelon. For fifty cents, each person gets about a quarter, more or less, of a
whole melon. Watermelon like this is very hard to find in local markets, at
least in markets in the Northern states. For one thing, they're full of seeds,
something you realize you have sorely missed from the ubiquitously
seedless—and increasingly tasteless—variety that has taken over markets
everywhere. Rush Springs' melons are at the peak of ripeness, and the
flesh is dense, meaty, and succulent, bracingly sweet and cool. The custom
of the festival is to take your chunk over to an open pavilion where rows of
tall wooden counters have been knocked together, and sprinkle the flesh
with a lot of salt. Beyond an odd pleasantry to neighbors and kin, no one
talks much as they lean over the counters and concentrate on the sheer
goodness before them, hungrily scooping out lumps of melon, unable, it
seems, to get enough. Seeds are spit on the ground or daintily into napkins, and chins are wiped clean of the juices with the back of hands. Nearly
everyone finishes their slices down to a thin crescent of rind, then they
toss it over the side of a Dumpster beside the pavilion, where it lands with
a satisfying thud on top of many other rinds and momentarily disturbs the
fat bees circling lazily over the sweet mound.

Thoughts from Our Country Fairs

The other reason I decided to head to Rush Springs instead of Rocky
Ford was because Oklahoma would put me in the vicinity of some of the
great midwestern country fairs. A piece from the Michigan office caught
my attention with this small description of such fairs:

The women came in for their share of attention by presenting handiwork. Jellies and jams, apple butter, pickles and large jars of canned fruits were exhibited before critical neighbors, who knew from experience just how a pickle should be placed in a jar to avoid display of a white spot and who knew how to select a cucumber in order to bring out its best qualities.

The men took this occasion to show off the results of their husbandry. Well-selected potatoes—not a little one in an entire sack—carefully graded apples, corn, both dry for stock feed or ground into meal, the biggest squashes they grew the summer before, and a variety of other commodities that would excite the envy of a modern storekeeper were all there on exhibition for the edification of their neighbors.

I wanted to see the modern competitions and maybe sniff out what was cooking these days on family farms. Country fairs used to be the place where farm families would first hear of, or see, such wondrous things as mechanical threshers, electric lights, antibiotics, vacuum cleaners, moving pictures, even the first silky panties on a vaudeville girlie act. Fairs became so popular that families scheduled their work so they could take time off when they opened. For a few nights or even a couple of weeks, fairs would be the center of the universe for rural people: they were the place to show off the fruits of your labor; to buy and trade livestock; to find or court a sweetheart; to lighten, for a moment, the struggles of a hardscrabble working life.

Most states and counties continue to hold fairs where you will find exactly what the federal writers did: presentations of husbandry and homey culinary skills. Nowadays, though, livestock competitions spawn a healthy business in breeding, at which thousands of dollars in stud fees are at stake. And the homemaking and culinary skills on display carry a heavy scent of nostalgia rather than the common everyday necessities they once celebrated.

At all the fairs I attended—and I ended up at many of them straight across the Midwest—I certainly ate a lot, but I don't think any of it was a reflection of cooking in a modern farmhouse. After a few weeks of traveling from one fairground to the next, the exhibition halls filled with prized tomatoes, pumpkins, gingerbread houses, and Spam casseroles all began to look the same. States became distinguished in my mind by their enormous cows sculptured out of butter (loved the sloe-eyed Illinois

A woman before her prized preserves, Gonzales County Fair, Gonzales, Texas, November 1939. (Russell Lee)

rendition; was perplexed by Iowa's scrawny-rib version). I got to milk a very forgiving cow, and hooted and hollered for a very sweet spotted pig who took to nibbling at my sneakers through the show corral fence while waiting for her blue ribbon ("light on her feet and so happy to be here," exclaimed the judge as he handed the ribbon to the pig's owner, a proudly shy eight-year-old girl). A week in, I was a sworn admirer of how many beautiful breeds of chickens there are in the world, and found myself being able to accurately distinguish among different kinds of cows and pigs out grazing in the fields I passed.

I steered clear of much of the fair food. This was made easy by a strapping young man holding a variety tray filled with fried Twinkies, Snickers bars, and peanut butter cups. His direct words were, "Yo, this sucks ass, man," then he proceeded to impart a definitive critique on all the offerings. If a kid with a cast-iron stomach feels this way, it's good enough for me. Besides, there were other things to eat—sweet cobs of roasted corn and steak, pork, and lamb chops, lightly salted and grilled just right, usually by aproned members of the Beef, Pork, or Lamb councils.

In the various culinary halls, canned fruits and vegetables; shelves of jams and preserves; layered cakes, pies, and cookies were exhibited in display cases as if they were museum pieces from another era—made for competing but not for regular eating. The 4-H and Future Farmers of America clubs continue to teach their young members the fine art of canning and jam-making, and many folks perfect their skills throughout the year to be able to vie for a cherished ribbon. Still, it is not apparent that any of this cooking is done as it used to be—as an important part of the care and feeding of a family. In fact, what was consistent at all the fairs was a great lament for the general demise of home cooking. Hurbert Schmiedu, an old-fashioned master chef demonstrating how to make stuffed deviled eggs at the Indiana State Fair, stopped what he was doing in mid-egg to lean across the counter and impart an impassioned plea.

"It's a crime what's going on in this country that we do not teach our children how to cook for themselves anymore. Our dishes are disappearing because you ladies don't take the time to pass them on."

A few days later, I met Leisa Ely at the Iowa State Fair while waiting for the "Famous Dave's BBQ sauce" competition to be decided. Her mother, Marjorie Rodgers, eventually came in second place with a recipe that managed to be a successful marriage of blackberries and garlic, among other ingredients. Marjorie, herself, who's in her late seventies, wasn't up to pushing through the fair's crowds and was out in the car waiting to hear the results.

"She's a fabulous cook. Has a meatloaf to die for," her daughter said and rolled her eyes heavenward. "My parents had a farm until they sold it a little ways back. Every holiday, Mom would make chicken and noodles—even the noodles were homemade."

"Does she still make them?" I asked.

"Oh, no."

"What about you?"

"Well, I know how. I'm a single mother and I work, so . . ." she said, her voice trailing off in a small laugh. "I'm just glad my son had a chance to experience meals made like that with everything coming from the farm. Mom's even taught him some of her recipes and they've competed together at the fair. It's good he can cook for himself because, if you know how, it's easier to get a good fresh dinner on the table at night. Some of my friends don't cook at all anymore because they're working so much. They miss doing it and eating dinner with their families, but there's nothing they can do with how things are these days. And that's sad."

When she cooks, I asked, what kind of things does she make?

"Regular things, you know. I'm part of a gourmet club where each month my friends and I get together at one of our houses and make a special meal or maybe just spaghetti. We try to cook healthy. No one uses bacon grease or lard anymore, and we don't use as much sugar because there's so much diabetes."

There's so much, in fact, that the fairs have included cooking for the illness as a new culinary category, as if a diabetic layer cake is something to crow about.

The closest I came to home-cooked farm food was at a little restaurant out on Route 36 in Bainbridge, Indiana, called the BonTon Café. The cook in back was once actually a farm wife before the land was sold, and the menu reflected many of her dishes—homemade pies and casseroles being a speciality. Out in front, a boisterous bunch of old farmers with heavily creased sunburned necks, dressed in baseball hats and overalls, held court at the center table over plates of another house speciality: sausage gravy and biscuits. This dish may be purchased most anywhere across the United States these days, not just south of the Mason-Dixon Line, where it originated as a cheap meal to get you through the day. What you are usually served now is a plop of white paste passing itself off as a sauce, made lumpy by greasy sausage bits congealing over a biscuit that can surely break a window. To understand how this dish became so beloved, you have to eat it at the BonTon, where the sauce was light, the sausage flavorful and not greasy at all. The biscuits were fluffy and held their own under the gravy. A truly first-rate delicacy more than capable of getting you through the morning in fine style.

The fact is, the kind of farm cooking that lives on in our collective conscious as forming part of the backbone of our culinary heritage—and here, I'm thinking of chicken and dumplings or noodles, pot roast and ham loafs, serving bowls brimming with vegetables and fruits—freshly picked or from a tightly sealed canning jar—is rare these days. Farming, especially for the remaining family farmers left out there, is extremely labor intensive. The women who used to prepare all these wondrous, though time-consuming, meals are often busy now with a job in town that helps support the farm and their family. Kitchen gardens may still be planted but they are not the mainstay of the year's groceries. Instead of all the added work required to can and preserve, the pantries in many farm kitchens are stocked with more convenient and cheaper supplies

Visitors at the Gonzales County Fair, Gonzales, Texas,
November 1939. (Russell Lee)

from superstores, such as Wal-Mart and Sam's Club, which are in almost every farming community. Vegetables and fruits—even the odd potted meats—are still being put up in Ball jars but it has become more of a craft, a boutique industry that taps into our inclination for sentimental remembrance of a supposedly simpler era. And that's what attending our great country fairs feels like, as well: they're a nostalgic trip to a time when our family-farm heritage was more central to all our lives.

The Farmhouse Cellar
by (Mrs.) Mabel G. Hall, Maine Office

It is a favored guest who is invited by the housewife to inspect the farm-house cellar; no other member of the family may either issue the invitation to conduct the tour. The man of the house will go no farther than

"Mother, how about showing Martha and John your preserves?" If Martha is held in sufficient esteem the trip will be undertaken but John can expect that those hidden precincts are not for his eyes. Mother will find the easy excuse of being too busy if she thinks the evidence of her season's work will not be appreciated. More often the trip is made with a neighbor's child to relieve the monotony of a stormy afternoon. Going down the narrow and steep rough wooden stairs the housewife leads with lighted lantern, thinking of tired hot summer afternoons, kitchen sticky with syrup, and berry-stained hands, and of the boxes of soil with tomato and celery seeds which must be planted by late January and kept on the window sills till sundown and then put on the shelf behind the stove, high enough so that the dog won't get into them. The visitor, groping on the stairs, is greeted by the fragrant scent of apples. As she gets to the hard earthen cellar floor she sees great quantities of clean-skinned potatoes spread on a section of wooden flooring; these were left on boards outside the bulkhead door and covered with canvas at night until they were thoroughly dry and then taken down to the cool cellar. Off to one side are perhaps fifty dark green Hubbard squash and above them a swing shelf of small yellow sugar pumpkins. Toward the wall are dozens of barrels of apples, some green, some red, and the late winter russets. On the other side are barrels of cabbages, turnips, and carrots. As progress is made across the cellar with its single electric bulb in the ceiling, the stores of preserves, jellies and pickles are come upon unexpectedly. The lantern was brought along to furnish sufficient light to read the labels. The guide may have told from which trees certain barrels of apples were gathered, but she feels no particular interest in the vegetables which after all were harvested by the men folks. But when she shows her 2-quart jars of rhubarb, blueberries, mincemeat, and canned chicken and beef, and leads on past the quart jars of damson plums, strawberries, both cultivated and wild, raspberries and cherries, to the dozens of half-pint jars of greenish gooseberries and red currants and an entire cupboard of assorted jellies in glass, she tells of the locations and circumstances under which nearly every fruit and berry was picked by her own hands and the visitor needs only to supply the expected "ohs" and "ahs." And the guest will not come upstairs empty-handed.

★   ★   ★   ★   ★

Threshing hands eating dinner, Central Ohio, August 1938. (Ben Shahn)

Recipes

Root Beer

There are two ways to get the flavor of root beer—using root beer extract or herbs. The problem with using herbs is that the most essential ingredient, the plant that really gives the full taste, is sassafras root and its sale has been outlawed by the government since 1930, when it was discovered to be a carcinogen. The following recipe, from the experts at www.rootbeer.org, presents the correct proportions of natural ingredients.

> Approximately 2 ounces juniper berries
> Approximately 2 ounces fresh sassafras roots
> Approximately 1 ounce dandelion root
> 2 ounces fresh or dried wintergreen leaves
> 1 ounce ginger root
> 8 quarts boiling water

Tie the herbs up in a cheesecloth and steep in the water as for tea.

The following is a basic recipe using extract from Dr. David Fankhauser's Making Rootbeer at Home Web page: http://biology.clc.uc .edu/fankhauser/Cheese/ROOTBEER_Jn0.htm. If you've managed to track down sassafras and have succeeded in making a strong enough root beer–tasting tea, then substitute it for the extract measurement.

SPECIAL EQUIPMENT:

2 clean liter-size soft drink bottles with cap (or an equivalent
    made of glass or pottery, with a tight-fitting cork)
Funnel

INGREDIENTS:

1 cup sugar
¼ teaspoon powdered baker's yeast (fresh and active)
2 tablespoons root beer extract (Zatarains's, Hires, etc., avail-
    able at beer-making supply stores)
Water

In one of the bottles, combine the sugar and the yeast. Shake the bottle to mix together.

Add the extract, then fill the bottle halfway with water. Swirl the bottle to dissolve the ingredients. You'll get a thick, pastelike substance. Fill the bottle the rest of the way, leaving about an inch space at the top. Securely screw on the cap or stop with the cork and invert the bottle a couple of times to thoroughly dissolve the ingredients.

Leave the bottle at room temperature for about 3 or 4 days (no longer, or it may explode!). Move it to a cool place (below 65°F) or refrigerate overnight. The brew will last, refrigerated, for about a week.

Biscuits and Sausage Gravy

BISCUITS:

2¼ cups all-purpose flour
1 teaspoon sugar
2 teaspoons baking powder
½ teaspoon baking soda

¾ teaspoon salt
3 tablespoons unsalted butter, chilled, cut into pieces
⅓ cup vegetable shortening, chilled, cut into pieces
¾ cup buttermilk

GRAVY:
1 pound pork sausage
3 tablespoons all-purpose flour
2 cups hot milk
⅛ teaspoon hot pepper sauce (optional)

Preheat the oven to 450°F.

PREPARE THE BISCUITS:
Combine the dry ingredients in a food processor or mixing bowl. Strew the butter and shortening pieces over the flour mixture and blend in quickly (if you're using a processor, pulse four or five times; if you're using your hands, use just your fingertips and lightly, but thoroughly, mix the fats into the flour) until the mixture resembles coarse meal.

Add the buttermilk. Stir lightly until the mixture is moistened and begins to form a ball. Transfer to a lightly floured work surface. Knead lightly, then roll the dough to ½-inch thickness. With a cookie cutter or the rim of a glass, cut into 2-inch disks. Arrange on a lightly oiled baking sheet so that biscuits are not touching. Bake about 12 to 16 minutes, or until the biscuits have risen and are golden.

MAKE THE GRAVY WHILE THE BISCUITS ARE BAKING:
Cook the sausage in a heavy nonstick skillet over medium high heat until cooked through, stirring frequently to break up meat into small bits. Using a slotted spoon, transfer the meat to paper towels or newspaper (works better). Press to remove as much grease as possible from the sausage. Transfer to a small bowl and set aside.

Discard all but 3 tablespoons of the pan drippings. Return the skillet to medium heat. Sprinkle the flour into the drippings and whisk until the flour is lightly browned. Whisk in the milk (make sure the milk is heated just to boil—this will make the sauce smooth). Increase the heat to medium-high and stir constantly until the sauce begins to thicken. Stir the sausage into the gravy and simmer for 1 to 2 minutes until heated through. Season with salt and pepper to taste.

To serve: Place a biscuit or two on a plate and cover them with the gravy. Serve with the hot pepper sauce on the side. Serves 4.

Pickled Watermelon Rinds

> 3 pounds watermelon rinds, clean of all flesh, sliced or cubed
> 5 cups sugar
> 2 cups cider vinegar
> 1 cup cold water
> 1 tablespoon whole cloves
> 1 tablespoon whole allspice
> 1 tablespoon broken-up cinnamon stick
> 1 whole lemon sliced

Place the rinds in a large glass bowl and cover them with salted water (about 2 tablespoons salt per 1 quart water). Let stand overnight.

Drain the rinds, place in a large saucepan or stockpot, and cover with fresh water (don't rinse!). Bring the water to a boil, then lower the flame to a simmer and cook until the rinds are tender (a fork should be able to pierce the flesh with just a small bit of resistence). Drain.

Combine the sugar, vinegar, and cup of cold water in the pot used to cook the rinds. Tie the spices together in a small cheesecloth and add to the sugar water. Add the lemon. Bring to a boil and cook for 5 minutes. Add the rinds and cook until they're transparent, about 45 minutes.

Pack the rinds into hot, sterilized jars and add enough of the syrup to cover them (leave a little space at the top). Seal the jars tight. Set aside for 6 to 8 weeks in a cold, dark place. The rinds should keep for about 8 months.

★　　★　　★　　★　　★　　★　　★　　★　　★　　★

Threshers' Dinner
by Iola Thomas, Iowa Office

I

"Well, Hilda, we can expect threshers in 'bout four days. Anna, you take the broom up to the granary any time now and sweep off the floor." It was a hot August evening after choring time, and my father had just spoken laconically to my mother and me.

"When did you find out threshers was comin', Triggs?" Hilda asked, her hands on her hips. We knew that he had not been off the place for half a day.

"Oh, Arch MacLaren stopped just before dinner this morning," my father said indifferently. "He's runnin' the machine on the outfit this year."

"Trigg Ross," Hilda retorted, emphasizing each word as she spoke, "do you know—will you ever know—how much work it takes to clean this house and get food ready for threshers? If you'd told me this mornin' I could of got in half a day's work toward it."

It was always the same every year. Trigg would keep it to himself that threshers were coming until he had the names of the neighboring men who would help him, and the grain and hay wagons he would need, all firmly fixed in his mind. He had the satisfaction of being ahead of Hilda with his share of the threshing responsibilities. But when the threshers arrived, Hilda would be ready to serve the best loaded table in the neighborhood.

The day before the threshers came, my sister, Myrt, would reach the dusty dishes that were rarely used except for "best company" down from the high cupboard shelves, and we would wash them in hot suds—the hobnailed vinegar cruet catching the sunshine beside the fragile rose-petaled vegetable bowl, a present from Aunt Pauline. Company dishes were needed—and some of the neighbors' dishes, too—before 15 to 25 men and almost that many women and children had been fed at threshers' dinner.

The main purpose of our threshers' meal was to feed the men all they could hold, the secondary purpose (an unwritten household law) was to out-do our neighbors. Compliments about Hilda's ambrosial and palatable dinners swept the countryside. If Hilda concocted a crisp newfangled salad or a novel meat dish for our dinner, the next season every woman in the neighborhood would serve it to her thresher men. Trigg said he never knew it to fail.

Neighboring women were telephoned early and asked if they would help with the cooking, lest they be gaddin' or off to town on threshing day. "If Mrs. Magilly comes to make them scrumptious raisin and lemon pies of hers," Hilda said, "the three little Magillys will have to tag along, and there will be that many more mouths to feed, that many more young ones to let in flies. But that will just have to be, for no one in the neighborhood can make pies like Mrs. Magilly."

The telephone line churred with the weight of words. "Can you bring your big roaster along for the roast beef? That little one of mine won't begin to hold it. And those round cake tins of yours? Because Mrs. Rockrohr just won't make loaf cakes. She's got to have them round and three layers high . . . Mrs. T— had her sister out from town to help with her cakes, but the men said they tasted of bakin' powder."

"Mrs. Fenstermacher will have to come early in the morning on threshing day so she can get noodles made in time for them to dry," Myrt would remind Hilda. With all the women frogging out their arms at their work, I knew it would be impossible for the noodles to dry in the kitchen. But Mrs. Fenstermacher, as certain of her ingenuity as of her noodles, would dry the long, yellow shoestrings spread out on newspapers on the bed downstairs. "No one will be knockin' them," Mrs. Fenstermacher would explain. "And where else would I dry them?"

On the morning of harvesting day, the thresh machine snorted through the big gate, leaving wide, zigzag tracks of dirt torn up in the barnyard. Our brown Leghorns scurried for cover under the barns. Behind the machine came our neighbors—men, women, and children filling the hayracks and grain wagons in which they were riding. The waterboy trotted into the barnyard on his spotted pony with his jug, wrapped and padded with a brown gunny sack. The family dogs, panting behind the wagon of their masters, perked up their ears and stiffened their tails at the sight of each other. Their mistresses reasoned that since no one would be home all day, the dogs might as well come along and get in on a good supply of left-overs from the threshers' table.

Myrt and I were not sorry to see the threshers come. Goodness knows we had worked hard enough preparing for them. But on this particular day I remember we were happy enough to have reason for hippety-hopping. "No more *schmeercase* like we lived off of yesterday," Myrt whispered, and giggled in excitement. "A house full of food and living off of clabber cheese."

"It's 'cause we've been so busy a thinking of food for the whole neighborhood, we've not had time to cook for ourselves," I said. Myrt glared at me for explaining when she already knew.

"Listen," Myrt hissed, and pulled me over to her. "I'm not going to take care of that raft of neighbor kids today, Anna. I'm too big for that now, understand"—Myrt was older than I, fifteen while I was but eleven—"I'm going to spend a lot of time at the machine—and I might go out to the grain field."

"Trigg wouldn't allow you in the grain field," I said, and stuck my tongue out at her because I was sure I was right.

Then the women and children were bearing down upon us with their baskets of kettles and dishes. "Why ain't the machine goin'?" Katie Magilly asked. She was eight.

"Why should it be running and wasting fuel when the men haven't brought up the grain yet?" Myrt responded coldly. "Besides grain can't be pushed through a machine when the wheat and oats have dew on them." I thought Myrt was acting awfully grown up and smart. I took all the girls with me to the orchard to pick up apples, and left her standing in the yard. From the orchard we could hear the pans rattling in the kitchen and the overtone of the women's voices. I put my bare feet over a rotten apple and squashed it. Suddenly a flood of enthusiasm washed my body, and I wished that we would thresh every month of the year.

Jimmie Rockrohr ran back from the water boy near the thresh machine and stuck his head through the fence. "Does your Mom can frogs in her pickles?" he asked hesitantly. The little girls giggled. I knew what he meant. "Of course Hilda has pickled cauliflower in with her cucumbery ones," I answered proudly.

"I bet she hasn't," Jimmie argued.

Then the realization came to me that Jimmie was hungry already. He was conjuring up a trick to get some pickles. Pig, I thought. I turned my back on him and we girls marched into the kitchen.

"Now listen you children," Mrs. Magilly said. "I've got important work to do, and I don't want you under my feet." She had a great pile of dough on the kitchen table, and the muscles on her arm stood out when she pressed down on the rolling pin.

Major, the Fenstermacher dog, stood outside the screen door and looked in with his tongue hanging out. The flies, attracted by the odor of the food, were gathering black on the screen door, and when Gertrude Fenstermacher crawled up to the door and pushed it open with her grimy fist, a cloud of them swarmed into the kitchen, where they hovered about the sweet, spicy raisin pie filling on the range. Hilda came in from the cave with a dishpan full of canned things—jars of blue-yellow corn, saffron-colored peaches, ruby-red plums, scarlet beet pickles, cinnamon-bronzed crabapple pickles, blended green bread-and-butter pickles, and bespeckled red and green Dutch relish. Mrs. Cooper, a renter a half-mile east, hurried to take the heavy jars from Hilda's arms. She picked up a dishcloth and wiped the scum of dust from the jars so that their contents shone brilliant and defined. The pickles looked firm and refreshing. I searched the faces of the little girls. Suddenly I knew we were hungry! I whispered into Hilda's ear. The next moment she was unscrewing the lid from the crabapples with her strong brown hand. We girls gathered around her, and fished with our fingers into the jar for the dark stems of the crabapples. The round juicy fruit, piquant with spice, popped easily into our mouths, and encouraged us to make several trips to the jar.

When Hilda told us we could get down several glasses of jelly from the pantry shelf for the threshers' dinner, I stood up on the high kitchen stool and handed down the jelly to the girls. We had fun holding the red contents up to the light in front of the window and trying to guess which was wild grape and crabapple, or gooseberry, or raspberry. Although the pantry door was closed we could smell the saporous odor of the boiling beef, and I smacked my lips in anticipation of Mrs. Fenstermacher's fat noodles which would be cooked in its rich, shimmering broth. Katie Magilly giggled. Hazel Cooper quickly put her hand over Katie's mouth and hissed "sh-h-h!" Hazel had her ear to the pantry door, and looked full of information—and secretive. She was no older than I, but she knew much, much more. This superior knowledge enabled Hazel to hold the awe of the older children in the district school after she had moved with her family into the neighborhood in March. Usually the children of tenants were "looked down upon" by the pupils whose parents owned their farms and didn't have to move every year, or two.

I climbed down from the stool and tip-toed over to Hazel. "What is it?" I whispered.

"Git yourself to the keyhole, and you'll git an earful," Hazel whispered back with such a loud hiss in my ear that it hurt my head.

I listened.

"What 'ya hear?" Hazel asked, excited and pleased. The other girls looked questioningly. Mamie Fenstermacher, who was only four, wanted out of the pantry because she was too warm.

"Hilda was just telling Mrs. Magilly that she must take it easy, and not work too hard," I whispered. "Hilda said that if she'd known she would have got some other woman to do the pies. What's there strange about that, Hazel?"

"Silly," Hazel said, and pinched me.

"Stop it," I returned loudly. "I think you are the one who's acting silly, and about nothing, too."

"All right, Miss Smarty," Hazel retorted, and made her freckled face homelier than it was. "I suppose you think it's nothin' that Mrs. Magilly is goin' to have a baby."

Katie Magilly began to cry.

"Stop it," Hazel demanded. "Stop it right now, or you won't hear another word."

"I don't want to," Katie said. She stopped crying, but she looked hurt and bewildered.

There was a queer feeling in my stomach. I was eleven and for the first time in my life I knew that a woman was going to have a baby. I stared up at the cupboard shelves. They were bare and desolate because all the dishes were piled on the buffet in the dining room where they would be handy for setting the table. Mamie Fenstermacher pushed open the pantry door, and we filed silently into the kitchen, I felt embarrassed and could not look at Mrs. Magilly. It was very hot in the kitchen and the steam was heavy and suffocating. Mrs. Cooper was swatting flies and chasing them off the food with a clean dish-towel.

"What's come over you young ones?" Hilda asked. She was mixing dough in a large pan for her raised biscuits.

Nobody answered. A hot blast of air shot out for the oven when Mrs. Rockrohr opened the oven door to look at her cakes. Mrs. Fenstermacher had finished with her noodles and was peeling potatoes in the dishpan. She dropped each naked potato with a splash into a water bucket which was over half full of water. Hazel sidled up to the crock full of red kidney-beans ready for a salad, and helped herself to a spoonful of them, eating right out of the tablespoon, Hazel's mother pretended not to see her, but Mrs. Fenstermacher looked ruffled and gave Hazel an austere look.

"Have you been to the machine yet?" Mrs. Magilly asked all of us.

"Not yet," I answered, and did not look at Mrs. Magilly.

"For goodness sakes," Hilda said. "Now when I was a girl threshing was different, but us girls was always in on the whole kapush. I think you girls better run to the thresh machine. Find out how near they're done with the oats, and when they'll be startin' on the wheat. And find out if they're expectin' to stop at twelve sharp for dinner. Tell them we women folks are plannin' big on twelve. And, Anna, if you see Myrt tell her to get a hurry on, and get in here to set the table."

We went outside slamming the screen door behind us. "Now be careful about the machine," Hilda warned.

II

The threshing machine was setting just outside the barnyard because Trigg wanted the straw stack to be near the barn for bedding purposes. From the grain wagon behind the separator we could see the grain shocks in the fields, looking like muffins dropped helter-skelter among the stubbles. The Upper Twenty, where the men were pitching the oats on the hayracks, rolled and dipped, but the Lower Forty in wheat was flat like a long burnt-sugar loaf cake. I stood with my bare feet in the warm oats, while the kernels poured into the wagon spasmodically from the spout of the separator, and thought how beautiful the pasture looked with its green bluegrass, and vervain, and mullein stalks, beside the swarthy grain stubble fields. Only last spring the latter had been a great green river with breathing undulations, but the Fourth of July had come and Trigg was restless at the celebration, afraid the rain would come and beat down the aureous heads before he had cut them.

Some strange young boy was helping feed the separator, finished pitching his load, and came over to the grain wagon. Sweat, running down between his eyebrows, left clean streaks in the dust on his forehead. He took off his large straw hat, and fanned the chaff from his neck. Suddenly his eyes brightened, and putting his finger to his lips he motioned for me to be quiet. Then running on tiptoes, he grabbed up a handful of oats near my feet in the wagon, and thrust them down Myrt's back. Myrt screamed, and giggled ridiculously. She pretended to be mad, but I saw that she was only fooling.

"I shall never speak to you again," Myrt said, and drew herself up tall. I noticed though, that before the day was over she spoke to him many times.

The large separator throbbed and trembled as the canvas feeder carried the sheaves of oats into its hungry ribs. I had to shriek to make the girls hear above its noise. Mamie Fenstermacher was frightened and would not crawl over the barnyard gate. Katie Magilly, feeling very grown-up, said that it was just as well since some of the horses were afraid of the machine and might run away and go over Mamie. Despite the excitement, I would see Katie looking quietly at her feet now and then, and I thought she was pondering about the conversation she had heard in the pantry. Hazel was the most daring of all the girls. She climbed up on the separator although the men forbade her. When they made her get down from it, and she threw oats in their faces, one of the men turned her over his knee and paddled her rather forcefully. Hazel kicked him angrily, and went off with the waterboy and the gang of boys. I was grateful to be rid of her, but after a time she came back to the machine, soaking wet. The boys had pushed her into the water tank at the windmill.

Katie and I helped the man in the grain wagon keep the oats back from the spout. "You're the two best workers on the crew," he told us. We believed him proudly.

When the wagon was filled with oats, Katie and I rode with him to the granary. The Leghorns, having lost all their fear, were picking up the oats beside the wagon tracks at the granary. The oats made a funny little clicking noise in their bills, and their craws stuck out round and solid.

"You girls better chase the chickens away," the man said. "Those fowls will eat themselves to death. Frank Frederick had to operate on twenty of their prize Minorcas, after they threshed, and take the oats out of their craws."

Katie was thoughtful as she chased the Leghorns back toward the chicken house. "A nice man like him wouldn't story," she said, "Fed'ricks must have op'rated."

Suddenly I felt hungry. It was almost noon. The men would be ready for dinner at 12 o'clock. I had promised Hilda to set the wash tubs outside under the maple near the well, and to hang up the heavy coarse towels on the clothes line where they would be handy for the men. Taking Katie by the hand, I ran to the house.

Hilda met me at the door. "Anna," she said, "you will have to be Hilda's big girl today. Hazel says Myrt has gone out to the grain field. You will have to set the table. Now hurry like you never hurried in your life."

I did, while Katie took Mamie and went upstairs to put Gertrude Fenstermacher to sleep. On the long table, which had taken every spare board, I spread the second-best linen tablecloth. It would only reach half-way. I finished out with a red feather-stitched unbleached muslin one. "It looks beau-tee-ful," Hilda said, and never stopped a moment on her trip across the kitchen with seasoning for the vegetables.

There was no need for napkins. The men would wipe their mouths on their big red and blue handkerchiefs, and their dusty overalls would need no protection from a grease spot or two. On one end of the table I set the five willow ware plates, their two flying pigeons worn with much eating and scrubbing at family reunions and "plain home cookin's"; beside them I placed the white kitchen plates and pieced out the twelve places with the faded posy plates of Mrs. Rockrohr's. The drinking glasses ranged from mustard and dried beef ones to the frosted and thumb prints which Hilda had owned for twenty or thirty years. I was careful about setting down the long boat-shaped cut-glass pickle dish and the old sandwich glass cheese plate which had belonged to Grand-mother Ross.

Mrs. Cooper hurried into the dining room, sneezing from the pepper Hilda was shaking into the pots, and hastened out to the kitchen with the white opaque rooster dish to fill it with jelly. The women were whisking about the kitchen. Mrs. Fenstermacher, her face flushed from the heat, was whirling the mashed potatoes around in a large kettle on the back of the range. She stopped suddenly now and then to stir the gravy in the big roaster on the front of the stove. Hilda was chopping cole slaw in a huge wooden bowl, the crisp cabbage and pimentos crunching to bits under her sturdy blows, while she darted back and forth to the screen door, directing Mrs. Rockrohr how to make iced tea in the crock churn in the cave. She looked worried, as though she knew dinner wouldn't be ready on time. Outside on the cement walk, Mrs. Rockrohr was crushing the ice for the tea in a gunny sack with a sledge. Hazel came dashing through the dining room. "Wha-am!" she said. "Sounds like Mrs. Rockrohr is beatin' her husband. Gosh I'm hungry."

"Young lady, you stay out of this kitchen," Mrs. Fenstermacher said loudly. "We're busier than a bird-dog with two tails."

"I hope the men held off a few minutes longer," Hilda said. "Hope they finish out the loads before they come into dinner."

I took the two brown pitchers and ran down to the cave to fill them full of cream for the men's coffee. Mrs. Cooper, who had been down in the cave after cream for the cooking, had spilt some of it on the steps. It looked greasy and yellow like butter.

As I poured the thick, separated cream into the pitchers, the whistle of the thresh machine sounded sharp and shrill. The threshers were ready for dinner. I would have to hurry. Grabbing the pitchers, I hastened up the steps of the cave. But on the fourth step, I skidded, my knees doubled under me, and I slid back to the bottom of the cave, landing on my stomach. The pitchers rolled under the steps and their contents poured out and reached the front of my dress. (I had slipped on the spilt cream!)

Frantically I picked up the muddy pitchers and crawled to the door of the cave, and stood up. My dress felt wet and cold against my stomach. The thresher men by the machine were talking loudly, and were laughing—laughing because they felt good in anticipation of Hilda's dinner. Would dinner be ready? Would they have to wait? I wanted to cry and felt mean toward Myrt for leaving me with so many responsibilities.

The women in the kitchen were almost running now—slicing ripe, crimson tomatoes, making coffee, turning the pans of crusty brown scalloped corn in the oven—but they looked happy. Hilda was chuckling for no apparent reason. She saw me and burst into loud booms of laughter.

"Look at the young one," she said. "Bless her. Run upstairs and change your clothes. Dinner is ready. It will be on the table red-hot by the time the men wash. Run. We'll get the cream."

III

The twelve places at the table were filled with men when Katie, Mamie and I came downstairs. The other threshers were outside drinking their glasses of wine which Hilda had poured for them at the last minute.

Trigg was of Scotch descent. His folks did not serve wine for threshers' dinner. But Hilda was of German people. "Trigg Ross," Hilda had said emphatically, years before, "you tend to your share of the threshin', I'll tend to mine. Who would want to set thresher men down to a table without a glass of something to wash down the dust in their throats?"

I marveled at the way Hilda had found enough chairs for the twelve men when we only had five in the dining room. She had brought in the piano stool from the front room and the homely chairs from the bedrooms. The thresh men had made Mr. Fenstermacher sit near one of the plates of cheese because he was so fond of it. Even after it was passed around, they kept pushing it on his plate.

"How many bushels has the oats been goin' to the acre?" Mr. Cooper, who had been a pitcher in the field, asked Trigg. But I was too busy hankering for one of Hilda's bronze-crusted raised biscuits to hear Trigg's reply.

The men stacked the food on their plates in high pyramids and bulwarks, with as much a knack as they loaded the wagons in the fields. I fancied that they needed sideboards on their plates. Because Mr. Magilly liked noodles so well, the men kept sending the savory dish past him before he had an opportunity to help himself to them. Mrs. Rockrohr and Hilda, who were waiting on the table, finally secured the noodles and helped Mr. Magilly to a generous mound. Everybody was having a good time.

"That's mighty nice straw, a good shiny yellow, those cats are runnin'," a neighboring man told Mr. Rockrohr.

It was fun standing back of the men's chairs. Mr. MacLaren slipped Mamie a plate of biscuit with jelly. Mingling with the luscious and teasing odor of the food was the rancid smell of perspiration clinging to the men. Ceremony was entirely dispensed with; the main thing was to eat and to do plenty of it. The men made admiring comments about the roast beef, the gravy, and the pickles. If they disliked any of the dishes, they made no remarks about them—(tsk) there would be time enough for that at the next place where they threshed.

"Anna," Hilda whispered, "you girls are in the way. Better go outside now. You'll eat at the third table."

The third table seemed hours and afternoons away!

But there was excitement outdoors. Cooper's hound was in a fight with Rockrohr's collie. The latter's nose was torn, and Katie, clutching my hand, began crying at the sight of blood. Jimmie Rockrohr separated the dogs by kicking the hound in the ribs. The thresher men outdoors were teasing Myrt about the young boy she was "hanging around." It made me embarrassed and I wouldn't speak to Myrt. I thought she was acting very unlady-like. She had on her shoes but no stockings and her ankles were chaffed and bleeding where the stubbles in the oat field had scratched them. I wouldn't let myself feel sorry for her.

Mrs. Fenstermacher was out in the corner of the yard picking the feathers from a chicken and dropping them into a barrel. We were going to have fried chicken for supper—and I hadn't even eaten dinner. I could hear the horses beyond the fence in the barnyard, eating their dinner, crunching the new oats which they had helped to thresh. I counted eighteen of them tied around the hayracks, eating their feed from buckets and small wooden boxes set in the wagons. Katie was tired, and we flopped down on our stomachs on the grass and caught a grasshopper, while Mamie sat on the well-curb and paddled her bare feet up and down in a mud puddle.

We had been hungry too long now to care if the minutes passed like long, taut hours. There had been so much noise and excitement all morning; now the whole farm was pausing quietly for the noon. Even Hazel and the boys, who had been playing horseshoes out south of the barn, had stopped, and were sitting in the shade of the cottonwood, their chops in their hands—waiting.

I can remember now that the men of the first table came outdoors, picking their teeth and joking. I remember they sat around in a circle in the shadow and coolness of the porch, and smoked their pipes and talked. But at the time there was only confusion in my mind and the stupidity of the minutes. When the men of the second table had finished eating, I fancy they were whisked up through the hot chimney or dissolved suddenly into kitchen vapor. I was only conscious of the fact that we girls and boys were splashing water on our hands and faces, and sliding into our chairs at the table, revived miraculously—and still hungry. What if the bean salad looked a little dull by this time—the tablecloth spotted? What mattered if the men had eaten up every speck of potatoes? The noodles, and cream peas, and devil's food cake, and a dozen-and-one other things were licking good—and filling.

We heard the whistle blow, the machine start up, and the fading rumble of the hayracks going out to the fields. The women folk came in from the kitchen—smiling, but with all the hurry gone out of them—and sat with us at the table to eat their thresher[s]' dinner.

"The men didn't eat the beet pickles so good," Hilda said. "We'll give them dills for supper."

Mrs. Rockrohr reached over and ran her fork vigorously into one of the beets, as if to let Hilda know that she thought the pickles tasted good.

Suddenly Mrs. Fenstermacher raised her head from her plate. "Something's wrong with the thresh machine," she said.

We all listened.

"I thought a moment ago I heard something queer in the runnin' of it," Mrs. Fenstermacher said. "Then it got better, and now its—"

The machine stopped. We went on with our eating.

Then we heard Trigg shouting. He was calling Hilda. A neighboring man came running to the house.

"We gotta telephone for the doctor quick. Pete Magilly was caught in the machine. Hurt bad," he told us breathlessly.

The women were all on their feet together. Mrs. Magilly's flushed face froze white, and her nostrils trembled. She was out of the screen door before any of the women.

Hilda stopped in the dining room doorway, and turned sternly toward us children. "Don't one of you move from your place. And finish your dinner," she said commandingly.

Katie pushed her plate aside, put her head down on the table, and sobbed brokenly. "My pap," she cried. The boys and Hazel got up from the table and looked out the window.

Mr. Magilly died in the afternoon. It was very quiet because Trigg let the rest of the threshing go until the following morning. Everybody went home except Mrs. Rockrohr who stayed to help Hilda and Myrt with the dishes. Hilda and Mrs. Rockrohr didn't talk much. When they spoke of Mrs. Magilly's condition, they glanced at me to see if I were listening, and used words I didn't understand. Only Myrt seemed to be happy, in a far removed kind of way, though. I knew she was thinking of the new boy, and thought she might have remembered Mrs. Magilly, and the two Magilly boys, and Katie at a time like this.

Finally I could be silent no longer. "This is all so bad for Mrs. Magilly coming right at the time when she is going to have a baby," I said.

Hilda and Mrs. Rockrohr stared at me queerly for a moment. Then Hilda said to Mrs. Rockrohr, "She'll be twelve this fall." Mrs. Rockrohr nodded, and seemed to understand.

★ 4 ★

The Wild Shores

THE NORTHWEST

Annual Events
from the Washington State Office

Nearly every one of the 39 counties in the State of Washington contributes during the year some type of individualistic product which serves to bring together thousands of the residents of the particular county or community. Unlike so many other sections of the country, the contributions of Washington counties are not merely "dressed up in their best bib and tucker" for the purpose of display at some county fair, but rather are produced, assembled, cooked, and served free of charge to all who may care to fraternalize or partake of the hospitality tendered.

The diversity of climatic conditions throughout the State is conducive to an equal diverseness in the type of products. That portion of the State lying east of the Cascade Range is famed for the production of wheat, potatoes, melons, apples, and berries. Adams County and adjacent vicinity is often referred to as "The Breadbasket of the World" because of the wheat yield; Wenatchee, in Chelan County is known as the "Apple Mart of America"; Yakima "spuds" are rated as being surpassed only by the Idaho potato; Kennewick and Pasco produce strawberries and raspberries second to none; melons of all variety are successfully raised in the Yakima Valley. Southwestern Washington and the Grays Harbor district are raising and shipping cranberries and peppermint to eastern markets. The west coast and northern part of the State have long since passed the experimental stage in the cultivation and production of strawberries, peaches and grapes.

As an illustration to what extent some of these annual events consist, attention is directed to the most recent observation of National Apple Week at Wenatchee at which time the largest apple pie ever to have been baked was served to many thousands congregated to celebrate the annual occasion. An idea of the size of the pie can be gathered from the following ingredients used: One ton of apples; 10 pounds of butter; 160 pounds of sugar; 100 pounds of flour; 12 pounds of assorted spices. When removed from the specially-constructed oven with the aid of a tractor, the pie measured 10 feet in diameter and weighed 2,300 pounds.

Western Washington is extremely proud of its success in the production of strawberries as is evidenced by the numerous annual festivals held each year glorifying that most luscious of fruits. Worthy of mention herein is a recent strawberry festival held at Burlington, Skagit County, when 5,000 guests enjoyed free servings of an ice cream sundae consisting of 200 gallons of ice cream completely smothered by 1,000 pounds of crushed strawberries. In a specially constructed dish, 8 feet long, 4 feet high and 4 feet wide, located in the very center of town, the huge mould of ice cream was placed and served by 10 waitresses. Pitchforks, spades, hoes and other garden tools were used to shape and serve this spectacular dish. Every ingredient used in the manufacture of the delicacy was of local origin.

Bellevue, King County, endeavors each year to surpass the previous year's record in the serving of strawberry shortcake, ingredients of which also are entirely produced in the county. The 1941 festival held at this little community on the shores of Lake Washington had 15,000 guests, each of whom was served a portion of shortcake and a cup of coffee. Baked into individual biscuit-type cakes, this seasonal dessert required 100 pounds of flour, 364 quarts of whipping cream, 15,000 pounds of strawberries. Coffee, the only foreign product used, was quaffed to the extent of 54,000 cups.

An annual "Peach-a-Reno" is held at Buckley, Pierce County, in August, at which time shortcakes with fillings of locally-grown peaches are served free to the several thousands gathered there. The women-folk at the community do all the baking at home, each bringing her contribution to a central point on the day of the festivities. "Peaches" of the talking variety are also in evidence, with the "pick of the crop" being crowned queen at the close of day.

Denizens of the deep sea come into their own in many of the northwest annual festive days. Of no little interest in this respect is the annual

Mariner's Pageant held at Anacortes, Skagit County, in July. The competitive exhibition held earlier in the day, engaged in by several hundred contestants, culminates at noon with a big barbecue luncheon, the main course of which, (no pun intended) is the "net results" of the fishermen's prowess. One of the latest of these gatherings had 10,000 guests to sing the praises of the cooks who had barbecued the 4,000 pounds of freshly-caught white king salmon. A huge bonfire of alder wood was ablaze all forenoon on the main street of the town and as soon as the catches were made in Puget Sound, the fish were dispatched immediately to the array of chefs, who in turn quickly prepared them for the revolving spikes over the burning seasoned wood.

Clam bakes, oyster roasts, fish fries and crab gumbo dinners are just a few of the enticing festivals which annually or oftener have a complete quota of followers. Descriptions of some no doubt appearing elsewhere in this volume.

★   ★   ★   ★   ★

By the time I hit the Pacific Northwest, I was bug-eyed with all the harvest festivals I had attended. Even as I'm happy to report that most of the above festivals are alive and kicking, I didn't think I would discover anything different at them compared with the other festivals. What was unique was how many—and how varied—the festivals were throughout the Pacific Northwest, and how they reflect the incredible abundance of fruits and vegetables reaped throughout the region. Local towns swell with each fair and it's possible to fill every weekend from late April to October with a celebration of some regional crop, giving rise to the impression that half the population of Washington, Oregon, and Northern California are, or were in their youth, queens and kings of peach, strawberry, and apple fairs, to name but a few. The only thing I'll say about the modern-day festivals, as opposed to when the federal writers attended them, is, if you have your heart set on the huge strawberry ice-cream sundae in Burlington, it is no longer made. But Wenatchee still bakes a big apple pie each year.

What I was interested in finding, instead, was some aspect of the pioneer spirit that had brought so many immigrants out to this part of the country in the first place and that, in a way, is still luring settlers to the region. By this, I mean the essences of what all those harvest festivals are celebrating, namely the rich soil and commodious climate, the extended growing season throughout the region that results in anywhere from 150 to 270 days of farm production that help to support endless groves of fruit trees, vineyards, wheat fields, and sheep and cattle ranches. The rivers and streams, although tamed in part by dams that have compromised fish populations, nevertheless still roil with salmon and trout. A walk through the mossy forests yields baskets of hazelnuts, walnuts, chanterelles, black morels, and American matsutake mushrooms. Why, there are even truffles to be found!

With all this natural bounty, is it any wonder that so much good cooking is coming out of the Pacific Northwest? It's all there for the picking and the stirring, with much of the produce and meat of high quality, often provided by small farms using unique seeds and strains—making the area something of the epicenter for the trend in localism, and the envy of most everywhere else where it's difficult to obtain good fresh food within two hundred miles of home. Young cooks have been quick to understand the implications of this, especially since it's coupled with a fairly reasonable economic base in the cities and towns that allows newcomers to open up restaurants where they can experiment on a supportive community.

As if that's not enough, the cities in the Pacific Northwest have a reputation for a progressive, easy lifestyle, one sensitive to the environment and sympathetic to the bumptious nature of struggling artistic youth. If you're an inch past thirty and do not have a tattoo-filled arm or leg (preferably both), or various piercings or, at the very least, an interestingly complicated haircut, then you may feel a little lonely walking around Seattle and Portland. But you'll get over it fast because there are too many good things to eat and tasty wines to swill. Plus, you'll probably have your favorite indie band playing down the street, if not living next door to you.

And that is why, instead of visiting a harvest festival, I headed to a wild game dinner in Welches, Oregon, a bitty town nestled in the underskirts of Mount Hood, about an hour outside of Portland. The dinner, which inaugurates Wild About Game Week in Oregon and Washington State to help promote sustainable game as a healthy alternative to commercially raised meat, is organized by one of the country's major distributors of wild game, Nicky USA. It would be considered a corporate event, except Nicky is a small company that prides itself on the very personal relationships it maintains with its farmers and ranchers—all of whose properties are pretty small and mostly family owned. This gives the event the feeling of a family reunion: if the restaurateurs, farmers, and ranchers don't know

Pigs on a farm, Oregon, September 1991. (Russell Lee)

each other well, they greet one another with back slaps and vigorous handshakes once they realize this family raises the pheasants they cook or that is the guy who is always asking for more pork bellies.

Anywhere else in the nation, Nicky would be a cottage industry but, in this region, wild game fits in well with the territory: the animals are raised naturally, in small herds, and their meat is good for you—low in calories, high in nutrition. Plus, there's something about being so close to the tousled beauty of forests and meadows that makes you start craving a rabbit or pheasant for dinner rather than, say, chicken (unless it is a poussin [squab], which Nicky also distributes).

The folks in the room are a nice blend of the curious, the professional, and the manic foodie, with the manics appearing to be in the majority. The event is in something of a rustic resort hotel decorated in a heavy Scottish theme (plaid everywhere), which sort of goes with all the talk about wild boar, bison, and quail. Before the dinner, there are cooking demonstrations by some of the region's best chefs: at the moment, the guy at the stove is Gabriel Rucker, one of the rising stars of Portland. He's making rabbit arincini with squash mayo—basically a fried rice ball stuffed with rabbit meat. Apples, cinnamon, and some cognac are involved; the butternut squash mayonnaise is incredibly simple. As he cooks, the audience talks back to him, correcting his measurements, making sure he's doing things right.

"That's not a cup of rice," someone shouts from the back of the room as Rucker pours Arborio rice into a pan.

"More or less," he replies, not particularly warmly.

"More," shout others.

He sighs and continues the demonstration.

Away from the cooking, the room is filled with samples of what were until recently members of local herds representing Kobe beef and its cousin, Kurobuta pork, as well as squabs and pheasants. Tiny glasses of a fine Washington State pinot noir are for the offering, too. The small room echoes with exclamation points: "Oh, God!" and "Damn, that's good!" No one is shoving but there's lots of over-the-shoulder reaching, even for the Kobe beef hot dogs that are a revelation in their juicy beefiness, even to a confirmed Nathan's hot dog girl.

Geoff Latham, the owner of Nicky USA, wanders about the room making sure everyone is happy. He's short and a little plump, like a good fryer, and patiently genial even in the midst of so many people vying for his attention. But he stands still for a minute if given the chance to tell the story about how he started selling game.

Rabbits. That's how the business began: Latham selling rabbits raised by a local farmer named Orbest. Latham would pick the rabbits up in his hatchback and peddle them door to door—or restaurant to restaurant. That was in 1990. After a while, some of the chefs he was selling rabbits to asked if he had anything else, say, quail or venison. He didn't, but he quickly found farmers who did or who were willing to consider adding an interesting small flock or herd. He now offers thirty-one different animals—everything from alligator to Tibetan yak (North American raised) to wild boar. Most of his offerings are locally grown, all are raised without antibiotics, and every animal that needs a pasture to graze gets one, chewing on grass and wholesome grains until it's ready for market.

Another cooking demonstration—this time chanterelle-stuffed duck necks—is riling the room. The impatient foodies just can't sit still and are hopping out of their chairs to see how each ingredient is being used. Latham strays off to see that the buffet of cured sausages, pâtés, and smoked duck is refreshed, and Gabriel Rucker wanders by muttering, "I lost my knife." He's trailed by a disciple who is clearly as worried about the knife as Rucker is. Once the knife is safely found, I follow the pair out to the hotel patio, where they quickly light up cigarettes and begin to pace, discussing a bit of trouble at a recent concert. All around them on the patio, people are arguing, dissecting, minutely breaking down the food before them and what they have recently eaten. Corn mush is vigorously debated; the foie gras controversy is aired if only because there doesn't seem to be enough of it. Foodies in other parts of the country are as animated, but somehow not as aroused, and it seems to be tied to how easy it is to find beautiful fruits, vegetables, and meats in these parts. There's just no excuse for bad cooking—or bad eating—when so much goodness is within easy reach.

Rucker's arms are tattooed with fluttering birds. Both men sport cool hats. They stop their pacing long enough to be polite to me. What is endearing about Rucker, who grew up in Napa and came to Portland only a few years before, is that when he talks about cooking in the region, he takes on the demeanor of a child in toy heaven. There's so much he can do here that would be harder to accomplish anywhere else, if only because the food he loves to cook with—sweetbreads and tongue, for starters—is available from small local farmers, such as the nice lady who slips him some eggs and pork liver whenever she comes to town. He calls his style "dirty cooking" for his use of so much offal, but it really is a harkening back to the region's beginnings, when people ate anything they could get and left nothing to waste—including testicles and innards.

I'm happy to tell him this as I launch into some stories about *America Eats!* and the federal writers. I figure he might be interested to know what the pioneers in these parts ate:

> We ate prairie chickens, prairie dogs and rabbits, and roasted wheat bran and corn meal bran for coffee.

> Anybody could have turkey and squirrel whenever he wanted it. The creeks were full of fish and you didn't need to be an educated fisherman to catch them, all you needed was a hook and line and you'd catch all you wanted.

> The cane-brake was full of wild hogs. In the fall after mist had fallen and the young shoats were fattened they were often killed by anyone who wanted fresh pork.
>
> —*OREGON OFFICE*

But Rucker's eyes sort of glaze over and wander past me. He's actually more interested in telling me about a dish he's in the midst of creating: foie gras profiteroles.

"You know what profiteroles are?" he stops to ask. Smart-aleck responses spring to mind but I let him off. Then he starts talking about how he's pairing all these fancy ingredients with what he terms "ghetto produce"—essentially white bread, Coke, and Dole pineapple chunks. And that pretty much ends our tête-à-tête.

There's more fun to be had talking to the Ericksons—Todd, Cheroyl, and their fifteen-year-old son, Todd Jr., known as TJ. For the last five years, they have been raising fallow deer (*Dama mesopotamica*). When TJ was nine, he thought it would be cool to start tending wild game herd for market. His parents owned a nursery about twenty-five miles south of

Salmon in trap at hatchery, Astoria, Oregon, September 1941. (Russell Lee)

Portland and they had some unused pasture land they could fence. They thought about reindeer but couldn't imagine the big animals on their property. They would have liked to raise elk but Oregon strictly regulates the wild game business, fearing that, if any got loose and mixed with the really wild population, the natural gene pool would be tainted. For this reason, people have to receive a license from the Department of Fish and Wildlife (instead of the Department of Agriculture) to raise any wild game and it is strictly limited: only fifteen farmers at any one time in the entire state are allowed to raise elk. Since all the licenses were taken, elk was out for the Ericksons.

Then TJ saw some fallow deer in Texas and fell in love with their petite size and the broad antlers on the males. The Ericksons fenced off sixty acres of pasture and woods on their property and bought eighteen does and one buck from a farmer in Iowa. They now have a herd of about 110.

"Boy, did we have a long learning curve when we got them!" Cheroyl says. The family nods their heads in unison, looking like they're remembering a handful of nightmares.

"There's a really interesting story about fallow deer," Todd Sr. says. He's big in all ways and ready to laugh at almost anything, especially this particular story, whose veracity he's not quite sure about. In any case, the story involves the last shah of Iran, who had a private herd of purebred Mesopotamian fallow deer. A German man by the name of Georg von Opel was desperate to obtain at least a mating pair because purebreds are so rare and their meat so tasty. So, upon hearing about the shah's herds, he planned a sort of covert mission involving guns, helicopters, and a cargo plane. The German and his accomplices succeeded in rustling a few of the deer into the helicopter but, just as they were being loaded into the cargo plane, the shah's soldiers attacked. Amid some gunfire, they managed to take off with a few, and now the deers descended from this stolen and probably very traumatized herd are known as von Opels, after the German, and are considered the purest bred and most expensive fallow deers. Corroborating accounts are nonexistent as far as I can tell but I agree with Todd Sr. that it's a good story.

One of the things I've noticed as I walked around the event was how often people were trying to assure me that what I was about to nibble wouldn't be "gamy" at all. I ask Todd his thoughts about this and he stretches back in his chair and smiles at his wife, who grew up on an Oregon farm that raised rabbits and lambs (she confesses that she still can't eat lamb because of the smell of sheep).

"Well, people like the idea of wild game but they don't want that wild taste—it's too weird for them. Nicky's stuff isn't really wild in that sense because the animals are raised consistently—well fed and looked after. But the truth is, the only reason game that you hunt taste wild is because people don't know how to properly field-dress the animals. They're not quick enough and the meat starts rotting. That's why the meat becomes strong tasting. Or if you take a male during the mating season—testosterone and hormones will make the meat high and wild."

This all makes me want to go out to the Ericksons' farm to see fallow deer up close. The family is gracious enough to not blow me off. Cheroyl gives me driving instructions and we set a time for the following afternoon, when TJ will be home from school and able to show me around.

In the meantime, there's the wild game dinner to attend. I have a small hope there will be cougar meat, if only because that was on the menu at a dinner the federal writers wrote about:

Wild Parties
from the Washington State Office

According to a news item appearing in a Longview, Washington newspaper several years ago, the city firefighters of a sister city, Kelso, had been guests the previous night at a banquet whereupon the "piece de resistance" of the meal served was—perish the thought—wildcat meat!

That the main dish of this dinner tasted a "little like veal," but stronger in odor, was all that the participants could remember or cared to release for publication. But this incident was the impetus for the recollections of other days long passed, when "cougar meat" was consumed by some of the residents of the same community.

The consumption of cougar meat at these repasts, was impelled more from a standpoint of "reprisals" than from a cultivated appetite for the animal. As the story is related, a woman by the name of Minnie (Christian name unimportant) was attacked and partially devoured by one of these deadly prowlers of the woods. The surviving relatives of the family, even to the third and fourth generation, have vowed to relentlessly track down all the future offspring and descendants of the offending cougar and to give vent to their wrath by eating the prey when trapped.

As cougars are not too plentiful now-a-day even in the wooded country of Cowlitz County, it is quite doubtful that the family is able to provide such an animal often enough for them to become tired of the fare. But when they do enjoy such a repast, 'tis said, the family always refer to the meal as, "eating Aunt Minnie."

It is unlikely that cougar meat will become a standardized article on the menus of the rest of the populace of the State, particularly in those families which do not have or ever have had an aunt with such an unfortunate surname.

★   ★   ★   ★   ★

Cougar meat is *not* on this wild game dinner menu. It's not even offered for sale by Nicky USA. Which is just as well because there are great quantities of other meats to taste, including bison, quail, squab, elk, Kurobuta pork (baby back ribs and spiral-cut ham), lamb osso buco, duck leg confit, and pheasant. At this dinner, a flank steak from a grass-fed steer has an anything but common flavor. None of the meat tastes like veal—or even chicken. Instead, running through the meaty flavors is a rich grassy note that is just addictive.

I am somehow seated among the young chefs (Rucker is holding court at the next table) and their partners who are also in the restaurant/food business. They are a chatty bunch about the restaurant community in Portland—small enough that everyone knows each other, supportive in a more generous way than in other cities they've worked in. No one, in fact, is actually from Portland, having all arrived in the Northwest on rumors of how cool and cheap it is and how good the ingredients are. The couple next to me is a good example: Rodney Muirhead backed his way into cooking Texas-style barbecue after being laid off from a robotics company and working in a couple of restaurants and studying at the French Culinary Institute in New York City. When he came to Portland, he worked at a pizza place, and on the one night the place was closed, he cooked barbecue there and called it LOW BBQ for "Laid Off Workers BBQ." His wife, Elizabeth, worked as a decorative painter but shifted into making chocolates flavored with the chilies her dad grows in the Mojave Desert. Rodney now owns a cool restaurant, Podnah's Pit Barbecue, which is generally so packed at lunch that it runs out of meat by three P.M. Elizabeth's tiny chocolate shop, Pepita Papa, is famous for the different chocolate barks she makes from fruit, chilies, and nuts.

The conversation wanes, though, after everyone comes back from the buffet with overflowing plates. For the next half hour or so, little is heard but single-word judgments about the food: all of it great, except for the elk, which everyone decides is a little overdone. We've all made pigs of ourselves, our bellies protruding over jeans, but happy in the knowledge that wild game is good for us: leaner, higher in protein and vitamins, lower in calories. Another bottle or two of wine is procured. We're all good friends now as we pull ourselves up for a second helping.

It took me all the next morning to find the Ericksons' farm. Not that Cheroyl's directions weren't good but it's amazing how quickly the highway gives out to country roads leading too quickly in and out of small towns. To be sure, with so many people moving to the area, urban sprawl has become a worry. Signs all along the road underscore the locals' fear of it, asking for votes for one ordinance or another to keep the flavor and character of the Northwest what it has always been—rural and untame. I'm not so sure anything can stop the growth now. But, still, by the time I get close to the Ericksons' home, the roads have lessened to a two-lane highway and, when I slowly ascend a hill, there are the deer, standing under a grove of trees, watching the logging trucks and four-by-fours whizz by.

On closer look, the deer are strange little creatures, their hides chocolate-colored or spotted white, their eyes bulging out on either side of a very long nose. You could take them for scrawny if they weren't so healthy looking. The does top out at a hundred pounds and stand maybe thirty inches tall at the shoulder. The bucks are much bigger—they can edge up to 170 pounds and stand three feet tall.

TJ is working on his truck but he comes over to begin the tour as soon as I park the car. We start at one of the fenced-in pastures where a herd is standing around wanting to be fed again, even though they had just barreled through a bale of hay. They see us and start chattering, the does and

Orchards in Hood River Valley with Mount Hood in background, Oregon, September 1941. (Russell Lee)

babies mewing back and forth to one another, the bucks growling like bears, all of them turning their backs and trotting away to the covering shadows of some trees.

TJ apologizes for their rudeness. "They don't like people unless they've been bottle fed."

We go into the barn and he begins to show me the series of chutes and stalls necessary to corral the deer. The deer are extremely hard to manage, so TJ and a friend built a wide enclosure that acts as a funnel, gradually narrowing to force the deer to go where he wants them to go—either to a holding pen to be tagged or have their antlers cut (bucks can kill one another with them during the rambunctious mating season) or to the truck to be taken to market. TJ climbs on top of the partitions and beckons me up the ladder to balance across the series of doors, so he can explain the whole process. I don't personally know a fifteen-year-old boy who can construct a solid, well-thought-out structure, but I trust him and climb up after him. He's gracefully hopping from the top of one gate to another, sliding open and closing big doors while I try to keep up with him in my middle-aged way. The barn is cleaner than my house and smells of sweet hay: TJ is up at five each morning working with the deer, making hay, cleaning out the barn. Then he goes to school and afterward comes home to work some more. Somewhere in the middle of our climbing and mucking about, this sinewy boy tells me he recently shot a four-point elk and carried it for six miles, draped across his shoulder. He can field-dress, then butcher and turn a venison steak into dinner with a little wine sauce on the side.

And Lord, does he raise happy deer! They have a large pasture to roam about in and all the grass, hay, and fresh fruit they could want. The Ericksons do not use antibiotics or hormones and the deers hang out together without too much stress being put on them. We spend some time pitching over the fence apples and small watermelons from the Ericksons' kitchen garden while TJ tells me about the business end of things: they're not quite up to breaking even on their original investment but they're close enough, and he has already mapped out future plans (actually, they're part of his Future Farmers of America project) that will increase the herd by artificially inseminating them with strains of pure-bred von Opel semen (TJ has fifty strains in a frozen container in the barn; each strain is worth about two thousand dollars). He's a tough businessman, right up to when he tells me how his favorite buck was mortally wounded when his antlers got stuck in another buck's antlers and a third buck rammed his side. TJ found the injured deer just in time to hold his head in his arms and say good-bye to him. Then he shot him.

As we walk away from the herd to my car, TJ says, "I love them." And you can hear the affection in his voice.

Which brings me back to Gabriel Rucker and his restaurant, Le Pigeon. After hanging out with TJ in the country all day, I'm starving and I need a place to eat. What's more, I'm craving pig's feet and venison, although I feel a little guilty about the venison. I hail a cab and am picked up by a nice young woman who is in the indie band Junior Private Detectives. She's lived all over the place, including New York City where she was a nanny before running screaming back to Portland and the band. That's Portland for you—that, and how she says she'll be glad to pick me back up after I'm finished eating.

I'm on the verge of asking her to join me, but then she's off and I'm left on a windy little street corner with a few others who are hoping to squeeze inside a small storefront for something to eat. It's Monday night, for God's sake! but the room is full. I get as far as the hostess and am told to come back in a half hour. There's a dark, laid-back, funky bar down the street with a friendly bartender who pours me a big glass of a really great red wine from Chehalem Vineyards in the Willamette Valley. Four sips in, Le Pigeon is ready for me so I give the bartender my glass and hightail it back up the street, where I am ushered to a stool that overlooks the cooking station where three raffish-looking men stand sautéing, stirring, and sprinkling herbs and sea salt all over the place. In between cooking stints, they lean against the counter and stare out over the room in a way that is very reminiscent of how curious zoo animals gaze from their pens: you can't tell who is watching whom.

There are restaurants this cool looking all across the country. That's not what is interesting about eating at Le Pigeon. It's the menu, indeed filled with Rucker's dirty food: beef cheeks, trotters, sweetbread, marrow, pig's tails. It's an earthy menu the likes of which were once very common on tables across this country because people appreciated and knew how to cook with these now-overlooked animal parts. They knew them to be richly flavorful, even better sometimes than the prime cuts when done right. This was especially true in this part of the country, where a strong European stock took hold. Cheroyl Erickson was telling me about her German grandparents coming across from Buffalo, New York, and arriving in Oregon City at the end of the Oregon Trail, where they set up a farm that is still being run by her eighty-year-old father. She, herself, still cans and preserves—fifty quarts of pears and twenty of peaches, among other things, this summer alone that she'll use through the winter. It's that holding on to traditions of hunting and gathering, and a reverence for sustaining those traditions that seem to permeate the Northwest— helped in many ways by young chefs such as Rucker who make good use of the surrounding land to turn old ideas on their heads.

If you ask him, Rucker would tell you he's cooking in an French-American tradition but, really, Cheroyl's forebears would recognize his cooking, full of fruits and vegetables and flavorful meat, such as TJ's beloved fallow deers.

Rucker has taken the night off. But his ideas are all over the place and the cooking is exquisite. It has to be admitted that he comes to his arro-

Indians fishing for salmon at Celilo Falls, Oregon, September 1941.
(Russell Lee)

gance honestly. And, look, foie gras profiteroles are on the dessert menu! Well, they have to be tried: the deep buttery sweetness of the foie gras complements the airy golden dough—a surprising perfect fit. And a good end to a wild dinner.

Recipe for Barbecued Salmon
from the Oregon Office

One day at Yachate we were preparing a huge salmon barbecue. Our local "character" Dunhorst requested the privilege of preparing the salmon. He said that he had a method that came from Germany and he had never seen it used in this country. Naturally we allowed him the "privilege" he desired because it meant less work for the rest of us. But we all watched the procedure.

First the salmon (five of them) were cleaned. Then "Dunk" dissolved a lot of brown sugar in a big tub of water. The salmon were then "dunked" (in more ways than one) in the sweetened solution. After about half an hour they were removed and placed in the barbecue pit and covered with ferns and grass.

The result of this treatment was a dish that was hard to beat. The salmon retained all its rich salmon flavor but had lost its "fishy" taste. A further result is that all Yachate housewives now wash their salmon in water sweetened with brown sugar before they cook it.

★   ★   ★   ★   ★

A modern translation:

> 4 salmon fillets, about three inches wide
> 2 cups brown sugar
> ½ cup water
> Ground pepper
> Maidenhead fern leaves, or other edible fern leaves, gently
>   washed (optional)

Wash the salmon fillets in cold water and pat dry. Place flesh side up in a flat-bottomed glass dish. Mix the brown sugar with the water to form a paste and spread it evenly over the fish, using your fingers. Add a few grinds of pepper. Cover and refrigerate for 4 to 24 hours.

When ready to cook, make a hot fire in the grill. Place the fillets on the grill, skin side down. If you are using fern leaves, arrange them over the fillets. Close the grill lid. Open the lid after 5 minutes. Use a metal spatula to remove the fillets, leaving the charred skin and fern leaves behind. The brown sugar should be caramelized over the fish to form a crust.

Serves 4.

★   ★   ★   ★   ★   ★   ★   ★   ★   ★

Crawfish Feeds Past and Present
by Patsy M. Teepen and M. W. Rowley, Oregon Office

"Come to our house Saturday evening for a crawfish feed," Helen invited over the telephone.

Helen knew that nothing short of an appointment with F.D.R., or possibly Eleanor, would keep me away from one of their crawfish feeds. To be invited you must be one of the initiate, or a very close friend to one of the initiates. The occasion and the crawfish are considered too precious to be wasted on any but the most appreciative. You are certain to meet a most interesting, if miscellaneous collection of people. Whether the taste for crawfish has anything to do with [it] I am not certain, but I am inclined to think it has.

I was introduced to the crawfish as a food shortly after my arrival in Oregon. Much to the disappointment of some friends who had taken me to a well known crawfish place where I was served a measly dozen of nondescript crustaceans, I was not properly impressed. They had no particular flavor that I could detect nor was there any prescribed technique for assimilating the food from the rather forbidding shells.

At Jack's it's different. When he ushers you into his basement rumpus room you are greeted with an ambrosian odor that is a mixture of all the spices of Araby and of the summer kitchen when Mother made piccalilli. If you are one of the initiate you say, "Jack, how are the crawfish?" and he is apt to reply, "Well, they're not too good this time." Then he leads you to the corner where two huge lard cans, the size you see in the butcher shop, stand cooling on the gas stove. He lifts the cover of one and you stare as if hypnotized at the sight that meets your eyes. Great red crawfish the size of young lobsters fill the can to the brim. Your eyes water and your nose wrinkles like a rabbit's at the sight and smell of the feast in store.

After Helen has covered the long table with an oil cloth and placed upon it paper plates and dishes filled with pickles, cheese and crackers, the guests—about twenty in number—are seated. Jack sets on the table several large platters piled high with crawfish. Mugs are filled with beer and the fun begins. If you haven't attended one of these feeds before, the proper procedure, a sacred rite, is explained.

First you twist the finials from the end of the tail, and elevating the crawfish and throwing your head back, you quickly suck the soup from the end of the tail, which acts as a straw. Next you lift the large shell off the body and scrape out with a knife (the only implement used) a gooey looking substance which you spread on a cracker—caviar never tasted like this! If it is the season for eggs you are doubly lucky. Your neighbor who doesn't find any eggs drools with envy.

Finally you twist off the large claws and crack them with your hands or your teeth and eat the delicious white meat. Large checked dish towels are used for napkins and since manners are neither possible or desirable, you make as much noise and eat as fast as possible. This adds to the confused gaiety.

Between bites a guest asks, "Jack, how do you catch the crawfish and where did you learn to cook them?" Another inquires, "How does it happen that Oregonians make such a specialty of them?"

"One at a time," says Jack. "Perhaps I'd better tell you the story. When I was just a kid my older brother and I had a saloon in Portland and I learned the recipe from our old French cook who had once worked at The Quelle restaurant which made Oregon crawfish famous back in the gay nineties."

"Whatya mean—gay?" someone shouts above the clamor. "What's the matter with the gay forty's?"

"Sure, gay, fat and forty, that's me."

Jack proceeds, "Well, chefs in those days were both fat and famous. One day Herr Kummli, chef of the Portland Hotel, and Max Schmidt, owner of the Vienna Café, were having tea, or possibly schnapps with Fred and Louis Sechtem, owners of The Quelle, when a fisherman brought in a sack of crawfish for sale."

"Those names sound like the Versailles treaty."

"Well, history was made at The Quelle, too," Jack says, "for none of them had ever tried to cook the vicious squirming creatures that filled the sack. But they decided to experiment. The crustaceans were a challenge to their creative ability.

"Schmidt recalled that in Germany they were cooked in salt water, flavored with caraway seed. They tried this method but the crawfish were flavorless. The other cooks suggested adding various ingredients, onions, bay-leaf, and allspice but the crowning touch came when Father Sommer of the German Catholic church dropped in and suggested putting white wine in the mixture."

"Is that what you use, Jack? I thought it was vodka."

"Anyway, the effect was dynamite," Jack replied, "and soon The Quelle was the favorite hot spot of Portland's elite and crawfish was their favorite food. Lillian Russell, who was appearing at the old Marquam Theater, gave a crawfish party at The Quelle and the orchestra that played for her performance furnished music for the guests. They really did things in the grand manner in those days."

"Me for the gay nineties," says Fat and Forty. "That's when a gal with a figger was really appreciated."

"You would have been if you had met the Baron," Jack consoled her. "The Baron loved the ladies as much as he did crawfish. He was the chef for The Quelle and was quite a personage in Portland. His real name was John, but he got his nickname from a beard, parted in the middle, and a long tailed coat which he wore with great distinction."

"Sounds wacky to me," says Fat and Forty, "but go on."

"Crawfish from Oregon became famous," continues Jack, having hard going with his story. "In 1900 The Quelle sold 35,000 dozen crawfish and shipped thousands of dozens to all parts of the United States. For twenty four hours before they were cooked, the crawfish were kept in huge vats of the 'soup' or seasoned stock in the basement.

"When William Howard Taft, perhaps our greatest epicure among presidents, came to Portland he ordered several dozen crawfish sent to his hotel suite, and when Kolb and Dill, famous comedians, were playing here they gave crawfish parties every night at The Quelle. They, too, spread the fame of Oregon crawfish on their tours."

"I'll bet they couldn't beat your crawfish, Jack. Tell us your recipe."

"Well, it was a secret then—and it still is," Jack answers.

"Where did they get enough crawfish to supply the demand?" another queries.

"Crawfishing was a real industry in those days," he replies. "One man owned a few acres of lowland on the Willamette River which he flooded with running water. He had traps or floats built which would hold 10,000 crawfish as he could market them at any time in any quantity."

By this time when every belt is let out to the last notch, and every crawfish is consumed the thought of so many crawfish is overwhelming.

"Did you ever hear the story of the traveling salesman," someone asks. So from there on—well, it is sure a swell party! The Quelle didn't have anything on this, I'll bet!

★ 5 ★

The Groveling Season

Political Gatherings

Women Stop the Meat from Breathing
from the Mississippi Office

If a Mississippi candidate for any office of importance is in earnest about winning his campaign he knows that he not only has to give a barbecue, but it has to be done just right and according to the accepted tradition. Speeches have to be accompanied by eating, and the eating has to be what is expected. Therefore, having full knowledge of these facts, he always hires Bluebill Yancey as the pit artist of the day.

Bluebill is what is known as a "bluegum" Negro, and they call him the blood brother of the Ugly Man, but personal beauty is not in the least necessary to a barbecue cook. There are some peculiarities that must be dealt with, however—Bluebill works according to the stages of the moon, and he has been known to call off entire barbecues at the slightest sound of thunder on cooking night. Moreover, no woman must come within smelling distance of the pit, for the meat won't "breathe freely" with a woman cook around. Not even Dicey, Bluebill's wife, is allowed to be present until after the cooking is done, and all his assistants are male.

They labor all night and on into the morning over a ten-foot pit with wire mesh stretched over the fire, at last coaxed down to smokeless coals. During the last and final stage of the barbecuing Bluebill paces ceaselessly—up one side to turn the meat, down the other to baste it with his sauce and mop. And, as the brown hunks of meat approach perfection, Bluebill grows as proud as a monkey with a tin tail. As the main speaker booms forth, his sonorous voice damning taxes and the Republican party, the fourteen hours of preparations come to an end, and the attention hitherto given the candidate is divided between him and eating. While the speaker is describing his opponent as a "shallow-brained, slack-jawed liar, a bull ape of Mississippi politics, a big baboon cavorting like a fat pony on high cats," teeth are already sinking into fresh bread, thick slices of beef, and Bluebill's incomparable sauce, the ladies are seeking glasses of lemonade from Uncle Si Curtis' stand, and the men are passing out the corn liquor.

Speeches over, the speakers move over to the table themselves, and the crowd makes way a little, but just a little. Dead enemies, who were a moment ago blackening each other for all eternity on the platform, meet, help each other to the delectable, tantalizing beef, the bread, and the potato salad, sample each other's whiskey and chat as if food and drink have eradicated all differences—at least for the moment.

★   ★   ★   ★   ★

It is close to noon and, as the day heats up, blistering the swampy land to a dry scab, the two sisters take a break from shelling beans to listen to the politicians swirling around the pavilion in Founders Square at the Neshoba County Fair. Whether it's an election year or not, if you want to be within fifty feet of a politician and hear a political speech, then the Neshoba County Fair is where you end up traveling to. The square is packed—almost standing-room only—with people who have come down for the day to listen to the political speeches and with those who live in rows of wooden cabins or in trailers on the fairground for the week. The sisters have been attending the fair since 1936, when Marie, the elder sister at ninety-three, was a bride. She proudly points back across the square to what looks like nothing more than a two-story shack leaning in a line beside other shacks.

"That's Dr. Jay Stribling's cabin," she says, speaking proudly of her husband's father, both men long dead. Marie turns back and looks around the square, trying to recall how many speeches she's listened to over the years. "My mind's not as sharp as it used to be." She smiles and shakes her head a little, indifferently brushing a white curl away from her forehead. She turns to her sister for help. "How many do you consider, Cecilia?"

The barbecue pit, Greene County, Georgia, May 1939.
(Marion Post Wolcott)

Her sister deliberates for a moment, then replies, "Oh, I don't know. Too many, that's for sure," and they both laugh softly together.

The bench where the sisters sit near the pavilion is fast becoming hemmed in by all the politicians and their assistants and managers and handlers, and oftentimes spouses and children. The audience under the corrugated metal roof of the open-sided pavilion is crowded close together on plain wooden benches rubbed smooth over the last century by people listening to whoever is talking at the simple podium on the slightly raised stage. The crowd is a fine mix of generations, from grandparents holding grandbabies to middle-aged parents corralling boisterous teenagers along the pavilion's perimeter. Everyone in sight is all dressed up and milling mirthfully about as if the Mississippi heat and dust aren't commanding presences at all.

"It's something you do," Marie says. "All of the politicans come down, make some noise and, to be polite, you come out and listen to what they have to say."

"You have to make a speech at the fair, you see, if you want to get elected in Mississippi," Cecilia adds.

"Look at my hands." Marie spreads her long knotty fingers across her lap. They are stained dark with bean juice. "I've been shelling beans since sunrise."

"It's probably enough for now," Cecilia says calmly, either about the beans or the political speeches. But after helping her sister to her feet, she begins to walk slowly back to Dr. Stribling's cabin with Marie's arm linked securely under her own. The women cry out greetings to people who wave fondly back at them as they pass.

"Oh, you're welcome to stop by later for some lunch," Marie calls over her shoulder. Cecilia waves to me as if to underscore the invitation, then guides her sister the rest of the way across the square to the cabin.

Food and politics—and a generous, open-door policy toward visitors—are legendary at the Neshoba County Fair. In political circles, it is taken as gospel truth that, if you're looking for the best eating, you steer clear of national races where there's money for catered events, and hit only the local circuits—say, a school board or, at the highest, a city council. This is where you continue to find a turnout of great home-cooked pies, fine tuna casseroles—perhaps, just perhaps, although it is growing rarer, even a real live barbecue as in days past.

The fair, billed as "Mississippi's Giant House Party," raises the bar for politics and food to a whole other level. Every year, two full days are set aside for politicians to come down and make a speech before an interested gathering of fair-goers. Throughout the week, different cabins host all kinds of feasts and invite everyone to attend. And there's always the carnival food along the midway around the amusement rides. But come the days of the political speeches, there is almost always at least one slow-cooking barbecue being fired up, as well as a whole slew of covered dishes and special desserts spreading across tables around the square. Most Mississippian candidates, both local and state, feel it is necessary for their careers to show up at some point. National candidates do, too—everyone from Michael Dukakis and John Glenn to Ronald Reagan (the last of whom proceeded to commit a famous political faux pas when he opened his presidential campaign at the fair in 1980). It's been this way ever since Governor Anselm McLaurin, the last Confederate veteran to run for office, spoke at the fair in 1896.

For good and bad, nowhere else in the United States comes close to having the Neshoba County Fair's steady impact on the political and social life of its constituents. Maybe the fair could only be maintained this long—and in much of its original shape—in a state where it is cosseted by a rural landscape and nurtured by a strong regional fondness for old traditions. For anyone else, however, whether they are Northerners or Southerners, so long as they are living outside Neshoba County, Mississippi, it helps to have a good idea of the fair's history, to understand why politicians continue to consider the parched field just down the road apiece from the town of Philadelphia so essential to their official welfare.

The fair began in 1889 as a typical agricultural gathering for local farmers to show off their produce and livestock. Two years later, it was organized into a private association and moved to where it is now, beside a little road through some pretty hardscrabble, almost barren, swampy land to what is pretty much the middle of nowhere (if you ask a travel agent to find accommodations, he or she will invariably get to asking just where in God's name it is you're going, since the town of Philadelphia, and the fairground, itself, despite being on the National Register of Historic Places, is about the size of a tick on most maps). It was about then that families started camping on the fairground for the whole week of the fair. Soon enough, they were building more substantial places to sleep, nothing more than thin sheets of wood or logs nailed to some posts over a dirt floor, and setting them so close to one another that one family could touch the next family's cabin if they put their hands out the window—if they had windows, which many did not: they had a front door and a back door and maybe some openings near the ceiling to give the searing summer heat a place to escape. The association saw the fair as a cross between a farm fair and a religious camp meeting so, in 1894, in addition to the cabins, they built the pavilion for such things as meetings and sing-alongs, planted some oak trees to shade the roof from the blazing sun, and called the area Founders Square.

Eventually six hundred cabins were built, first by people who came to the fair each year, then by their descendants, to the point where you can walk around and get a good sense of family lineage in Mississippi just by reading the names nailed to most of the cabins' front posts. If there isn't a family name attached to the post, there's a cute title given for the hovel, such as "The Fox Den" or "Ye Old King's Kastle." The most desirable cabins ring Founders Square; others meander in more or less straight lines from the square, creating streets, alleyways, and cul-de-sac neighborhoods labeled things like "Happy Hollows" and "Beverly Hills." Other streets are named for prominent families who have houses there. By now, many of the original cabins have been added on to or improved to accommodate more commodious modern sensibilities, but it's been done in such a way that the original bones are still apparent. Some have added electrical power for air-conditioning and a refrigerator (in the old days, they used to dig a hole in the middle of the dirt floor, line it with canvas, then pour in ice), as well as indoor plumbing, although both Marie and Cecilia fondly remember the unisex privy—a beauty at twenty seats—with a boardwalk path. It was in use well into the 1950s.

More dramatic improvements—including tear-downs—have been met with a combination of awe and mild unease as possible signs that the fair is getting away from its past, when everyone—the county's doctors and lawyers, as well as farmers and store owners—lived equally in modest dwellings. Some of the new cabins, in fact, would fit well into a suburban subdivision, complete with manicured landscaping hugging their tiny foundations. These are a firm display of their occupants' wealth, considering how much cash was laid out for a place that is generally used for just one week out of the year. No matter if the cabins are new or old, though, they are all decorated and painted in a cornucopia of colors, banners, streamers, flowers, flags, and twinkling lights.

So what happens at the fair that makes it such a potent draw? Longtime fair dwellers will tell you it's about the sense of community, the coming together of extended families and old friends, the celebration of Mississippi's olden days when things weren't so complicated. Life, indeed, seems very uncomplicated during fair week. A newspaper that is printed each day of the fair's operation always has good news to report—and even its bad news is not so bad (a three-year-old boy escaping from his family's house in the middle of the night and wandering the fairground until he is found; a mule losing his footing during one of the races). The world's crises are suspended, at most fodder for front-porch lectures and slide shows—as one man who worked for a contractor in Iraq gave, trying to explain the Iraqi people to his Mississippi audience by passing around pictures of Middle Eastern food and chaotic street scenes, his fellow contractors posing in the photos in military fatigues.

With so many people living so closely together, it's perhaps not so strange that life at the fair is incredibly *domestic*. In fact, almost every household chore is glorified and ritualized—from home decorating to carefree child-rearing to generous hospitality. Cooking actually seems to be one of the main occupations of the day: many of the dishes are started weeks before and arrive frozen, then are finished at the fair. But others, including pies, cakes, and elaborate banquets, are made from scratch—many in modest, if not rudimentary, kitchens—and take all day to complete. For entertainment, residents also take great pains to plan elaborately themed festivities, such as luaus (where at least two hundred-pound pigs are roasted), ice-cream socials, and pie-eating contests that are open to all the residents—all of which gives rise to the conviction that the fair is anything but a relaxing retreat for whoever is doing all the cooking.

The other occupation of the cabins seems to be drinking, which in a state with so many dry counties is something to see.

"There's more drunks up in those cabins than all of New Orleans during Mardi Gras," claims the lady making the nonalcoholic Piña Coladas at a stand on the midway. She hands me a festively shaped purple plastic glass filled to the brim with a lip-puckering frozen concoction and nods back at the cabins. "Just go back there and someone will throw in something with a kick."

Sure enough, as I roam again among the cabins, now with the purple glass, I receive offers to punch up the virgin Piña Colada with rum, tequila, or (not kidding) peach brandy. It seems rude to decline such generous overtures, especially when no one seems to take seriously my Yankee phrasing of, "Okay, really, that's plenty."

Between (or actually running concurrently with) eating and drinking, people may try out the tame carnival rides, or attend a concert or a harness race at the grandstands. Neshoba is the only place in Mississippi where it's legal to race horses (betting is done in a quiet, private way in the stands, but on a still, hot summer's day, the obvious winners and disappointed losers are easy to spot). The concerts present up-and-coming country singers or gospel groups, most of whom seem to be known already by everyone but outsiders. The harness racing commences with a prayer from the announcer: "Praise to God who gave us Jesus to die on the cross for us. Thank you for this beautiful fair where we gather with our family and friends. Lord, may you protect our troops and Jerusalem and all that is going on in that city these days. May you bless the goings-ons here that are about to begin. For thine is the kingdom and power,

Man eating oysters at a political rally, Jackson, Mississippi, between 1939
and 1941. (Standard Photo Co.)

Amen." Before the harness racing starts, mules are raced by different age groups—children as young as five whipping their charges for all they're worth, teens, and adults—with the crowd-pleaser one day clearly a young man who comes in second but who rides casually back on his saddle with his shirt open, as if he is driving down a country road in an old '65 mustang instead of on an ornery mule. When he passes the fence before the grandstands, the genteelly, linen-clad lady sitting next to me who takes pains to say she is just visiting friends who own a cabin and that she grew up in New Orleans, lives now in Jackson, and finds all that's going on at the fair a little, well, *"rural,"* whispers, "Now I know why they race mules around here." When one mule insists on going the wrong way around the track, the announcer explains: "Horses will let you race 'em all you want, but a mule demands you negotiate."

Late at night, after the races and the concerts are over, children take a few more turns on the rides or run amok through the makeshift streets virtually unsupervised by the adults who sit on the porches sipping and talking, or singing and strumming an instrument. Nothing from the outside world appears to perturb the fair, not even the most heart-wrenching incident in the county's recent past—the murder of James Chaney, Andrew Goodman, and Michael Schwerner. Through the summer of 1964, when the young civil rights workers were missing, many prominent people across the state were of the opinion that the men's disappearance was a hoax. They continued thinking that way right up until the moment their bodies were discovered not two miles down the road from the fairground.

"Philadelphians are busily preparing for their annual fair which is called 'Mississippi's Giant House Party,'" the *Guardian* (Manchester, England) reported on August 8, a few days after the bodies were found:

> A Southern journalist writing in the *New York Herald Tribune* today reports a Mississippian as saying that the Fair will be the greatest celebration in Mississippi's history. He quotes:
>
> "For six weeks we have had to put up with invading enemies—agitators and Communists and writers like you who hate us and spread lies about us. Now we are going to entertain our friends and the sweetest music for everybody in this county is going to be hearing George Wallace pour hot lead into the pants of all you South-hating writers. And even sweeter music will be hearing Barry Goldwater junior [*sic*] tell us how police power ought to be returned to the Neshoba County and to the Mississippi State highway patrol."

Certainly, things have come a long way here in Neshoba County since then, with justice finally served and concrete strides made to improve race relations. And yet all of the cabins at the fair are still owned by whites. Anyone is free to buy a cabin when one comes up on the market, it's just that they are usually snapped up by family members and, besides, they're pretty expensive, with the cheapest cabin—a tear-down on one of the back streets, for instance—going for $65,000. A passably new cabin on Founders Square was sold recently for $285,000. Then there's the fact that final approval of the sale rests with the fair association's board of directors and not the seller. All of which may—or may not, depending on who you are talking to—explain why, in a county that is one-third black, the only African Americans (or, for that matter, any other racial/ethnic groups) at the fair are not sitting on one of the nice porches eating pie but, rather, racing or tending the horses and mules, and running the carnival rides.

It would be easy to dismiss this tiny, anachronistic patch of back-road ground if not for the fact that politicians continue to show up and make some pretty important platform speeches. State and local officials come in part because Mississippi's primaries are held in August, so the fair's timing at the end of July—or at the latest, the first week in August—is perfect for one more final go-round between the candidates. What draws national candidates may be the old-fashioned forum it provides, and the homogeneous demographics of its residents. When Ronald Reagan appeared at the fair shortly after the Republican National Convention in 1980, it was because his advisers saw the Neshoba County Fair—or, as it has been called, the "Republican's Woodstock"—as the perfect place to court Southern votes, which he did, but not without drawing criticism. After saying he would "restore to states and local governments the power that properly belong to them," most of the nation's press and the NAACP voiced loud protest. They took what he said to mean that, under the Reagan presidency, Mississippi would be given more power to undermine laws guaranteeing equal rights for African Americans. Republican senator Trent Lott was so pleased that he forecasted Reagan would easily carry the state, which he did by 49 percent.

"This is Mississippi politics at its best," exclaims Mick Bullock, the executive assistant to the state auditor, as he nods toward the pavilion where the state treasurer is speaking. Mick doesn't appear to be anywhere north of thirty and neither does the pretty woman he is cozying up to, who also works for a state politician. Despite the heat and the sawdust that never tames the pale dirt, Mick and his companion are *really excited* (they both exclaim this with wide smiles and bright white teeth) to be at the fair with their bosses. Asked why, Mick gives the standard answer offered by Neshobans: it is, he says, merely part of a great "tradition. Even people down south along the coast listen to what's said at the fair. If you're from up north, it might be hard for you to understand or to explain to you, but it's as simple as that to us, ma'am."

There are enough news cameras and reporters hugging the stage to make sure everyone in the state hears the candidates. Sitting on the Striblings' porch waiting for the bean casserole to finish baking, Cecilia remarks that, in the old days, there were more regular people—from miles around, not just in Neshoba County—who came to hear the speakers. Now, with the television, she says, they don't have to.

"Everyone speaks here because we take our politicians seriously enough to want to see them up close," she says, then adds, sounding just a little bewildered, "How can you vote for someone you don't know?"

There is something to be said for that, and for the overall energetic interest in political matters that is churning around the square. These people are anything but blasé about their elected officials and they expect not only a good speech but the chance to question, criticize, and often laugh at them, too. They sit as still as they can under the pavilion's blazing roof, fanning themselves slowly with paper fans as each candidate has his or her ten minutes on the stage. Meanwhile, the square is almost impossible to walk through, with all the young campaign workers and fledgling candidates greeting one another, hugging and kissing, kidding around in the heat like frisky pack animals.

Marie, who is too busy in the kitchen to sit down, opens the screen door and says, "You know who you should talk to? Sid next door. Everyone stops and talks to Sid."

"Oh, yes," Cecilia seconds. "Sid's a talker. All the politicians come to his porch to talk to Sid."

Sid is a popular columnist and editor at the local newspaper, the *Clarion-Ledger*. It is declared that he knows pretty much everything anyone would ever want to know about Mississippi politics and the Neshoba County Fair but, the truth is (and where confessional journalism now makes a very small appearance), so many people are crowded around his porch—including the governor, Haley Barbour, who is joking about his problem in coming to the fair when he's on a diet ("For me, a balanced diet is a pair of pies in each hand," he said earlier, to great applause, in his pavilion speech)—that it would take more strength than is currently available without Marie's casserole to push on through to Sid. The sisters remark that a stop later might be wise. Sid will surely still be talking, Marie implies slyly and then hustles back into the kitchen with a smile still lingering on her face.

So instead of joining the people on Sid's packed porch, I meander down to the pavilion to listen to some of the speakers. It's clear Hurricane Katrina has changed the proceedings slightly. Most of the people standing at the podium are uncharacteristically nice to one another; hardly an insult or innuendo is hurled about. People are in no mood for partisan sniping while the state still struggles to recuperate from the disaster. The long-overdue completion of recovery efforts is on the minds and loudly on the lips of a lot of folks sitting on the pavilion's benches. The only official who comes in for some serious drubbing by the audience is insurance commissioner George Dale, who says rather proudly, "Both sides are mad at me so I must be doing something right."

Still, the audience seems rather disappointed with all the good manners onstage and only rallies briefly from the heat-induced stupor when the lieutenant governor says she has decided to quit politics for a while and a judge condemns the Supreme Court for staying the execution of a local man convicted of murder. Governor Barbour gets a mild *tsk* when he claims there will be no new taxes—a former tobacco lobbyist, Barbour has steadily opposed raising Mississippi's cigarette taxes (the lowest in the country), despite the wishes of a majority of its residents and the need for revenues.

After their time is up, almost all the politicians make it a point to walk around the fairground—with few going any farther than the porches around Founders Square, although their workers are discovered everywhere, including on the amusement rides, nibbling on sticks of fried

Cooking a fried supper for a benefit, Bardstown, Kentucky, August 1940.
(Marion Post Wolcott)

chicken or alligator (the other *other* white meat in these parts—and quite tasty, at that). It's hard to walk a few feet without something being thrust into your hands, such as a paper fan with a politician's name emblazoned across it, a bumper sticker, or a button. As I make my way back across to the Striblings' cabin, I gladly accept all the fans thrust upon me.

"How's the beans?" Cecilia asks Marie when she comes out again. Marie says they're fine: she's now working on the marinated carrots (raw carrots, onions, bell peppers mixed with Campbell's tomato soup and chilled).

"I'm so tired!" She laughs.

"Then sit."

"I will," she promises and then frowns. "Oh, dear, here comes one of them. I can't listen to another one," and she pops up again and scurries inside just as a politician climbs the two steps to the porch with his hand out to shake.

A Word or Two about Barbecue and Politics

Barbecue is as American as American food gets. It is a subject where the heart rules more than the brain, and sometimes even the stomach. Its place in the national psyche is unshakable, rich in lore—both of the true and tall nature—and redolent of all that our cooking sensibilities hold sacredly dear. By this, it is meant that barbecue is a simple meal, nothing more than meat (mostly) cooked over glowing wood and coals for a long period of time and generally flavored by highly individual and regional tastes, all of which are hotly debated among the different populations.

Today, if you live in any good-size city, it is possible to find representations of almost any region's style of barbecue, with the result that its ubiquitous presence has muddied our understanding of what exactly barbecue is. The federal writers wrote at a time when barbecue was still a fairly localized speciality, with distinct regional differences in ingredients and preparation methods. A Northerner, for instance, had to go south of the Mason-Dixon Line or down around Texas and through the scrubby pastures of the Southwest to taste what pulled pork was, or to sample slowly roasted, spice-rubbed, and thickly sauced steer or mutton. The stories they subsequently wrote impart about as fine a sense of the different regional preparations—as well as an exacting primer on how to barbecue—as you're liable to find anywhere else.

A good handful of these barbecue stories start at a political rally if only because politicians, understanding the potent symbolism of such a national dish, felt that providing the community with a good feed and then sitting down among them to eat a mess of meat and ribs made them appear more like common folks—and thus more likely to be voted for. Also, as one writer noted, barbecue was a good political meal because it took so long to cook that it provided something of a captive audience for people who were lured—and held fast—by enticing smells, and thus willing, at least in body if not spirit, to listen to some speeches.

These days—and even through an extremely busy and highly contentious political season—it is hard, if not impossible, to find a good old-fashioned political barbecue of the kind described in the papers. Fancy Farms, Kentucky, has held a political barbecue for the last 128 years on the first Saturday in August. But it is nowhere near the kind of feed, recorded by *America Eats!*, that Oklahoma Governor Jack Calloway Walton provided in 1923:

> A battery of three 10,000 gallon coffee pots required steam from six fire engines to keep them boiling, along with 300,000 tin cups and three carloads of coffee, and more than a mile of trenches for barbecuing the meat. The official checkers counted over 250,000 guests, who consumed one carload of Alaskan reindeer and a trainload of cattle, chickens, rabbits and buffalo, with a carload of pepper and a carload of salt for seasoning.

Hardly a pit is dug or a steer slaughtered anymore for a political gathering. Time is probably the main issue, followed closely by local zoning rules about digging milelong trenches and filling them with smoldering wood—on public property. Then there are all the health regulations that were not in place in the 1930s, things that encompass such barbecue essentials as killing an animal and cooking and serving its fresh carcass in what has to be admitted were probably less than controlled sanitary conditions.

And yet, it surely must be considered one of the sorriest facts of modern life that, for the most part, public consumption of barbecue has been relegated to restaurants—or if one is very lucky, unassuming shacks on the side of the road. To entice someone, somewhere, to put on a proper public barbecue that has all the spirit it should have, here are excerpts from a few of the federal writers' own accounts on what community barbecues were like. Read them. Grow hungry. Raise a civic voice for digging a trench.

Barbecue Samples
from the Georgia Office

Southern people will give a barbecue for any occasion at all—a political rally, a civic club meeting, a celebration of harvests, or just to show a visitor a good time. The calves and shoats are killed a day or two before; if lamb is served, it is usually bought from the butcher, for the Southeast is not a sheep-raising country.

For some reason, the most celebrated barbecue cook of a community is usually a man. He may be a white man or a Negro. But, however he may differ from his fellow artists about such things as sauce and condiments, he is sure to insist on a slow fire. Having arranged to have the pit dug the day before, he is up at dawn to start the green hickory wood burning. The clean grey smoke curls up with a pungent smell on the fresh morning air and falls to an even bed of ashes.

You will see all kinds of people at a barbecue. A generation ago it was not uncommon for a farm landlord to reward his tenants by this form of celebration, and the oak grove near the house would be filled with blue overalls and sun-bonnets of the tenants who had "got their crops laid by." Or there might be a barbecue given for a small-town belle and her visitors, and there would be boys and girls laughing and calling down the long trestle tables spread under the scuppernong arbor. A stag barbecue is sometimes held in somebody's pasture, and the men sprawl comfortably along the green slopes to eat.

If the guests at a political barbecue are seated, the speakers of the occasion are "spotted" among them, so that the audience is addressed from every angle. After such a meal, the people are likely to be drowsy, and the speeches must be as fiery as the barbecue sauce to arouse them to attention. And usually they are. Here the oratory of the old South comes back. Shouted exhortations, stinging irony, anecdotes with local humor, the sentiment that strikes close to home and heart—all are there.

And you must not think that because the speeches are flowery they are not sometimes packed with meaty observations. When the guests waddle toward their automobiles, they usually find that the political issues have been thoroughly covered and know exactly how they ought to vote when the time comes.

The only trouble is that the rival candidates, too, may decide to give a barbecue.

from the Alabama Office

The barbecue is no place for daintiness in eating. Greasy fingers, greasy chins, and a liberal spray of dust from hundreds of churning feet, are just more items to make the occasion special. If the fingers get too greasy suck them or use a paper napkin.

When the appetite palls with barbecued beef, try the chicken; enough of that and try the pork. By the time the eating has all been done, most of the eaters have made stuffed pigs of themselves and laid up nightmares for the coming evening.

In former years of alcoholic prohibition, there were always those who carried hip bottles of scorched white mule, and charcoal yellowed low-bush corn to wash down the meal. Since legalization of drinking many now drink beer, but there are still stacks of corn and rye bottles to be gathered after this mighty gustatorial bout.

> It's a good old Southern Custom;
> Feed until you nearly bust 'em;
> Barbecue and drinks and pickled;
> Stuff yourself or face ridickle.

from the Kansas Office
(written by W. L. White and collected by the FWP from the Emporia Gazette, *August 15–16, 1939*)

Consider, for instance, how the Floyd Ranch, at Sedan, Kansas, recently entertained several hundred visiting cowmen on the beef tour of Chautauqua county.

The cowboys first cut out from the Floyd's herds a pair of the fattest 2-year-old steers. These were slaughtered, and the quartered carcasses hung in the cooler for proper aging. The day before the celebration a huge pit was dug, and in the early morning of the feast seasoned hickory logs were piled high in it and set ablaze. By mid afternoon it had burned down to a thick bed of red-hot coals. The two carcasses now come out of the cooler, the quarters are cut into 30 pound chunks and buried deep in the coals, which first sear the outside of the meat, sealing in the flavor, and then cook it slowly and succulently, the smell of baking beef and hickory smoke coming up through the coals and perfuming the country to attract discriminating eaters for miles around.

Thick pine planks set up on saw horses become serving tables. The big juicy chunks one by one are raked from the coals and carved on the tables with bits of charred hickory still clinging to their outsides, and the thick slices are slipped into buns. But first the meat is drenched in barbecue sauce, for which each ranch has its own recipe and about which there is much controversy. This sauce is as much part of the Latin heritage of the Southwest as are the crumbling Spanish Missions. Along the Rio Grande, it is a dark crimson blend of tomatoes and chili peppers with the latter so hot and strong that a drop of it, spilled on the plank table, will leave a charred spot after it is wiped away. But as you come north the chili peppers weaken and finally disappear, until near the Canadian border they offer you nothing stronger than a watery scarlet store catsup.

from the Indiana Office

Center of attraction, of course, is the barbecuing pit, where expert amateur chefs, men with years of experience and a firm scorn for mere woman "cooks," have been busy with preparations since early morning. The pit is usually about four feet deep and five feet wide, its length depending on the number of animals to be roasted. It is lined with stones, filled with brush and seasoned logs and a fire is kindled. When the logs are burning nicely the pit is filled again, this time with green wood—preferably hickory—which is allowed to burn down to form a bed of hot coals.

Meanwhile, another contingent of the cooking staff has prepared the animals. Veteran barbecue men contend that only an expert can perform this task, and that if the meat is dressed improperly half the flavor will be lost. In dressing mutton, for instance, the fleece must never be allowed to touch the flesh; if it does, the meat will become strong, according to local belief. After the kill, plenty of time must be left for "cooling out"—allowing the animal heat to leave the carcass—and the cleaning and jointing must be skillful and thorough.

In years past it was a universal practice to impale the whole animal on a spit for barbecuing, but today the carcass is more commonly cut into convenient portions which are roasted individually. This lessens the time required for cooking and insures a more even degree of doneness. If a turning spit is not to be used, the pit is covered over with a heavy, woven-wire netting held in place by green poles set upright in the pit. The meat is placed directly on this wire netting.

Much of the artistry of the presiding chef lies in knowing exactly when it is time to put the meat on to cook, for the bed of coals must be neither too hot nor too cool. Under his watchful eye, the pieces are turned over and over to prevent either side from becoming burned or over cooked. Seasoning, other than salt and pepper, is not ordinarily used; the succulent barbecue sauces of the South are said to obscure the finer flavor of the mutton or beef itself. . . . By the time the meat is nearly ready, the delicious odor of its broiling has served as dinner-bell for the entire group, which gathers in a body around the barbecue pit to watch the work and shout advice to the cooks. As soon as it is finished it is whisked to the tables, to join the other delicacies. . . .

From the wide choice, an average allotment for a healthy male may consist of three or four thick chunks of roast mutton; two kinds of potatoes, green beans, baked beans, tomatoes, and cole slaw; half a dozen slices of home-made bread; a couple of eggs, pickled, deviled, or hard-boiled; a piece of chocolate cake; a quarter-slice of apple pie; assorted cookies; and four or five cups of coffee.

from the Nebraska Office

Mr. S. R. Danekas, who lives at Thedford, Nebraska, Thomas County, has considerable reputation as a master of ceremonies at barbecues. Invited by letter to describe his system, he responded as follows:

In the particular barbecue you asked information we happened to use two buffalos.

After the carcass has been thoroughly chilled and cured, the bones are removed and the meat rolled into uniform pieces, no piece to excel 25 pounds.

Then for seasoning, I like to use just plain salt and pepper rubbed into the meat, the amount used depending upon the age of the meat animal and degree of seasoning desired.

The meat is then wrapped in clean muslin or cheese cloth, then wrapped in clean burlap.

A well-drained location should be selected for the pit. A pit 4 ft. deep and 3½ to 4 ft. wide and 4 to 5 ft. in length should be allowed for each 200 pounds of boneless meat.

The best fuel is hardwood broken up into uniform pieces. I list a few of them in order of their preferences: hickory, oak, ash, hard maple, elm, willow and cottonwood. Pine or fir or other resinous, pitchy, or turpentine trees cannot be used as they injure the flavor of the meat. The same is true of walnut and other woods which produce an offensive odor in burning. Even cedar, cypress and the like should be avoided if anything better is available.

The fire should be started 20 to 30 hours before serving time. Seven to 12 hours time is necessary to get a bed of live coals three feet deep, depending on the dryness of the wood, the draft of the pit, etc. Ten to 20 hours cooking time must be figured.

The next step is leveling off the bed of coals and removing all unburned pieces. Then one to two inches of coarse dry sand is spread evenly over the coals. The bundles of wrapped meat are then placed on top of the sand, allowing an inch or so between the bundles so that the heat can penetrate each chunk of meat uniformly. As quickly as possible the trench is covered with sheet iron or some durable materials supported by iron rafters or pipes to hold up the 12 to 16 inches of dirt that is to be put on top of the sheet iron. The heat is thus retained and all meat juices are under seal.

The meat is left in the pit 10 to 20 hours. When a small portion of the pit is uncovered, with the aid of a pitchfork, I hook a chunk of the wrapped meat and place it in a tub ready to unwind the burlap and muslin. Then place the savory smelling chunk of cooked meat on the slicing table. The meat is sliced cross-grained into slices to be put into buns or bread. From 350 to 400 servings can be expected for each 100 lbs. of boneless meat.

Recipes

Bluebill's Sauce
from the Mississippi Office

Naive strangers have asked Bluebill for his recipe for the sauce, but no one does it twice, for his answer is always as evasive as it is violable. He recites it like a grocery list: vinegar, bay leaves, lemon, paprika, pickling

Man slicing barbecued meat, Gonzales, Texas, October 1939.
(Russell Lee)

spices, onion and garlic. To make it "good and delicious" Bluebill says go heavy on the garlic and paprika. If he is really annoyed he will recommend generous use of a butter substitute. If only mildly he will suggest using cow butter. But catch him off guard and he will confess that he really uses nothing but chicken fat. Then, having made what he calls his "politeness," he returns to mopping his beef, and offers no details.

Rodeo Barbecue Sauce
from the Alabama Office

No less than 14 ingredients are blended by old hands at its making. Carefully proportioned, they are, tomatoes, green peppers, cayenne pepper, black pepper, cloves, allspice, onions, garlic, thyme, parsley, butter, vinegar, sugar and salt.

★　　★　　★　　★　　★　　★　　★　　★　　★　　★

Candidates' Barbecue
by E. O. Umsted, Arkansas Office

"My opponent will address you while we eat," roared tall Justice of the Peace Porter from the speakers platform. "But just because the food is good, don't get the idea his qualifications are any good."

The candidates' platform of raw lumber reared alongside the creek under the cypress trees. In front of the platform stood several hundred people, some interested, some bored, all hungry. Some of them kept glancing back at the elm grove where the wives and daughters of the candidates scurried around the long tables, ready to serve the big biennial candidates' barbecue dinner.

About a dozen other speakers sat on the platform behind Porter. He leveled a bony finger at one of them.

"I've made a good J.P. for two terms," he roared. He straightened his neat black coat, ran a slender hand over his neat, graying hair. "I've married your children for you, got your husbands out of trouble, ladies. I've dealt with wrongdoers in an honest and dignified way. Speaking of dignity, look at Mr. Bufford, my opponent. Don't he look dignified?"

Mr. Bufford, who sat where the bony finger was pointing, squirmed. The truth was, he didn't look dignified. A day's growth of reddish beard littered his freckled face, his trousers had never yet been pressed, and his paunch depended untidily from a wide belt.

"He's slouchy and seedy, Bufford is," declared Mr. Porter. "He lets things go to rack. All he can do is eat—just watch him at the table in a few minutes. But don't elect him your justice of the peace, folks. He'd ruin our township in sixty days. Just look at his old wreck of a car, over yonder."

Porter pointed toward an old mud-covered sedan with two bent fenders and a missing hub cap.

"Look at the way he keeps it!" Porter pressed. "Won't even get him a hub cap. Wouldn't he be a fine, orderly something for a J.P.?"

Porter sat down amid applause. A man fishing on the creek bank laughed. Bufford stood up, red-faced and angry. He looked down at his baggy pants.

"Mr. Bufford will now address us on behalf of his candidacy," the master of ceremonies announced. "But first, ladies and gentlemen, let's proceed to the tables and begin the feast which these generous office-seekers have provided."

The crowd swarmed about the tables, seated themselves on the long, backless benches. The women began passing out paper plates. Then ten of them brought out trays of hot fried fish.

Everyone wanted fish. Catfish, caught that same morning from the creek. Yesterday's fish wouldn't do.

The best local cooks had prepared the fish. First, they'd removed the scales by scraping with a dull knife from tail to head, rinsing the knife occasionally. Then, holding the fish by the tail, they had made a lengthwise incision down the belly, scraping out the insides, and cut off head and fins. The inside cavity was washed out with salted water. Then the fish was cut up into chunks the size of a man's hand and fried in deep fat.

After the fish came the roasting ears, boiled in big pans of salted water. Then hard-boiled eggs, the guests peeling their own and dunking them in salt. A Negro boy passed a platter of sliced Swiss cheese, and there was beer to go with it for the men—if they wished it and dared drink it publicly. There were tubs of lemonade, and coffee boiled in enormous, fire-blackened pots and served in new tin cups.

And then the pit barbecue!

The pit was dug yesterday: three feet wide, three deep, and ten feet long. The fire was lighted in it at five this morning, and thereafter fed watchfully, just enough to keep the coals red and a little flame spurting.

At six the cooks laid the hogs—skinned, cleaned and split into halves along the backbone—upon the iron rods that cross the pit.

Dad Crummit has presided over every barbecuing here for thirty years. He has mixed the sauce personally, using vinegar, brown sugar, Cayenne pepper. A little garlic. He makes a swab by tying a clean rag around the end of a clean stick. With it he smears the sauce over the top side of the half hog. After the meat has cooked a little, Dad forks it over, so that the sauced side is toward the coals, and he swabs more sauce on the other side. After six hours of saucing, turning and cooking, the hog is ready to be cut and served.

While the other candidates and the guests have been helping themselves to the meat, Candidate Bufford has stood alone on the speakers' stand. The idea was that one of the speakers should entertain the crowd while they ate, and Bufford had unfortunately drawn this period.

Bufford realized that barbecued pork is heavy competition for people's attention. He also realized that if he did not hurry, he would himself get little to eat, and Bufford was a hearty eater.

He began his speech. A big-voiced man, he brought the diners' heads up for a moment or two. But they soon fell back toward their plates. Bufford wondered if they were going to leave any of the Widow Creary's famous apple pie. She'd baked twenty pies for this occasion. Bufford had particularly wanted a slab of her pie because he was rather sweet on the widow—as was Mr. Porter, dang him!

At the thought of his opponent, Bufford snorted: "What we need is a honest J.P. I don't mean Porter ain't honest, but everybody knows I am—and you can draw your own conclusions. And as for me not lookin' dignified—well, I'm just one of the people. And if I was grabbin' off the money Porter is out of various J.P. collection schemes, I'd have a nice car too!"

He'd finished. He'd expected his final blast at Porter's honesty to get a big response, but nobody paid any attention. The crowd at the tables now considered his voice as merely so much sound.

Bufford descended from the platform and made for a table. On the way, he passed his car. It did look bad. Muddy as a hog, it was, with its bent fender and the one hub cap missing. He eyed the other cars parked higgledy-piggledy around it. They looked nice. Maybe he should have bought a hub cap when he was in the auto store the other day, but the things cost ninety cents.

He reached a table. Alec, a shiny colored boy often in the local jail for misdemeanors, was helping to serve. "Heah's you a place, Mr. Bufford," he greeted guilefully, pointing to a bench. "Ah been saving it for you specially."

Bufford set down. "You scamp, you ain't saving anything. I got no tip for you. Go long, now."

Bufford seized a paper plate. The others, he noticed, were well along in their meal. Then he spied the Widow Creary.

"Could I have some of your apple pie?" he asked.

A large, late-middle-aged lady, the widow wore an apron over her red dress, and a sun hat, made of straight pins and newspapers, covered her head.

"But you haven't even started on your meal yet," she said. "I'll get you some barbecue, you poor man!"

"Some pie first, ma'm. I'd rather have a small slab of your apple pie than all the rest of the meal put together."

Beaming, she brought him a whole quarter pie. "I'll get you some other food, too," she volunteered. "You're right flattering. Maybe I'll vote for you."

Bufford smiled as she walked away. He glanced a few places up the table. There was Porter, and Porter had overheard the widow's remarks. Porter sniffed, straightened his neat, bleak tie.

Bufford began to eat. Alec, the Negro boy, came along with a platter of corn bread. Bufford took a large piece. He noticed that Alec was eying his slab of pie covetously. The scamp!

Bufford glanced back at Porter. Porter stuck his nose in the air. "Watch my plate," Bufford said to a neighbor. "And especially my pie. Now, Alec, come with me a minute."

Bufford led the Negro over by the parked cars. "Look here, Alec," he said confidentially. "Do you still carry that screw-driver around with you all the time?"

"Yes, suh."

Cautiously, Bufford nodded toward his sedan. "My car's got the hub cap off one wheel on this left side, see?"

"Yes, suh."

Bufford forked a thumb at another car. "That blue car over there is Mr. Porter's. It's got all its hub caps on. It's the same make and year as my car. Understand, Alec?"

The Negro's eyes rounded. "Yes, suh."

"Now, my boy, isn't it a fact that you're kind of in the hub cap business? Haven't you got quite a supply of various hub caps at your house? Caps you've found, that have dropped off cars in the streets?"

"Yes, suh."

Bufford winked broadly. "You haven't any of your supply out here at the barbecue grounds, have you?"

"I keeps them hid out this way. I believe maybe I could git you one."

"Um-huh. You couldn't sell me one for a dime, could you?"

The Negro's eyes narrowed. "That Mr. Porter's the judge, boss. He can put a man in jail, if he want."

"I'm going to be the next judge, Alec. Do you install one of your hub caps on my car right away, or don't you?"

Alec wet his lips. "A dime ain't much. You know that pie you got watin' at the table? For the dime and the pie I might be able to find you a hub cap in my pile."

Bufford glowered. "That pie?" He started to thunder "No!" and then he remembered Porter's supercilious sniffs. "All right," he agreed.

Bufford returned to his plate. He wouldn't even look at the pie, it tempted him so. He finished off a gigantic meal. He couldn't see Alec. He couldn't see his car from his bench, or Porter's car. They were in behind some other cars. He looked at Porter. Porter sniffed. Bufford threw back his head and laughed. Porter, his grey eyes puzzled, stared witheringly and turned pale.

Bufford dropped his fork under the table. He'd done it on purpose. He crawled under the table after it. While there he pulled a small bottle from his hip pocket and had a drop of corn whisky. Then he sat up again, his appetite returned, and he called for watermelon.

Bufford ate two chunks of melon. Then some cake. Then some strawberry ice cream. He looked up and saw Alec. Alec grinned. "There goes my pie," Bufford thought with a pang, "but oh, boy!"

Several children were distributing cards. By now Bufford had received six cards. The one on top of his stack read: "Vote for your friend and servant—Tom ('Smiley') Teague for Assessor, Subject to the Action of the Democratic Primary, August 12."

Somebody was tugging at Bufford's sleeve. A four-year-old boy. "Vote for my daddy she'iff," he lisped, reciting a well learned formula. "Mama need it."

Bufford ate a lot more ice cream. It pained his forehead. Then Alec came up to him.

Bufford gave him a dime. Then the pie. Alec started away with the pie. Bufford heard an ominous sound around his shoulder.

The Widow Creary stood over him, her eyes blazing. "Why did you give him my pie?" she demanded.

"I'm—er—full," said the discomfited candidate. "I didn't gauge my appetite right!"

Alec escaped. "Be sure you don't ever ask me for pie again," stormed the widow. "Or my vote, either!"

She flounced away. Bufford looked up and saw Porter grinning triumphantly.

Bufford's lips tightened. "You're a fine one to talk about a seedy car in front of all these people!" he said aloud to Porter. "You're the one with the seedy car!"

"My car looks fine," growled Porter. "I wash it myself."

"I ain't talking about washing," Bufford said. "I've been checking up on how it looks. Come with me."

The two went to Porter's car. Several others, attracted by the loud talk

followed. Bufford eyed one side of Porter's car. Both hub caps were on.
Alec must have misunderstood. He'd secured the hub cap somewhere
else, then. Maybe he did have a supply of them cached out here somewhere.

"Anyway," said Bufford, pointing to the left side of his own car, "What
do you mean by telling these folks that my car looks bad? I admit it's a
little muddy, and one fender's a little bent, but I'll make you eat what you
said about hub caps. My car's got four hub caps!"

Porter swallowed. "Well, I just thought the rear one on this left side
was off. I was wrong. I beg your pardon."

"If you'd 'a' been honest, like me," Bufford said loudly, "you'd 'a' made
sure of your slurring remarks in advance."

Porter looked puzzled. "It couldn't have been the other side that had
the cap off, could it?" he asked.

"You know better," Bufford snapped. "Why can't you be honest?"

Porter frowned. He wasn't as large as Bufford, and he didn't want to
risk any trouble. Biting his lip, he started back to the barbecue table.
When he'd safely passed Bufford's car, he glared back at its owner. Then
his glance slid along the sedan's other side, and stopped.

"Come here," Porter said.

Bufford went over there. From that point his eyes followed Porter's
glance at the dented sedan.

The rear hub cap was missing.

Bufford's jaw dropped. His eyes raked the crowd for a sight of Alec.
There was none.

"That thieving scamp!" Bufford roared. "He got his dime and the
widow's pie. And he pried off and sold me my own hub cap!"

★ 6 ★

A Gathering in the Woods
NATIONAL HOLIDAYS

A Ton of Rice and Three Red Roosters
from the Florida Office

Each year on Armistice Day the small Florida town of High Springs cele-brates a Peanut Festival with a free chicken pilau and full day of ceremony. The 1941 program was at once typically American and Southern. Folk from all the surrounding country began arriving in High Springs early on the morning of Armistice Day. They came crowded into old automobiles and light pick-up trucks from which towheaded children dangled their legs. In spite of the area's large Negro population, the only ones in atten-dance were those who assisted in the preparation of the chicken pilau.

Long before 10 o'clock the main street through the town's small busi-ness district was lined with expectant people waiting for the parade to begin. Participants in the parade could be seen forming a line several blocks in the distance. Finally the line moved forward at a slow pace. The procession, extending some two blocks, slowly passed a reviewing stand and was led by an American Legionnaire and a cowboy on horseback. Be-hind them came a Legion color guard, and then the High Springs School Band, led by a shapely, high-stepping drum majorette clad in shining boots and short white satin skirt. Vying with the drum majorette for at-tention of the crowd were several flashy convertible automobiles bearing the colorfully-gowned entrants in the beauty contest to select the "Queen of the Peanut Festival." The main body of the parade consisted of giggling and self-conscious school children carrying small American flags.

The parade over, the crowd broke up and hurried to a vacant lot known as the municipal park, where it formed into a semicircle around the bandstand. Assembled on the stand were the speaker of the day, a minister, several Legionnaires, a master of ceremonies, and the beauty contestants. This phase of the program was opened by the high school band playing the Star Spangled Banner. The men pulled off their faded farm hats, and the entire crowd stood nervously at attention.

The minister then delivered a prayer in which he asked God's blessing on American's new efforts to establish a lasting and just world peace. Following this, three local Legion officials proceeded to read an Armistice Day commentary; each man reading a few paragraphs, and then passed the test on to the next man. The crowd pricked up its ears a few minutes later when the master of ceremonies introduced the speaker of the day, the Honorable Jim Cary, candidate for Congress. The speaker divided his words between customary Armistice Day observations and peanuts. He spoke highly of the role the lowly peanut has come to play in the economy of the region, and told of a recent talk he had had with the famed Negro scientist, Dr. George Washington Carver at Tuskegee Institute, "who has discovered so many uses for peanuts and all their by-products."

The master of ceremonies then proceeded to outline the coming activities. "Ya'll go right ahead and do all the dancin' and cuttin-up you want to," he urged. "If ya end up in jail we can't promise to get ya out, but we'll be glad to crawl in with ya. Now after we leave here you're all invited over to the peanut-oil mill—they've got a real show arranged for ya over there. 'Pee Wee' Jenkins and his Border Riders is gonna treat ya to some mighty pretty music. After that we want ya all to come back over here for a big pilau dinner with all the trimmins. There's been some talk goin' around that pilau ain't nothing but a ton of rice and three old red roosters, but I'm here to tell ya that ther's gonna be plenty of good chicken in that pilau an I know you're gonna like it.

"After we all git through eatin' we want to gather around the bandstand here and pick out the prettiest girl to be the Queen of the Peanut Festival, and what with all the pretty girls in the contest that looks like a mighty pleasant job. Then this afternoon comes the big game between the Alachua Indians and the High Springs Sandspurs. You folks who think there's rivalry between the university teams of Georgia and Florida haven't seen nothing yet till you've seen these here two high school teams get together. After the game tonight there's gonna be a big round- and square-dance in the high school auditorium with some more of that good music by the Border Riders. It's gonna be a fine dance, so you folks want to be sure to stay over for it. I reckon by midnight they'll all be dancin' the Elephant Stomp and by morning the band will be playing the 'Daylight Serenade.'"

Throughout the morning young girls have been handing out small bags of raw peanuts, which were not only eaten but also pinched open at the end and thus clamped on as earrings. In between the various events the men and women gathered in groups and discussed local matters, particularly the condition of crops and the weather, and some men engaged in games of horseshoe pitching.

Preparations for the pilau had been under way since early morning, by a group of townswomen who had volunteered their services. About 20 three-legged iron kettles were assembled in the park and two Negro men kindled fires under them and got them boiling. After being dressed the chickens were boiled in the kettles, and then the women began the task of

Fourth of July on St. Helena Island, South Carolina, July 1939.
(Marion Post Wolcott)

removing the meat from the bones. Meanwhile, huge quantities of rice were placed in the kettles and cooked in the water left over from the chicken-boilings. When the rice was done, the chicken meat was mixed with it, and stirred by a Negro man with a board. A woman with a spoon and boxes of salt and pepper went from kettle to kettle, seasoning each to taste. Nearby, a Negro man boiled coffee in a large metal drum.

Long before the pilau was ready to serve, a line of people was twisting serpentine fashion to the far reaches of the park. No one was given more than one plate, so entire families had to stand in the line. The pilau was served on paper plates, accompanied by a slice of bread, a pickle, and a paper fork. Coffee was poured into paper cups and evaporated milk and sugar were provided.

The Border Riders, having been delayed by the necessity of putting away their instruments, sought to break into the line near the serving tables. But the town policeman quickly ushered them to the end of the line. "Sorry, boys," he said, "but everyone has to wait their turn."

★　　　★　　　★　　　★　　　★

The guy answering the phone at the High Springs' Chamber of Commerce office is pretty adamant on the subject.

"There's nothing special going on for Veterans Day. We never had a peanut festival here."

When informed things might have been different in 1941, with a federal document to prove it, he is not impressed.

"Down in Williston. There's always been a peanut festival down there. But in October. November's too late for the crop to be in," he scoffs.

Williston is about thirty-eight miles down the road from High Springs and their festival started in 1988. It sounds like a good one, too, with the peanut honored in all kinds of ways (besides the usual raw, boiled, roasted and fried, they offer peanuts Cajun, hot, ranch, and garlic flavored, to name just a few, as well as served in pies, ice cream, cheeses, and milk). They also choose a peanut queen and king from among the peanut-size crowd of six-year-olds and under.

"Sweetheart, I'm telling you. Never happened here," he says and hangs up chuckling at the idea.

Well, all right, so there isn't a peanut festival with a pretty peanut queen and big vats of chicken pilau being served on Armistice Day in High Springs. I'm not going to judge whether the federal writers made it up or not. Maybe they were just confused by the towns. In any case, I found another bang-up national holiday celebration in Boalsburg, a tiny village on the outskirts of State College, Pennsylvania. They commemorate our other militaristic holiday—Memorial Day—with enormous style and some of the best food around.

Boalsburg claims to be the holiday's birthplace, staked by local residents on the fact that, in 1864, three women in the village decided to decorate the graves of their loved ones who had fallen during the Civil War. They continued to do so each year and, eventually, as the story goes, their tradition grew into the current national holiday.

We should pause here for a moment and consider the likely truth of the Boalsburg connection. To be fair, a little village in Virginia claims almost the same story, and another town in Georgia, where some other woman decided to decorate her relative's Civil War grave, is also said to have originated the holiday. Surely, a few other towns and villages out there swear they started Memorial Day and we should give them all their due, agreeing there are many truths (including that there just might have been a peanut festival on Armistice Day in High Springs, Florida, in 1941). Because, really, what does it matter?

Still, what Boalsburg has going for its assertion is a life-size bronze tableau of the three women in their hoop skirts bending down with flowers over a grave. It is situated on the edge of the village's Lutheran churchyard, which holds the graves of local men who have fallen in nearly every war America has ever stepped foot in. The Revolutionary War grave—its marble stone almost completely erased by time but marked by a bronze star and a small American flag—is nestled close to the old church walls; Brandon McCombre, a young pilot who lost his life in Iraq, lies far away in the last row, under a bronze statue of a small boy holding aloft a toy plane. In between, there are tombstones marking the fallen from the War of 1812, the Civil War, the Spanish-American War, both world wars, Korea, and Vietnam. Because it is a small town and a small congregation, family names are repeated over and over again, each generation forfeiting members to one battle or another for causes great and not so great. On the eve of this Memorial Day, American troops are engaged in bloody fighting. May has been a terrible month. Ten soldiers have been killed on this day alone. A lonely sorrow captures the heart as the church bells ring out and the early summer's light fades into evening—golden green then bluish purple—across the white stones and the young blades of freshly mowed grass.

The celebration that will soon take over the town encompasses many things. The village's residents decorate their houses and set up tables and chairs on their lawns, greeting neighbors in a tight show of community. Then there are the Civil War reenactors, both North and South, the Confederates just a little more dashing—and younger by decades—than the Yankees but whose campsite is relegated to the opposite side of the road away from the main celebration; a Lutheran evening service the day before the celebration that uses an eighteenth-century liturgy in which God is portrayed in prayer and song as abiding firmly on America's side; an early-morning foot race to open the day's events; continuous concerts staged in the gazebo on the town's square; a blacksmith's demonstration; a crafts display; and—most moving—a ceremony at sunset re-creating the Civil War women's walk to the cemetery and at the end of which flowers are placed upon all the soldiers' graves as a guest speaker talks to the congregation about the meaning of the day. The ceremony and the day's festivities conclude with the Civil War reenactors and a marine reserve honor guard's gun salute.

All during the day, though, there is the food to enjoy. First off, Boalsburg has this thing about soup—the townspeople offer for sale different kinds of homemade—chief among them chicken corn chowder, served at several booths, followed by the beef or vegetable, available behind the blacksmith shop. Each bowl tastes phenomenal and is hard to put down even on what is almost always a steaming hot summer's day. You'll find the first bowl of chicken corn chowder for sale near the entrance to the town, in the St. John's United Church of Christ meeting room, along with several good examples of homemade pies—shoofly, apple, cherry, pecan, lemon meringue to name a few—some made with exquisite lard or butter crusts. The beef or vegetable soups at the far end of town are notable because they are a blending of many pots; early in the day, villagers carry the soup they made at home to the blacksmith shop and pour it into two big, common cauldrons where the mixtures bubble away above an open fire. The soups turn thicker and more complexly flavorful as the different recipes meld together throughout the day.

Further along the sidewalk after that first bowl of chowder, the Knights of Columbus offer hot dogs and assorted sides such as potato and macaroni salad. But keep going toward the town square. Sharply at noon,

there is a pie contest—a good old-fashioned kind with neighbor competing against neighbor, and where any variety goes—from a fancy kiwi
whipped cream to a lovely lattice-topped strawberry-rhubarb. Two elderly women judges, who look as if they were born with rolling pins in their
hands, sit on a bench behind the pie tent where the entries are displayed
and nibble a little bit of each before they make their decisions. It's a hard
fit under the tent because everyone wants to be on hand after the judging
is complete to grab a taste of them—even of the pies that lose. It takes a
good hour for the decision to come in and about two minutes for the pies
to be devoured and the crowd to disperse, leaving little behind but a smear
of raspberry jam and a flute of a crust crushed on the ground.

In a side yard of a little white house a few doors down from where the
musicians are playing (watch out for those gathered to hear the music—
they tend to start dancing at a snap of a note), some middle-aged men
are standing around something that looks like an oil tank on wheels. It
is, in fact, an oil tank on wheels, jerry-rigged with a spout on one end
and with smoke pouring from its middle seam. Most of the men hold big
red plastic cups of beer as they mill around the yard or stare intently at

*Barbecuing beef and lamb for a picnic supper on the grounds of St.
Thomas Church, near Bardstown, Kentucky, August 1940. (Marion Post
Wolcott)*

the smoking contraption. They are all members of the Harris Township Fish and Game Commission. One among them, that would be Stan Lindsay, steps forward to open the tank's lid. A curtain of sweet smoke flutters up and inside the tank a glistening, almost topaz-colored roasting pig is revealed.

Stan started roasting pigs as a teenager twenty-eight years ago, when it somehow got into his head that cooking a whole pig over an open fire might be a fun thing to do. He didn't know much of anything of the traditional Southern pit barbecuing but, being good with his hands, he figured he could rig up some sort of thingamajig to cook the entire pig in. One night, he rounded up his friends and, being farm boys—or at least boys who knew about farms—they found a pig, took it to a field behind the high school, and in some fashion or another got it to die (he won't reveal how and there's a little shudder to his averted eyes to stop the curious from pressing the point too hard). Afterward, the boys dressed the pig. The cooking styles around these parts led the teenagers to simply place the pig in what would become the prototype of the oil tank without much—if any—seasoning. Certainly, no complicated recipe for a Southern-style mopping sauce, or even a Texas spice rub, was involved. Not that it mattered: after a long night of waiting, when the pig was judged to be done, it was such a delicious feast that Stan and his friends were hooked for life. From such serendipitous hijinks beloved traditions are born: for the last fifteen years, Stan and the boys who were with him that night (all of whom now work for the Fish and Game Commission) have continued to tinker with their tank and their recipe to produce a superb roast pig that, during the Memorial Day celebration, is turned into pulled pork sandwiches and sold to help support the work they do in the nearby national forests.

The pork sandwiches alone are worth the drive to Boalsburg. That and watching the men cook the pig, which actually starts at midnight the night before in the gravel drive behind the house. The pig and its fire need constant monitoring throughout the process. In the early hours of cooking, the coals in the bed of the tank are liable to flare up with the freshly dripping pig fat. On one occasion, the situation got out of hand and is recalled with humbled laughter and a clicking of red plastic cups full of beer. They now keep the tank out on the gravel until the skin and fat caramelize a bit, which would be about three, four in the morning—it's a tricky thing to gauge, especially if you're up that late and have been drinking beer. Then they roll the tank (hence the need for wheels) around the corner and up to the side yard, so the people celebrating in Boalsburg can be properly enticed by the smells of the roasting pig. All day long, for the sake of all the hungry folks milling about, the men have been selling pulled sandwiches made from pork butts they barbecued a few days before. The smell of the roasting pig just makes customers buy more, ignoring the example set by experienced Boalsburg attendees who stand about patiently waiting for the whole pig to finish cooking. From beginning to end, it takes about twelve hours to cook a pig to perfection—that is, to an internal temperature of 190 degrees.

"That's the best temperature for pulling," Bob Hoffman, who oversees the gang, says and nods his head rather seriously as Stan sticks a small thermometer in the pig's shoulder. "Any lower and you won't get the meat to pull right off the bone, and if it's any higher—like anything over two hundred—the tenderloin is too dry. You don't want the fat all cooked up; you want some left at the end to keep the meat moist."

All the men standing around the tank heartily agree with Bob and move just a little closer to Stan to read the thermometer with him. It's decided that another half hour would be good, then they take a drink from their cups. Red-skinned from their work outdoors, the men seem like the kind of people you'd want to meet in the woods if you ran into trouble. Muscular, even with middle-aged bellies, they are knowledgeable about tools, and fashioned the tank with an inventive V-shaped trough below the heavy-duty wire mesh grill that cradles the pig. The trough perfectly funnels the dripping fat away from the coals so the flesh never burns in a sudden flare-up but slowly and evenly roasts to a fine, moist crisp. Bob produces a little sketch to show the tank's inner workings:

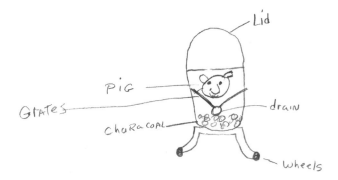

A half hour later, the pig is declared done and the men, noticeably looser after another round of beer, all cheer. Stan does the honor of carving the pig. He starts by running a knife down the middle of the back, then around the neck to loosen the skin (in the last two years, an Asian woman who moved with her family into the community has asked for—and received—the whole skin: "They eat 'em or something—the ears, too," Bob says, a little aghast). Stan slips the knife under the skin and loosens it around the head, pulling it back like a mask to reveal the cheek meat. With the tip of the knife's blade, he scoops out a little of the cheek meat and places it on the pig's forehead.

"Ohhhh, yeah!" an older man yells and quickly pinches away the delicacy before anyone else does.

When the skin is pulled back, the articulation of the animal's muscles is revealed. The meat comes off the bones in ribbons, pale pink and oyster white. The other men help out by carrying over deep aluminum trays for the meat, then take them to the sandwich booth, where they pull it into small heaping strips. As all the meat is scraped from the pig, the arching ribs and shoulders cave in together, a graceful ruin over the

Making barbecue sandwiches for Labor Day picnic, Ridgway, Colorado,
September 1940. (Russell Lee)

smoldering coals. No seasoning was used in the cooking; no sauce has been brushed across the skin. The flesh is sweet but gamey, luscious in its soft texture.

"I'll tell you the secret of a good pork sandwich," Bob says as he prepares a sample.

"You can't do that!" exclaims Stan, and the horror he displays is only half show.

Bob laughs, "The secret to a good pork sandwich is horseradish—not that weak store-bought stuff, I'm talking real fresh horseradish."

"We don't have any left," one of the men in the booth reports.

Bob winks: "We'll find you some."

After some rummaging around the booth, a container of fresh horseradish is unearthed and, it has to be said, it makes the pork sandwich a spectacular thing of beauty.

Homecoming, East Bend, North Carolina
from the North Carolina Office

The Fourth of July is celebrated at East Bend, a small town, 20 miles west of Winston-Salem on route #67, with a homecoming. Even with threatening skies over 500 attended in 1937. Former residents of Yadkin County and adjacent borders of Surry, Stokes, and Forsyth Counties bring good things to eat and assemble under the trees on the school grounds. Table clothes are brought to spread on the long row of tables of plank boards resting on saw horses. The people visit in groups until they are called to dinner, when after a prayer they all help themselves to the good things that have been spread out. Fried chicken, country ham, roast beef, chicken salad and slaw are heaped on plates or platters, cakes and pies are there in great variety. One year as many as 27 varieties of cakes were represented. Practically all of the food is home made including relishes and pickles. After eating they listen to one or more speeches. Following this prizes are distributed to the winners of races, bicycle, foot, potato races, also for various other distinctions such as the oldest and youngest twins, the boy and girl with the most freckles, the tallest man etc. The guests are entirely dispersed usually before dark.

Food Usually Found on the Table
at the East Bend Homecoming

Baked Country Ham
Fried Country Ham
Baked Meat Loaf
Fried Chicken
Roast Beef
Slaw
Pickled Beets
Cucumber Pickle (sour, sweet and grape leaf)
Potato Salad
Chicken Salad
Pimento
Pickle; Relishes; Sandwiches
Cream Cheese
Cottage Cheese
Deviled Eggs
Boiled Eggs
Twenty-seven varieties of cake
Apple Pie
Sweet Potato Pie
Peach Pie
Custard Pie
Berry Pie
Lemon Pie
Pumpkin Pie
Cocoanut Pie
Baking Powder Biscuits
Beaten Biscuits
Sliced Light Bread
Lemonade
Iced Tea

★　　★　　★　　★　　★

We're such an individualistic country that the United States doesn't really have national holidays. The federal government is allowed to establish official holidays for its employees and the District of Columbia, but it can't tell—let alone force—the fifty states to follow suit. You would think Independence Day would be the one exception but, historically speaking, it isn't, with states sometimes celebrating it (although not without protest from purists) on the third or the fifth if the fourth arrives inconveniently on a Sunday, when some citizens feel religious services should take precedence. But whenever it is celebrated, it's safe to say the day is filled with parades and fireworks. You can also count on parks packed with picnickers, while backyard barbecues work overtime.

In East Bend, North Carolina, pretty much everyone in this itty-bitty town comes together in the same way the federal writers observed but with one important exception—there's a deep religious undertone to the songs and speeches, and food is decidedly sparse.

Welcome, then, to East Bend's God and Country, Fourth of July Celebration! It is hard to tell if the residents of any other surrounding county continue to join in the day's festivities as they did back in the 1930s, but the parking lot before the East Bend elementary school is full almost to capacity. People call greetings to one another as they pull themselves slowly from their cars, hauling out small children and elderly relatives who loudly hope room will be left for them under the trees. There is cause for their concern: the stand of tall oak trees behind the school on a little rise overlooking the playing fields appears to be the only place with a shady breeze, and it's already crowded with those who followed behind the parade earlier in the day. The annual parade consists of the mayor, perched uneasily on the backseat of a flashy convertible, and a ragtag troop of flag-waving old soldiers and young children, followed by snappy marching bands with twirling batons and an armada of handsome floats that compete to be the most patriotic, or the most inspirational, or the best decorated by a local kid. The town's fire trucks bring up the rear, decked out in banners and ribbons, gleaming bright tomato red in the morning's sticky sunlight. As soon as the parade gets within shouting distance of the school, a focused, somewhat good-natured rush for the trees commences. A jostle of canvas camp chairs and squeaky aluminum folding chairs snap open to secure prime spots near enough to the little stage to see everything, yet far enough away from the sound system to make private conversation possible.

It's eleven now and, more or less on time, the celebration's entertainment is starting with a hearty, off-key rendition of the national anthem and a fine welcome from the mayor. Then the talent contest for the town's children gets under way. It's a mini *American Idol* show, as the MC, who has all the beam and bearing of a former beauty queen, keeps repeating. First up is a plump nine-year-old girl who shyly takes the microphone and, after a quiet start, lets rip her voice bellowing into the trees, "Are You Washed in the Blood of the Lamb?" By the time she reaches the final verse, she's pacing the edge of the stage like an ol' time minister and has nearly everyone who is able standing on their feet and singing the hymn with her.

Next comes a six-year-old, swinging a long blonde ponytail beneath a red cowboy hat, to belt out Shania Twain's "Man! I Feel Like a Woman!" Many of the men jump out of their chairs and begin clapping and hollering, coaxing the little girl on as she swings her tiny hips from side to side: the women, their bodies turned a little from the stage, whisper neighborly remarks to one another, a lot of their faces broken by a stiff smile until the little girl hands the microphone back to the MC.

A couple more gospel songs, pop tunes and country standards later, Little Shania wins a prize. A boy of about eleven who crooned a Johnny Cash song as if he was Johnny's son, earns the top award: tickets to a Kelly Clarkson concert, an *American Idol* CD, and fifty dollars.

The entertainment goes on throughout the day with bluegrass and string bands, and local gospel groups that hawk their private-label CDs and their next appearances. As time meanders along, some in the audience stretch out in their chairs and pull their baseball caps down over their eyes for a little nap, lulled asleep by the cooling breeze raking through the trees' high branches. Others wander down the small hill to where a few carnival rides have been set up, along with booths displaying the handiwork of local artisans. Across from the petting zoo full of baby sheep and llamas, and a hefty rabbit hopping freely around the children's legs, a fully decked-out Humvee is attracting teenage boys by the score. The Humvee and the table beside it are manned by a sergeant in the North Carolina Army Reserves who reports he's having a productive day. "Good leads. A lot of good leads," and he smiles as he watches two boys trail their fingers over the vehicle's camouflaged flank.

Those town people who come later in the morning—say, close to lunchtime—have to make do by crowding their chairs before the concession stands. A half-dozen old picnic tables, their soft wood inscribed over the last decade with names and such legends as, "Remember you can always talk to God!" and "Jesus ♥ you very much!" are being shared by several different families or piled high with teenage friends. There isn't a picnic hamper or cooler in sight. Not a pickle relish or cake, and certainly no pies among the audience. Instead, all the food at the celebration comes from the concession stands sponsored by local churches and organizations. After my being primed by the federal writers for a good homemade feast, the concession stands are at least tolerable because almost all of the offerings for sale are homemade. The local Quaker Meeting House and the Yadkinville Christian Ministry supply hot dogs and hamburgers and fine vinegary cole slaw and silky potato salad. A counter set up by a local diner offers kielbasa sandwiches and slices of country ham—salty and sweetly smoked—on a hamburger bun. The celebration's committee women sell fresh lemonade and, for dessert, there is shaved ice in all kinds of flavors, funnel cake, and—the one commercial vendor—a Hershey ice-cream truck. No one but me with my heart set on tasting many of those twenty-seven varieties of cake the federal writers promised, seems to be too upset about this state of affairs. After all, the proceeds from the concessions benefit their sponsors, so some good is being done and, as one woman at the diner stand notes as she slathers mustard on her kielbasa sandwich, "It sure is a sweet day to be doing nothing." This has to be made sweeter by the prospect of having others cook up a storm for the holiday.

Later on, when it gets toward evening, some families do show up with the remnants of their private celebrations—some pies and watermelon halves—to finish while they learn whose child has written the best essay for this year's Mayor's Citizenship Award and listen to the day's guest speaker (this year a starting quarterback and honor student from Wake Forest University) wax on what God and Country means to him. Finally, there comes a last blessing from one of the town's pastors and, with the first fullness of darkness in the sky, fireworks.

In their chairs under the trees, those who have seen many such celebrations smile at the luminescence suddenly blooming over the trees. Parents stretch back and cradle sleeping infants on their shoulders, while their older children skip down to the playing field and spin cartwheels across the thick grass. The town's teenagers—an old Prince *Purple Rain* T-shirt the single mark of a rebellious nature among them—have long since drifted back to the gas station where, with feline paces, they haunt the deepening darkness along the shoulder of Route 67 as sparklers stream jubilantly across the July sky.

A Word about a Changing Agricultural Landscape

After celebrating July Fourth, if you continue on in either direction on Route 67, you'll pass towns not much bigger than East Bend. Amid wide fields of soybeans and corn, sturdy brick modern homes and fancy double trailers share ground with the hulls of old farmhouses and sheds, their wood gone gray, the ribs of their tin roofs buckled, blood brown with rust, their frames shrouded almost to oblivion in kudzu vines.

What are mostly gone now are tobacco fields. Not only are there fewer farms cultivating the crop but the garden plots—whose yield cotton mill workers, carpenters in the local furniture factories, school teachers, and shop clerks sold each year to the big tobacco producers—are all but absent. Tobacco was a reliable way to make some extra money, a sort of living insurance against layoffs, slowdowns, and other crop failures; against a crippling illness or accident. But overseas competition and the vigorous campaigns against smoking in this country combined to make the market fall and, beginning in 1997, people across the tobacco belt were faced with the prospect of losing their land and way of life if they couldn't find another profitable crop to grow.

Which is why now, when you drive through the valley, you spy on either side of the narrow country roads field upon field of grapevines. Indians and settlers, especially in the eastern part of the state, used to concoct a sweet wine from the native scuppernong grapes, a meaty fruit that also makes a mean pie filling. Concord grapes were cultivated elsewhere and turned into wine, but Prohibition—along with the region's deeply conservative religious leanings—shut down the wine industry for the rest of the twentieth century.

Recently, though, winemaking has come back into favor. When tobacco prices fell, the government, joined by tobacco companies settling lawsuits, began to encourage farmers to grow a healthier crop. In nearby Dobson, Surry Community College was spurred to offer classes in viticulture by two local guys who were tired of the construction business in Charlotte and wanted to return home to establish a winery. Farmers and local residents heard about the classes and, with the support of the college and its

faculty, took advantage of the buyout offers and began to turn their tobacco fields into vineyards. Along with the native scuppernong, North
Carolina farmers are planting *v. vinifera*, French-American hybrids, and
native Labrusca-type grapes.

Making the change is not a cheap proposition. The Crates family has
farmed their land for five generations and, when they decided to turn a
portion of their tobacco crops over to grapes, Terry Crates estimates it
took about twelve thousand dollars an acre to do so. That was back in
April 2003. Their winery, Buck Shoals Vineyard, is just starting to produce because it takes three years before the vines mature and bear fruit,
then it's another four years before the wine develops into anything approaching drinkable. And that's if you're lucky. While the Yadkin Valley
and the surrounding counties are technically ideal, with a clay-loam soil
and temperate climate for growing grapes, the Southern humidity and
occasionally heavy seasonal rainfalls can play havoc on the vines.

Another factor to take into consideration is the culture itself in this
part of the country: frankly, it's not what anyone would call conducive
to a bacchanalian way of life. Many of these highly skilled tobacco
farmers—men and women who have maintained thriving family farms
for generations—happen to be upstanding Baptists and Methodists, people for whom hard work is next to God and drinking anything with an al-
cohol content over .01 percent is next to Satan. Many of the counties in
the North Carolina wine-growing belt are dry and they've been dry for
decades without much protest from anyone but the local teenagers (and
the occasional thirsty and disgruntled writer driving for long hours
through the state). The prospect of these folks establishing vineyards and
wineries plainly smacked of desperation.

But by the late 1990s, many farmers were desperate.

"If I hadn't done something, it was either going to be a shopping cen-
ter or a trailer park," Frank Hobbs, the owner of RagApple Lassie
Vineyards—one of the best and oldest vineyards in the valley—told me.
"I didn't want either of those things happening to my family's land."

So now along with his acres of grapes, in the back of the spanking-new
Tuscany-esque stone building where his wine is made, Hobbs and his wife,
Lenna, preside most days over a marble-countered tasting room festooned
with silk flowers and faux-country antiques, where tourists happily spend

an hour or two sipping their way through his stock. There are currently twenty wineries in and around the county, with about fifty-five statewide. A whole tourist industry has grown up around the vineyards. Festivals and tours are sponsored by the counties; upscale restaurants are opening in nearby small towns; and old antebellum homes, once on the verge of being abandoned, are now serving as handsome bed-and-breakfasts.

The buyouts have preserved family farms and the agrarian landscape, and they have helped to revive the local economy that has suffered not just with the decline of tobacco production but with the closing of factories and mills. Yet, at the same time, the burgeoning wine industry is slowly transforming a core strand of the region's rural life. As they chase tourist dollars, the counties are becoming less insular, a little more like everywhere else. The local Baptist minister has even been known to bless a new winery's tanks and, at Sunday services, it's no longer frowned upon to speak of one's fondness for a nightly glass of Cabernet.

F. M. Gay's barbecue given on his plantation every year, Alabama, between 1930 and 1941. (Photographed as part of the America Eats! project)

If the area's distinct culture is slowly being diluted, the benefit of the buyout program is not an arguable point: it's better to keep the land thriving and in family hands than to see it plowed under for a Wal-Mart parking lot. It is also decidedly pleasant to sip wine in the late afternoon sun in a bucolic garden overlooking beautiful, flourishing vineyards. It will be a long time coming before the Yadkin Valley comes anywhere close to the Napa Valley and yet it's heading that way. That's both a happy and something of a sad turn of events.

Recipes

Since the *America Eats!* papers did not include a recipe for chicken pilau, I looked for a recipe that closely reflects what was described in the papers. The following recipe is from the *Historical Cookbook of the American Negro* (reprinted by Beacon Press, 2000). The chicken corn chowder is an amalgamation from various cooks in Boalsburg, and the pie is my own.

Chicken Pilau

> 1 pound whole chicken
> Salt and pepper
> 2 thick slices of salt pork, diced finely
> 1½ cups rice
> 2 medium-size onions, diced finely
> ¼ cup celery, diced finely
> 2 tablespoons minced fresh parsley

Clean the inside cavity of the chicken well and season with salt and pepper. Place the chicken in a stockpot, cover with water, and bring to a boil. Lower the heat to a simmer and cook the chicken until the meat is tender, 25 to 30 minutes. Transfer the chicken to a plate and let cool, reserving the broth. When the chicken is cool enough to handle, cut the meat into serving pieces. Discard the bones.

Fry the salt pork in a large skillet until it is slightly browned. Add the rice and cook over a medium-low flame until the rice is golden brown. Stir in the onions and celery, and cook for a minute or two. Then add the chicken and 1½ cups of the reserved chicken broth (add water if needed to make 1½ cups). Season with salt and pepper and cover. Cook for about 20 minutes, or until all the liquid is absorbed and the rice is tender.

Serves 4.

Chicken Corn Chowder

> 6 slices bacon, diced
> ½ cup finely chopped onion
> ½ cup finely chopped celery
> 1½ cups water
> 2 cups cream-style canned corn
> 2 cups cooked diced or shredded chicken
> 2 cups chicken stock, preferably homemade
> 2 tablespoons butter
> 2 tablespoons all-purpose flour
> 2 cups hot milk
> Salt and pepper

In a stockpot, fry the bacon until crisp. Remove the bacon and drain all but 2 tablespoons of bacon grease from the pot. Sauté the onion and celery in the bacon grease for about 3 minutes. Add the water, corn, chicken, and chicken stock. Bring to a gentle simmer.

Meanwhile, in a small saucepan, melt the butter, then add the flour and blend to a smooth paste. Add the hot milk and stir until smooth.

Add the thickened milk to the chicken mixture, stirring until well blended and heated through. Add salt and pepper to taste.

Serves 6.

Memorial Day Pie

> **CRUST:**
> 3 cups sifted all-purpose flour, chilled
> ¼ cup sugar
> 8 tablespoons (1 stick) salted butter, chilled and cut into
>   8 pieces

⅓ cup lard, chilled and cut into pieces

6 to 8 tablespoons ice water

FILLING:

1 cup frozen strawberries

3 tablespoons sugar

2½ tablespoons quick-cooking tapioca

1½ tablespoons cornstarch

2 cups fresh strawberries

2 cups fresh blueberries

1 teaspoon lemon juice

EGG WASH:

1 egg

MAKE THE CRUST:

Combine the flour and sugar in the bowl of a food processor fitted with the metal blade. Sprinkle the pieces of butter and lard over the top, then cover the processor and pulse a few times until the fat forms small clumps in the flour mixture. Turn on the processor and quickly add the ice water in increments until the dough begins to form a ball. Turn the dough onto a sheet of plastic wrap. As you wrap the dough in the plastic, form it into a disk. Refrigerate for at least 30 minutes.

MAKE THE FILLING:

Preheat oven to 425° F.

Line a 9-inch pie plate with half of the pastry and set aside in the refrigerator, along with the unrolled half, while you make the filling.

Thaw the frozen berries and drain off the juice—pressing on the berries to crush them into the juice—into a medium-size saucepan. If you don't get 1⅓ cups of juice, add water to make 1⅓ cups. Stir in the sugar, tapioca, and cornstarch, and heat rapidly until the mixture begins to thicken. Set aside to cool.

Pick over the fresh berries and wash thoroughly. Let dry.

Reserve some of the berries to sprinkle over the top, about 1 cup combined. Add the rest of the berries and the lemon juice to the cool, thickened juice. Pour the filling into the prepared pie crust, then sprinkle the top with the reserved berries.

Roll out the reserved dough for the pie top. A lattice top looks pretty with this pie. If you use a single sheet of dough, cut vents. Flute the edges. Break the egg in a small bowl and whip with a fork to blend, then brush the egg mixture over the top.

Bake on the lowest rack of the oven for 30 minutes, or until a good golden brown.

Serves about 6. Great with ice cream.

★　　★　　★　　★　　★　　★　　★　　★　　★　　★

Conch Eats Conch and Grunts
by Stetson Kennedy, Florida Office

When "[C]onch eats conch" nothing like cannibalism occurs, because the Conchs are a group of Anglo-Saxon people of Bahaman descent now living on the Florida Keys, who have come to be so called because of their fondness for eating the conch shellfish. Some 5,000 Conchs live in Key West, Riviera, and along the Florida Keys, most of them eking a living from the sea by following their traditional occupations of fishing, sponging, and turtling. It is not surprising, therefore, that they are partial to seafood.

On days "when the wind is walking right" Key waters are "as crystal as gin"—to use expressions of the Cockney-speaking Conchs. On such days conchs can be sighted at great depths on the ocean floor. Spongers, peering through glass-bottomed buckets, are able to bring up conchs with their sponge hooks from depths as great as 60 feet. But most Conchs are excellent swimmers, and capture many conchs by diving for them.

Some Conch fishermen and spongers are fond of eating the conch raw, as soon as it is caught. With a chisel or screw-driver, they pierce the shell near the spiral tip, and by inserting a knife blade they sever the muscle that binds the flesh to the shell. Grasping the protruding "heel" of the conch, they then draw out the mass of flesh.

Strips of the best parts are pared off, and dipped over the side of the boat to season them with the salty sea-water. Then the strips, perhaps still squirming a bit, are chewed and eaten with great gusto. It is popularly believed that eating raw conch has a pronounced aphrodisiac effect.

Conch meat is also eaten raw as a salad, with a dressing of lime juice, olive oil, vinegar, salt and pepper. Similarly seasoned, it is made into sandwiches. It is also prepared as steaks, but the most popular conch dish is chowder made with tomatoes, onion, garlic, salt, and hot pepper. Conch in all these forms is served in most Key restaurants, and is popular with both natives and tourists, even more so than another Key delicacy, the "turtleburger," made from ground turtle meat.

Countless souvenir shops along U.S. 1 maintain heaps of conch shells which they sell for 5¢ each, or give free to their best customers. Other shops make the shells into attractive lamps and similar curios. This market for conch shells so depleted the supply of conchs that the Florida Department of Conservation was forced to restrict the business. Strange to say, the Conchs who supplied the demand for conch shells believe that they bring bad luck, and will not allow them to remain in their houses.

"Besides conchs, grits and grunts is our favorite eats," the Conchs say. "We can't afford much else, but even if we could, I guess they would still be our favorites." The grunt's popularity is by no means confined to the Conchs—it is one of Florida's most important food fishes. In Key West, waterfront fish markets keep their grunts and other fishes alive in pens along the docks. Customers peer into the water, point out their preferences, and the fish are scooped up with a dip-net and sold either dressed or alive.

In former days, when ships piled up on the dangerous and then unchartered Florida Straits, the Conchs plied the lucrative trade of salvaging; and when a ship ran ashore the message was carried from one Key settlement to another by means of plaintive blasts blown on conch-shell bugles. One wrecker became so prosperous that he took his wife to New York City and established residence at the old Waldorf-Astoria. His wife soon tired of the hotel's rich French cuisine, and announced indignantly that if he did not wire Key West immediately for "a sack of grits and barrel of grunts" she was going to return to the Keys "where she could get some decent eatin." The grits and grunts were sent for and, in keeping with the tradition of American hotels to cater to the whims of their guests, were cheerfully prepared and served by the Waldorf-Astoria.

The grunt, it should be explained, is a small bottom-feeding fish (*Haemulon plumieri*), which derives its local name from its habit of emitting several loud grunts upon being pulled from the water. In other parts of Florida, this fish is known as a "croaker." Because of their small size, usually from 5 to 12 inches, a considerable number of grunts are required to feed a hungry Conch family. Fortunately the grunts are numerous, and are quickly and easily caught on small hand-lines.

In preparing grunts for the frying pan the Conchs scale and clean them but leave the heads on. They are then dipped in meal, and fried in deep fat until they are a crisp, golden brown. Heaping portions of grits (finely ground hominy) are placed in plates or soup bowls, and the grunts are stacked high on a platter in the center of the table. The grunts are seasoned with "sour," a bottle of juice from the small, fragrant Key Limes, and the grits may or may not be eaten with butter, depending upon the family's income. The grits are eaten with a fork or a large spoon, while the grunts are eaten entirely by hand.

The Conch develops his skill at eating grunts at an early age, as his speed determines the number of grunts he gets from the platter. For this reason, speed, rather than ceremony, keynotes the meal. Competition is keen, and the piles of bones mount very rapidly.

The Conch's knowledge of the grunt's anatomy is truly amazing. First the head is snapped off, and by dexterous plucking with the thumb nails the cerebral cavity is laid bare and the brains are sucked out. Before being discarded the head comes in for a nibbling which removes the fleshy strips and tasty crust. The body of the grunt is then manually dissected. The backbone and dorsal fin-bones are removed, leaving two slabs of virtually boneless flesh and the crispy tail and fins, all of which is consumed. The number of grunts that can be eaten at a single sitting by a single Conch is almost incredible—a conservative estimate would exceed 30. The bones are picked so clean that Conch cats are notoriously undernourished.

★ 7 ★

At the Lord's Table

Church Suppers

The Salzburger Gathering
from the Georgia Office

The open grassy lawn surrounding Jerusalem Church is the scene of the annual gathering held by the progeny of the Salzburgers. Religious services begin the morning activity in the little church with its memories of colonial times. Then the officers of the Society address the gathering, speaking on the history of the group, eminent citizens who have gone forth from its ranks, and the future plans of the organization. After the meeting comes the climax of the day, the spreading of basket lunches under the trees of New Ebenezer.

Last year a newly married member of the society had his inquisitive Western bride on tiptoes weeks before the annual spring gathering.

"You must bring a picnic basket," he told her. "All the women do."

"Ham sandwiches, pickles, lemonade," she enumerated, but he shook his head.

"They bring all kinds of cooked things, rice and fried chicken and stuff."

The young wife compromised by frying two or three pullets and baked several lemon pies, but on the day of the meeting when the services were over she became eagerly interested in the great covered utensils that were set out on the long picnic tables. Three kinds of rice were there, the famous chicken pilau, a pork pilau, and mulatto rice.

"Why do they call it mulatto rice?" she whispered.

"Because it's yellow-red," answered her husband. "It's easy to make and I'll show you how sometime. You just throw some bacon in a pot and fry it brown, then you throw in a couple of cans of tomatoes and some onions and cayenne pepper and salt, a little parsley, and maybe a little garlic. Throw in a couple of pounds of washed rice and let it all steam for an hour. It's great."

"What are these big red things, whole shrimp? I've never heard of serving whole shrimp with the heads on!"

"They're prawn," said the groom. "Every year the judge brings a bushel of these giants. All you do is peel 'em and eat 'em."

From cold sliced barbecue pork to potato salad and cornbread the bride went nibbling, nibbling. Hot coffee and iced lemonade were served, and dessert was a variety of home baked pies, cakes, and preserved fruits.

"Or ice cream," invited the young husband, "if you would like some real home-made Southern custard cream."

The girl accepted a paper plate heaped with the South's favorite dessert. The ice cream was like velvet on her tongue and she immediately demanded to know what was in it.

"I haven't had to help make any at home for years," answered her husband, "but as I remember it, Malinda, the cook, used to spend half a day at the job. With seven kids in the family she had to make gallons of it. She'd use three quarts of milk and three pints of pure cream, half a dozen eggs to make it strengthenin', about two pounds of sugar and some gelatin and a cup of flour."

"Flour in ice cream?"

"You see, the custard has to be cooked. Malinda used to boil most the milk and then stir in the flour mixed first with cold water, then add the gelatin and sugar mixed up with the rest of the milk. Then she'd take this off the stove and beat in the eggs, though they'd already been beaten separately until they could hardly stand it. After that she'd throw in a dash of salt, cool the custard, put in vanilla flavoring, pour it into the big churn, pack it with ice, and call us boys to churn. We had to churn it slow and steady to get that smooth texture, and it took three of us to satisfy Malinda. She wouldn't let us stop until the handle refused to budge."

"I'm glad she taught you how," said the bride, "because it's the best cream I've ever tasted, and this is the best picnic I've ever been on. Let's

Grace at Sunday school picnic, Jere, West Virginia, September 1938.
(Marion Post Wolcott)

see, I've had rice with pork, rice with chicken, and mulatto rice, cold barbecue, fried chicken, prawn, corn bread, pickled artichokes, Lady Baltimore cake, coffee, and custard cream, not to mention marshmallows and
benné candy and Georgia pecan pie."

Shortly thereafter the woods resounded with the voices of the
Salzburger descendants singing a final hymn. The last car disappeared
through the trees, and Jerusalem Church was left to the slow dusk of the
tidewater land.

★　　★　　★　　★　　★

Even when it seems that everything in the country is changing, church
suppers remain pretty much the same as they always have. Or at least they
feel as if they have, and that is just as good. Maybe this is because, beyond
their service as a place of worship, churches function as the repository for

a community's history and people. Often, they are an anchor holding people in place, keeping the community straight and guiding it through the perils of everyday life. Other times, outliving the original congregation and their needs, the buildings, themselves, remain the only evidence left of a people's passage through the country, their customs, physical embellishments, and churchyards keys to past traditions and lives. It's one of the most profound contradictions of our country that, for a nation expressly founded on the notion that church and state should have little, if anything, to do with each other, nevertheless, it is often these theological structures that provide the nation's citizens with an abiding community center—a place looked upon as much for governance as solace. For all these reasons, and others beside, churches wield a mighty pull that can draw back even the most tattered flock. They may even, if only for a few hours of prayer and fellowship, create a new one.

Given our nature to have food about when we gather together, suppers have always been among a church's most potent tools for creating and maintaining a fold. In a strict culinary sense, the great thing about church suppers, whether they are fund-raisers or celebrations or get-togethers for the parish, is that they tend to showcase and maintain local dishes—and, of course, cooks—to their best advantages. The dishes may be regional favorites, such as the chicken and biscuits with baked beans served on winter nights at the First Congregation Church in Fair Haven, Vermont; or the pancakes, boiled ham, doughnuts, and apple pie offered at the Oaklawn Baptist Church in Cranston, Rhode Island, for its century-old May breakfasts; or the superb mutton burgoo used as a potent fund-raiser at St. Pius X Church in Owensboro, Kentucky. Other dishes are reminders of the immigrants who built the church (and the community), as evident in this notice in a local Wisconsin newspaper, touting the offerings at various denominations: "Catholic fish fries, Lutheran lutefisk and lefse dinners, Greek Orthodox banquets, German pork hocks and sauerkraut feeds, and Italian spaghetti suppers."

An outstanding church celebration occurs each year centered around Our Lady of the Immaculate Conception Church in New Bedford, Rhode Island. The parish is home to the Portuguese congregation's Feast of the Blessed Sacrament, and every August the Club Madeirense S.S. Sacramento sponsors a rousing weekend-long shebang, the highlight of which is the abundantly glorious food. First of all, there is the handsome stone barbecue pit that runs down a good third of the lot where the fair is held. Across the pit, people suspend five-foot-long stainless-steel spikes (you get to rent them for ten dollars apiece) upon which they have impaled cubes of salt-marinated beef to grill while they sip cup upon cup of fine Madeira wine imported by special arrangement between the parish and the ancestral island. Some people bring vegetables to add to the spikes for one impressively long shish kabab, but that practice is frowned upon by the sponsors. After the meat is cooked, the spikes are maneuvered over to a table that has a metal brace to pull the meat cubes off and into a paper basket. It's rare that the basket remains full until it arrives at a nearby bench or table—a state of affairs that starts again the process of filling the spike with more meat and barbecuing it to satisfy those who missed out on the first round.

For those who do not wish to grill, there is a banquet hall from which vast quantities of unbelievably tasty food cooked by a battalion of local men (most having been certified to be of Portuguese descent from their father's side) is served. On the menu there are goat, rabbit, and lamb stews; cod in a spicy tomato sauce; garlicky fava beans; tuna ceviche; escarole soup; and pork butt marinated in a vinegary wine sauce—you can go back for seconds but the teenagers dishing the portions out are so generous, few really feel the need to, although the desire may linger. The feeding goes on late into the night—although the later the hour, the more formidable those long steel spikes become in the hands of some glory-seeking young men. Rock and salsa bands fill the three stages, folk dancers spin across the asphalt lot, and many in the audience join in with them, imitating the complicated dance steps or spinning off in loopy renditions of fox-trots, waltzes, and boogie. With all the wine and liquor being drunk, the heady food—especially the addictive *malassadas*, a fluffy, fried bread sprinkled with sugar—is a sobering tonic.

In all probability, the parish is not as big as the congregation celebrating the feast—and certainly the motorcycle club members who come out in force for the event are not among the regular churchgoers—"Look how many pretty women are here!" exclaims a decidedly senior biker from his perch on the back of a huge Hog—but for at least this weekend, a lot of people in New Bedford and beyond belong to Our Lady of the Immaculate Conception Church parish and turn themselves into proud expatriates of Portugal.

Everywhere I went across the country, I stumbled upon a multitude of dinners hosted monthly, if not weekly, and during special holidays, for all kinds of faiths and creeds. Potlucks precede Bible study classes in many Baptist churches. A mosque in Brooklyn whose worshippers are from a wealth of different nations observes the end of Ramadan with a dinner that includes dishes from each homeland, as well as a roast turkey for their adopted land. In Saint George, South Carolina, someone from the Indian Fields United Methodist Church always has a barbecue for the gathering around the Tabernacle during the annual fall camp revival meeting. And August would not be August without the clambake for the members of the Allen's Neck Quaker Meeting House in Dartmouth, Massachusetts.

The Salzburger gathering outside Savannah, Georgia, over Labor Day weekend is a little of everything—a celebration of the role the Lutheran immigrants played in the settlement of the area; a public showcase for re-gional cooking and crafts; and a reunion of parishioners—current and past members, all of their descendants, and a few of their friends.

The church is on a bluff above the Savannah River, built in 1767 of red clay bricks made by the Salzburger settlers. (The present church is the congregation's third; the first church, built in 1741, was at a settlement a couple of miles away that proved to be too swampy and unhealthy, al-though it had the honor of being the first church constructed in Geor-gia.) The bustling village of New Ebenezer once surrounded its thick walls and white wooden steeple, but now, after driving for a while down a narrow two-lane road, the first sign of civilization is the churchyard scratched out of the sandy soil where salamanders scurry across the old cracked stones. Yet, each Sunday, the congregation gathers from miles around in the old pews and they continue to be buried in the cemetery when their time comes.

On this hot Labor Day, a gentle wind combs through the kinky strands of moss draping from the stately fir trees as the parishioners call out greetings to one another while walking into the church, where a sign on the door reads, ENTER WITH REVERENCE.

In this sun-filled simple structure, the orderly pews fill rapidly with people who have descended from the original settlers from Salzburg, Austria. Young boys leap over the pews in the balcony for seats shielded from any grownup's view; the middle-aged men and women who occupy the front row are costumed for the occasion in their ancestors' eighteenth-century tan britches and bright red skirts with black, tightly laced bodice vests. They are members of the Georgia Salzburger Society that helps to maintain the heritage and legacy of the church's Lutheran founders. A man who appears to be the minister is dressed in severe Lutheran vestment and powdered wig, playing the role of Pastor John Martin Blotzius, who began constructing the present church but who died in 1767, two years before the church was completed. He's here, he says, "through the miracle of living history," and then proceeds to give a sermon, admonishing the parishioners about how they've changed in the twenty-first century—not always for the good.

"We are not as conservative as we were in my day," he says with a halting Austrian accent. "Parents, you must teach the catechism to your children and not allow them to take communion before making a good confession."

He's given a round of appreciative applause and cedes the pulpit to his modern replacement, Pastor Eleanor Russey, who looks out across the gathering and defines the legacy of the church as, "You, dear saints. It is this long train of people that stretches back through the centuries."

After the services, and as the bells in the old belfry chime noon, lunch is served—not at tables set up under the trees but in a handsome new (and perhaps more important, air-conditioned) parish hall. Lunch is ten dollars and tickets have been sold out for days. Latecomers are woefully out of luck and stand looking forlornly at the women bustling about the open kitchen and pulling from the ovens baked hams, trays of biscuits, and loaves of raisin bread. They're mixing up a big bowl of egg yellow potato salad and cutting into serving slices pretty pink and green squares of what's known in these parts as congealed salad—and to the rest of the country as Jell-O mixed with various fruits or vegetables. (Asked if the salad is a regional speciality, a woman in her seventies laughs, "I've made congealed salad my whole life and never thought of it as regional. It's just congealed salad.")

Across the dining room, two young women unseal homemade cakes from their Tupperware holders and unwrap tinfoil and plastic wrap from pie tins. The women start to cut them into neat pieces, arranging individual servings in rows on a side table. Every now and then, they sneak tastes from what clings to their knives—moist crumbs, rich fillings, flaky crusts, buttery icing.

"I made that one," one of them says, pointing to a perfect lemon meringue pie, its peaks so high and swirling brown above the white mounds it could be a model for a ski run.

"Gee, that looks good," her companion says, her voice a bit muffled by the edge of a crust she's just popped into her mouth.

Another woman brings in two red velvet cakes and is anointed with this judgment: "They look so good, we could auction them off and get a bundle!"

Martha Zeigler, a tall straight-backed woman, her gray hair cut in a girlish pageboy, is, at seventy-seven, something of a walking history book for the parish and relates how the celebration has changed:

"It started long ago as a thanksgiving for the harvest. The church was the host and the sponsor and they would set up long tables on the grounds and just have a feast cooked by the women. The food was something. And the lemonade! If you believe it, people came sometimes just for the lemonade.

"But about five or six years ago, we decided to open it up to everybody because, you know, darling, people just don't know where they come from anymore."

The educational aspect of the celebration includes a tour of the cemetery and a historical exhibit in the small house that was used as an orphanage for the children of parents who died on the passage overseas or who had succumbed to the mosquitos and heat of their adopted land. The orphanage now holds an art exhibition, and a poster contest on some aspect of the Salzburgers' history—this year it's their colorful dress. Out on the church lawn, beneath the shade of the fir trees, the Dasher family is putting on a demonstration of how sugarcane, a once important local crop, was made into syrup. Emma Lee, who married into the Dasher family, does the talking, while her husband, Clayton, sits by the bubbling pot of syrup in a open-sided shed set up on the church ground for this purpose. Beside it is a working cane "sweep": a rusting gear box nailed to the top of an old tree stump with a long tree branch attached to the top of the box. A mule gets hooked to one end of the branch and, as it walks in endless circles around the stump, the gears turn and pulverize the stalks of cane.

"It works like an old washing machine," Emma says, demonstrating how to feed a cane into it. You need a great pile of cane to make ten gallons of juice, which then gets boiled down to about one gallon of pure syrup. A lot of work, but when Emma pours a little syrup over a piece of bread, the distinct clear sweetness does make the effort seem worthwhile.

A young man standing nearby helpfully uses the back of a church program to sketch what the contraption looks like in full swing:

"My husband's family raised cane for generations, but now it's just a hobby of ours."

They keep a field of sugarcane for themselves while the rest of the farm is lent out to a neighbor to grow corn and graze cows. Over the last few years, the Dashers have harvested their small field in November and, as part of their Thanksgiving family reunion, they make cane syrup.

"It's a way that I can preserve our heritage for the grandchildren," Emma says.

A demonstration of silk making, a dream Georgia's founding father, General James Oglethorpe, had for the young colony and which the Salzburger congregation proved to be fairly adept at, is taking place in the old parsonage building. An elderly gentleman, sweating profusely in the woolen garb of the old settlers, holds an audience of youngsters in thrall as he lets a plump and pretty silkworm crawl across his fingers while he demonstrates how to pull the silken thread from the worm's cocoon.

For the folks who could not get into the luncheon, there's the consolation of a booth selling very tasty knockwurst, and some really terrific fresh homemade lemonade. Better yet are the loaves of homemade raisin bread for which the Salzburgers are famous. These are on sale at the Marktplatz—a white tent shading tables filled with other baked goods and jars of thick, tart, homemade wild blueberry jam.

"Yours is the best I ever had," a woman calls to Martha Zeigler as she passes by.

"Oh, darling, thank you," she says, then turns back and reveals the bread's secret: instead of packaged yeast, she uses a wild sourdough yeast starter her daughter Pam gave her. With giving out a little to family and friends over the years, Martha figures about two thousand people have some of that very starter by now.

Pam—not as tall but, in every other way, a mirror image of her mother—comes up beside Martha and rubs her back lightly. It looks like it's about to rain, the air heavier than usual with moist heat and the sky lowering to gray. Pam looks about at the gathering slowly drifting toward their cars.

"When I was growing up, I only knew Lutheran and German names," she says. "Now there are so few left in the area. The parents, most of them worked in the paper mills in town or were farmers and had always lived

Women of the congregation preparing for annual cleaning, Person County, North Carolina, July 1939. (Dorothea Lange)

around here. But they sent their kids to college and, once the kids left, they kept on going away. That's why this supper is so important to us now; it's a way of keeping our heritage alive."

The Big Quarterly
from the Delaware Office

The most enthusiastically attended Negro event in Delaware is the Big Quarterly celebration at Wilmington, which attracts members of the colored race from such distant points as Georgia, West Virginia, and New York. It is a day of intense religious fervor, mixed with feasting on foods prepared by some of the best Negro cooks in the State, and gaily taking over the streets of the city that have been roped off for the occasion.

Originally the celebration was a religious event marking the last quarterly meeting of the year, of the official board of the African Union Methodist Episcopal Church, established as the first all-Negro church in Delaware in 1805. It was the custom of slave owners in Delaware and nearby states to allow slaves to have a day of freedom quarterly to worship or do as they pleased, and many slaves were provided with carts and ox teams to make the trip to a common gathering place. The August meeting in Wilmington came at a time when weather conditions made traveling best, and throughout the years, attendance at Big Quarterly increased.

The modern trend of scoffing at old traditions exists but has affected Big Quarterly little. The celebration is more largely attended than in former years. It is now celebrated by Negro churches of all denominations, which hold special service, and make constructive effort to infuse the spiritual meaning of the celebration, without spoiling the feasting. These services are augmented by crusading missionaries, both men and women, who loudly exhort the passing throngs to Christianity from street corners.

Not the least of the attractions drawing the large crowds are the tables lining the sidewalks, where the savory aroma from sizzling dishes tantalizes the appetite. In addition to the sidewalk concessions, practically every house in the section is an "eatery" for the day. Feasting begins early in the morning, and continues throughout the day. The varied menu consists of fried chicken, chicken pot-pie, ham and cabbage, hot corn pone, greens and side meat, frankfurters, watermelon, soft drinks, pig feet, pork roasts, and baked ham thickly studded with cloves. There is no formality to the eating, most of the diners making their selections from the stands and feasting on the succulent morsels as they walk along the street, then stopping at the next stand that attracts the eye and palate. All the diners are not just promenaders, but many are singers, breaking forth with Negro spirituals at such times as their mouths are empty, while those who have seen the "light" of conversion are ready, between nibbles on the breast of fried chicken, to loudly proclaim their faith.

★   ★   ★   ★   ★

"Praise the Lord, everybody!" shouts the master of ceremonies.

Seated in lawn chairs or on blankets arranged under the London plane trees in Tubman-Garrett Park, the faithful raise their hands and shout almost in unison again, "Praise the Lord!"

"It's time to be saved," the MC announces to usher in a men's choir who, even before they bounce onto the stage, blast out a rousing hymn that makes almost everyone sway. Children, dressed in their good clothes, leap across the lawn, mindless of their elders who cry out, "Don't get dirty, now," even as they laugh at the somersaults and skips and fill the children's hands with coins for the amusement rides set up in a nearby parking lot.

The MC comes back onstage and exclaims, "We don't want the world to be making more noise than us, Amen."

"Amen!" people roar, loud and clear.

Then he asks, "Who danced before the Lord until his clothes fell off?"

"David!" comes the jubilant response. Onto the stage twirls a troop of praise dancers in long, flowing skirts and ballet leotards—teenage and middle-aged women, none of them owning particularly dancerlike bodies. But then the music starts and their light agility and elegance is a wondrous joy. The beauty of those everyday bodies flowing, pliant and lush, through graceful steps seems to pull all the faithful to their feet, their bodies rocking back and forth to the melodically pulsating music. Even the police officers assigned to the event begin to sway, all their equipment hooked to their belts—flashlight, handcuffs, the gun in its holster—smacking gently against their hip bones as the beat grows louder.

Somewhere after the fourth performance, a man standing by the stage cries out, "I want to be saved!"

The audience erupts in joyful hollers, while the MC and the minister playing the piano reach down to touch him.

"One more for the Kingdom!" the MC announces, as he straightens and people all around the saved man clap him excitedly on the shoulders.

If the August Quarterly is smaller than it once was, stuffed as it is into a little park in front of the train station beside the Christina River instead of taking over Wilmington's streets, it remains a stirring, deeply felt celebration. More important, if you look at it from its beginnings to what it is today, the Quarterly—how it has been celebrated, what it has meant to the people who have come to it for almost two hundred years—exemplifies the experience of what it has meant to be black in America. It is an event that on the surface is full of glory, of praises to the Lord and vigorous communion. It is an afternoon of hugs and backslapping and jiving music and plentiful food. It is a day that runs deep with the struggle to live free, to be heard, to break away from the limitations set by intolerance and inequality.

Peter Spencer, a freed slave, founded the Mother African Union Church about a half-mile up the hill from the city park. Before forming a church of their own, Spencer's small congregation was part of the white Asbury Methodist Episcopal Church but, as he wrote in a short history of why he felt the need for another church, "The Methodist Episcopal Church in this region thought proper to deny the colored members of said church the privileges guaranteed by the word of God and His liberal Gospel." By 1813, a church solely for the African-American population was established at North Franklin and Ninth streets, and the following August—a month when field labor was less intense and both freed and enslaved members could join together—the church held a celebration to commemorate its religious freedom. Preaching was always a major part of the event, but the Quarterly soon became important as one of the few times people could come together and possibly see their kin who had been sold or moved away. It provided a rare moment of personal freedom—and sometimes an entrance to the Underground Railroad, often with the help of Father Spencer and Thomas Garrett, Wilmington's train station master at the time.

After the Civil War, as poor blacks settled in Wilmington, the church became an important spiritual, social, and cultural touchstone for the inner-city community, and the Quarterly grew to be a massive celebration that emanated from the church and took over the surrounding streets in the downtown area. While the church, itself, was the centerpiece for the day's activities, itinerant preachers used street corners and store stoops to bring the gospel to the people. Many of the houses in the surrounding blocks opened their front doors and placed tables out on the sidewalk, where residents sat and enjoyed the crowds. Households made some money by selling from their doorsteps fried fish and chicken, roasted corn, baked ham, all kinds of long-cooked greens, pig's feet in red-hot sauce, and custard pies. The faithful promenaded up and down the pavement, often in clothes bought specially for the Quarterly. The whole neighborhood poured out into the streets, gleefully singing and dancing, being saved one way or another, late into the summer night.

Except for the two women manning a table for a politician running for a local office, I'm the only white person in sight. Some eyebrows are raised as I linger by the stage and one kind woman asks me if I'm looking for the train station across the street. But Bishop Albert Jarman greets me warmly and finds two empty chairs by the park's entrance. He is an elegantly turned-out man with a perpetual smile adorning his round face. He serves on the executive board for the Quarterly and remembers what it was like when he was a boy.

"There would be at least a hundred buses filled to bursting with celebrants coming from up and down the seacoast for the event. The original site of the festival was French Street between Eighth and Ninth streets, and going as far down as King Street. The black intelligentsia of the time lived along the thousand block of French Street and they were always a little uncomfortable about the Quarterly, about the social aspect of it, because, along with the preaching, there were people playing cards and drinking a little bit, you know, in front of their houses. You know Alice Dunbar Nelson? She wrote a piece that said the Quarterly brought disrespect to black people because it underscored stereotypes. So when the riots came, that part of our culture was glad to see it go."

In the 1960s, the Quarterly was considered by the police and city officials to be a stronghold of the Black Power movement and, with the riots that engulfed Wilmington in 1968 after the assassination of Martin Luther King Jr. and occupation by the National Guard for the ten months following, the celebration was shut down. After the riots, the neighborhood surrounding the church fell into decline. The building of Interstate 95 through downtown, in conjunction with urban renewal initiatives, shredded whatever was left of the once vibrant community. Today, a bronze statue of a man holding a sleeping child marks the site of the original church and the graves of Father Spencer and his wife Ann.

Bishop Jarman leans forward and nods his head. "You know up the hill where all the city and state government buildings are now? All that used to belong to Father Spencer's followers. I always say it took poor slaves to purchase the land and educated blacks to give it away.

"But, anyway, when we got the Quarterly back going in 1976, we had to rebuild it. Some in the community were still against it and the youths didn't know the history of it and didn't see a reason for it. We had to do a lot of teaching to our people about the Quarterly's significance. We had to talk a lot to city officials about how we could make it different, by moving it to the park and bringing in religious speakers and choirs. Sometimes in those years, there were few people among us to work for the Quarterly but the reason we did it and still do it is to remember our past. You can tell what a culture's values are when you look at their celebrations and the August Quarterly was the foundation of the building of our culture. We remember how our forebears not only persevered, but made the best of a worse situation than any of us will know."

A big part of the August Quarterly today is getting people to know its history, to have them understand that they are part of something bigger. For this reason, a second day dedicated to reaching out to teenagers has been added to draw them into the fold and, just as important, to expose them to educational and cultural opportunities they may not come in contact with beyond their everyday city life.

Sitting near the bishop at a table full of literature about the Quarterly, Valerie McCoy, the cochair of the August Quarterly planning committee, nods her head at what he has said. She looks out for a moment at the park, now close to bursting with a great gathering, and says, "People may not know why they're here, but they know what they are doing here."

The stage is never empty of singers and performers for long, and more prayers are shouted to the heavens, and more souls are asked to be saved. No houses are opening their doors; today the food is provided by a handful of vendors who set up shop before the rail station. With all the singing and dancing working up an appetite, they are doing a brisk business. Before the Quarterly was shut down in 1969, folks may have cooked food redolent of the South; the vendors now—with a nod toward more recent immigrants and some relocation from the Gulf Coast states after the hurricanes—are selling dishes flavored with Caribbean and Creole spices, which is not to say there aren't some mighty fine crab cakes and fried trout from local waters available, too. What must also be tasted is the very creamy, egg-rich homemade vanilla ice cream and tropical ices, and what appear to be vats of concoctions that are popularly known by their colors, not their flavors (as in, "I'll take a small red drink, please").

"Hello, sugar," the young woman behind a table under a makeshift awning says to a customer. It's almost five o'clock and she still hasn't fully set up her station because people have been interrupting her since she arrived, too impatient for her food to wait. She has a couple of large coolers filled with salads and marinated meat that she prepared the night before in her kitchen. A little camper stove and a toaster oven are at hand to warm up her jerk chicken and—if she gets a moment—to prepare macaroni and cheese. She only has her sister and a young daughter to help her and most of the customers who are standing impatiently before her table are like Keith, a conductor for the railroad who spent his half day off at the Quarterly.

"You know what I want," he smiles at the woman and she gives him a fierce, no-nonsense smile right back.

Keith hangs his head contritely and nods up the street. "I've been to that other place up there and they tried to give me some of what they call potato salad but that's not any potato salad I'd eat."

"Then try some of this," she says and goes to one of the coolers, digs out a big plastic container, and spoons out a taste for him. The salad is clumped together, flecked with celery and big chunks of potatoes. Keith hasn't even swallowed what he hungrily snatched from the spoon but he's smiling, completely enraptured.

"You're all right with me, girl! That's the stuff. That's potato salad. Give me that and some jerk chicken, and you know I'm hungry, so don't skimp."

As she walks away to prepare his plate, she calls over her shoulder, "You are something, man."

*Outdoor picnic during the noon intermission at an all-day meeting of
ministers and deacons, Yanceyville, North Carolina, October 1941.
(Marion Post Wolcott)*

"I know I am. And hungry, too."

When she comes back, she hands him a container brimming so high
with food she can hardly close the lid. It contains the jerk chicken and potato salad plus a large heap of silky, spicy cabbage.

Keith takes the container and says to the rest of the customers waiting
their turn, "The Lord has made me a happy man today. A happy man!"
and he walks off to find a spot to eat near the singing before he reports to
work again.

Religion and the Federal Writers

The stories devoted to religious events in *America Eats!* reflect the de-
mographic of the federal writers, themselves, and America in general
at that point in our history: meaning a much more homogenized
population—certainly in its religious practice—than now. By and large,

the stories revolve around Protestant sects: revival meetings, foot-washings, and Household of Ruth dinners; church suppers in New England's Congregational churches and camp preaching out on the open Oklahoma prairies. In this context, the Mormon Church is viewed as exotic, but its celebration runs just four perfunctory paragraphs, with this one being the kernel:

A Mormon Ward Reunion
from the Idaho Office

A representative feed held recently in a north Idaho town by 58 Latter Day Saint members featured chili beans, salads, several kinds of desserts, crackers, candies, etc. These meetings are described as entirely democratic, where barber and banker rub shoulders. Followers of this faith do not believe in drinking coffee and only beverages such as punch or lemonade may be served there.

★   ★   ★   ★   ★

A Jewish Seder is the only other religious meal described in the archived papers and it was classified under "Foreign Group Meals." The story comes out of the New York City office, which was asked to assume responsibility for collecting material about foreign groups because, relative to other places in the country, the city was where most immigrants had settled or at least come through and stayed for a time before heading out to live more permanently somewhere else. A memorandum to the city's supervisor asked for materials that: "Indicate the influence of foreign foods and mass cooking on the eating customs of the region . . . [such as] a Jewish Seder, or other ceremonial meal of foreign-born groups. Although the emphasis of *America Eats!* is on American food and social group eating, we cannot overlook the influences spreading from the larger immigrant groups."

Two Seders are documented in the city's files. One is a straightforward account of the main Seder meal with a history of the holiday; the other explores the ritual and dietary restrictions associated with the holiday and the burden on the housewife who prepares the meal.

Because the writers wrote similarly of the Seder's rituals, I have merged the accounts, taking the best passages from each writer.

A Passover Seder

by Jean Greenberg and Arthur Zipser, New York City Office

There are really two "Seders" associated with the eight day holiday of Passover. The first takes place on Passover eve, the second on the evening of the first day. But the first Seder, which introduces the holiday, is considered the most important, and even non-pious Jews who might ignore many other Passover customs, always manage to be present at their parents' home on the "First Seder" night.

Considering that many pious Jews will not even dine at the table of their non-pious children, then it may be easily imagined how anxiously they avoided the non-coreligionist. And this may serve as an explanation that strengthened and kept intact the Jewish family attachment, for which the Jews receive such general praise.

Passover (Pesach) which falls around the end of March has even greater limitations and hardships for the Jewish housewife. For the Passover, the kitchen is a veritable burden for the housewife.

For a whole week an entire new assortment of cooking utensils and plates are required, and the dishes are in main prepared from matzoth (unleavened bread), eggs, meat, soup, potatoes, in which nothing leavened must be used. It is easily understood that such a limited choice in the menu calls for inventiveness.

When the members of the family arrive after attending the evening synagogue service, they find the table laden with horseradish, onions, maror (bitter herbs prescribed for the occasion), dishes of hard-boiled eggs, sliced and soaked in salt-water, matzoth wrapped in a large white napkin, soup, chicken, and large glasses of sacramental wine. Before each plate there is a prayer book containing the prayers to be recited before, in between and after the meal.

The old father first blesses the wine, and intones several prayers. For the youngest male member the high spot is the moment when he must ask the Four Kashas (questions). He inquires, without a glance at his Haggadah, for he knows this part by heart:

"Wherein is this night so different from all other nights of the year? Why do we eat bitter herbs? Why do we eat unleavened bread? Why do we dip the parsley in salt water and the bitter herbs in haroset?"

His childish voice, pitched to a chant, is answered by his father's deep rumble, in the same singsong key: "To remind us of the time when we were slaves in Egypt."

When the long introductory ceremony is finished, the group happily falls to the lavish Passover meal which runs to many courses and will often include such dishes as gefilltte fisch (stuffed fish), chicken soup with knaydlech (matzoh meal dumplings), boiled chicken with potatoes and legumes, stewed fruit, sponge cake made of matzoh meal and eggs, and the traditional four glasses of wine to wash it all down.

Long after the meal is eaten the family lingers around the table, stuffed, relaxed, and happy. They nibble at sponge cake, eat nuts and sip wine or brandy while Grandpa reads aloud from his Haggadah the familiar and ever-fascinating history of the Passover. The younger folks who may not be able to read Hebrew follow the parallel English text. The very youngest, becoming restless, wait for the joyous end when every one joins in the singing of the traditional round, Had Gadya, with its endless stanzas about "an only kid my father bought for two suzim." Then all the children are sent off in search of the afikoimen—a piece of matzoh which has been hidden in advance. The finder is loudly hailed as a truly blessed hero and on this gay note the Seder ends.

★　　　★　　　★　　　★　　　★

Recipes

When the Salzburgers settled in America, they attempted to adapt their native Austrian dishes to the plants and animals they found in southern Georgia. Martha Zeigler's daughter Pam recalled that, when she was growing up, their table was filled with mostly rice and vegetable dishes.

"They made sauerkraut out of collard greens," she said—and with a look of sheer bafflement crossing her face. "It stinks so bad when you open the jar, my daddy wouldn't let Mother open it in the house!"

The following recipe (somewhat adjusted for clarification) comes from a collection of old Salzburger recipes.

Collard Sourkraut

> Collards (greens will shrink considerably, so figure 3 times whatever you think will fit into the container you will be using)
> Salt
> Wooden keg or bowl for storage
> Pestle

Clean and wash the collards. Stack several leaves on top of one another at a time, roll lengthwise (jelly-roll fashion), and slice as finely as possible with a sharp knife. Repeat with the remaining collards, leaving four or five whole ones.

Place an inch or two of the shredded collards in the wooden container, sprinkle with 1 tablespoon of salt, then press the collards down with the pestle until tightly packed. Continue this procedure until you have packed in all the collards. Add water to cover and then enough salt to make the water really salty.

Cover the top with the four or five whole collard leaves. Fill a sealable plastic bag with water, seal tightly, and place on top of the leaves. This will seal the surface from exposure to air and prevent the growth of mold. For extra protection the bag with the water in it can be placed inside another plastic bag. Place a clean plate that fits snugly over the crock and weight it down just enough to press the leaves further but not enough to burst the bag of water. Leave the crock to set in a cool place for a week, then remove the weight, plate, and bag of water and check on the fermentation. This process may take another week or so.

The sauerkraut is done when it's tangy enough for you.

Raisin Bread

> 1 (1-tablespoon) envelope active dry yeast
> 1½ cups warm water
> ⅓ cup sugar
> 1 teaspoon salt

2 pounds all-purpose flour
3 tablespoons lard
1 to 1½ cups raisins

Preheat the oven to 350°F. Dissolve the yeast in the water.

In a large bowl, mix together the dry ingredients. Cut in the lard and mix quickly. Make a well in the middle of the flour and add the yeast. Mix to form a dough. Turn out onto a lightly floured surface and knead until the dough is smooth. Add the raisins. Let the dough rise until it doubles in size, then punch down.

Divide into two loaves. Bake in greased loaf pans for about 40 minutes, or until golden brown.

Emma Lee Dasher's Syrup Bread

1 teaspoon baking soda
½ cup boiling water
1 cup cane syrup
½ teaspoon salt
1 teaspoon grated nutmeg
1½ cups flour

Preheat the oven to 350°F. Grease a 9-inch cake pan and set aside.

Dissolve the baking soda in the boiling water, then add the rest of the ingredients and beat well until the dough is smooth.

Pour the mixture into the prepared pan and bake until lightly brown, 35 to 40 minutes.

Revival Cooking

Religious revivals took place in mid-August, during the small respite in farm work that occurred between the first and second harvests. From then until the end of the month, people had the opportunity to gather together to listen to sermons from local ministers and traveling preachers. Come the afternoon, long tables would be set up around the church or pavilion (called a tabernacle) constructed for the occasion in a nearby field, and women would bring out the special dishes they had cooked at home. Vegetables and fruits were at their ripest; the young chickens at a good weight for frying. While no one would admit to the sin of pride, enough care was taken with each dish that even the worst cook in the congregation put out a nice spread. Revivals gave families an excuse to call on relatives and invite friends from far away and, for those few short weeks before the hard labor of the major harvesting commenced, everyone got a chance to feast and visit in the Lord's name.

The following is a list of dishes for a revival supper:

A Revival Menu
by T. S. Ferree, North Carolina Office

FRIED CHICKEN—Young fat chickens off the farm, slaughtered, plucked and salted down for a few hours. Rinse, pat dry, then cut into choice pieces and roll in flour, sprinkle with black pepper. Heat up about two inches of lard in a pan and drop the chicken pieces in. Fry until both sides are rich brown.

SWEET POTATO BISCUITS—Take four medium sized smooth sweet potatoes and wash them, then cut into pieces and put them in a pot with a little water to boil. When they are soft, drain, and peel them, then mash them up well. Sift flour over the potatoes, cut in shortening. Mix well, then pour in some buttermilk. Mix again until all is blended together real well. Drop by tablespoon onto a greased sheet and bake in a hot oven until they are brown.

COCOANUT PIE—Mix together shredded cocoanut, butter, eggs, sugar, and corn starch, then pour it into a lard pastry crust on a pie pan and bake.

RELISHES—Pickled cucumbers, beets, peaches, and pears.

★　　★　　★　　★　　★　　★　　★　　★　　★　　★

May Breakfast
by Rhoda Cameron, Connecticut Office

Someone crowded into the bus seat beside Elizabeth Bradley. Stout persons invariably chose the place next to her, as her spare frame filled less than half the seat. Without looking up, Elizabeth pressed closer to the window. But the new passenger was a friend.

"Why, Mrs. Bradley, how are you? I *am* an early bird, if I've caught your bus. Do you know, I was speaking of you only last night to my sister. I said to Hattie, 'Hattie,' said I, 'do you realize that it's almost spring again? Mrs. Bradley will soon be flying around getting up another of her marvelous May Breakfasts for the church.'"

An added weight seemed to fall upon Elizabeth's spirit. The May Breakfast. Why had Mrs. Cartwright reminded her of that, today of all days? Her mind had been full of household problems. How was she to get her spring cleaning done, the garden made, the family wardrobe renovated? She couldn't count much on Bernice, her fourteen year old daughter. Bernice had small liking for domestic work. Charles, the boy, was really more of a help, though he was only eleven. But after all you couldn't expect a boy to do a woman's work. As for Ben, her husband, she had long ago resigned herself to the fact that the less you expected of him, the less likely you were to be disappointed in the end. Ben's inability to cope with life, his unimportant, ill-paid job in the lumber yard, had made it necessary for her to go to work in the factory.

Mrs. Cartwright rattled on.

"And Hattie said to me, 'Marian,' she said, 'do you know our church is the only one hereabout that still carries on the old custom of the May Breakfast. One by one the others have all dropped it. And I'm sure the only reason that Emmanuel keeps it up is because we have Mrs. Bradley with us. If anything happened to her, there'd be no one else capable of carrying on in the same way.' Not, of course, that Hattie was thinking for a minute anything would happen to you, Mrs. Bradley. Everybody knows how your folks live to a ripe old age, and I said as much to Hattie. But we both feel that our church is certainly lucky to have you for a member."

"I consider that a great compliment, though I'm sure I don't deserve it," Elizabeth said politely; and she smiled and nodded in simulated interest for a dozen blocks more, while Mrs. Cartwright recounted a story concerning her small granddaughter. She was relieved, however, when her neighbor left the bus as they reached the shopping district. She wanted a chance to think.

Funny—she had just forgotten that May Breakfast time was coming. After managing it a dozen times herself, and helping her mother and grandmother ever since she could remember. Always the first Sunday in May after the Sunrise service. Doing it herself ever since mother died. Of course it would have been Mattie's job, her being the oldest, if she hadn't gone to California with her husband. Elizabeth had never quite gotten over Mattie's going away like that—leaving Connecticut where the Phelpses had always lived since 1635. It had made her sick, when Mattie went, real sick so she couldn't eat for awhile. It seemed so like going back on all those other Phelpses, who had stuck it out even when times were bad. All of them buried right here in Connecticut.

Elizabeth differed in various respects from the other factory employees at Stafford Loud Speakers, Inc. A tall, spare woman with grey threads showing in the abundant brown hair which she parted in the middle and drew back to a generous bun at the nape of her neck. A clean print dress of dark blue; black oxfords with sensible heels: that was Elizabeth in her working garb—rather austere in her lack of feminine finery, but beautifully clean and neat. After a hard day at the factory she would emerge at 4:30 from the employees' door in a crowd of wilted, wrinkled, perspiring fellow workers, looking exactly as she did when she entered that same door at 7:30 in the morning.

She differed, too, in the amount of work which she accomplished. Supremely indifferent to the antagonism of the other women who worked with her in the big room, she wound an average of four hundred and fifty coils a day, her long, deft fingers moving rhythmically about the flying wheel with never a false motion. Most of the girls averaged no better than three hundred. For this reason, she kept her job in the slack season as well as during rush times. As for the dislike of her fellow-workers, it worried her not at all. What had she in common with these noisy, rude young women of foreign extraction?

All day, as Elizabeth's hands flew about her wheel, her thoughts kept returning anxiously to the May Breakfast.

"I must be getting old before my time," she told herself in disgust. "I got up the Breakfast those other years without any great fuss, and if people enjoy it as much as they always say, it's selfish of me to begrudge the time spent. Mother did it cheerfully, and so did grandmother. Maybe it was done by her mother, for all I know. When I'm gone—"

But no amount of imagination could conjure up the picture of Bernice preparing a May Breakfast. The girl couldn't be trusted to turn a pancake without disastrous results.

That evening, when the supper dishes were done and the house put to right for the night, Elizabeth began planning a menu for the May Breakfast. Her fruit cellar still contained a wide variety of jellies and preserves, many of them put aside at the time of their making, for this particular event. The wild strawberries, preserved under glass by the best of the sun's rays, for instance, were a delicacy which the family had enjoyed only at Thanksgiving and Christmas breakfasts. Eight jars waited in the darkest corner of their shelf for the May morning when they would be unwrapped in the church kitchen, and their delightful aroma would be greeted by a chorus of ohs and ahs!

Elizabeth's sun-preserved strawberries were one of her greatest culinary prides; but only second to these came her watermelon-pickles, which emerged from their jars still the pale greenish-white they had been in their raw state, still with their edges as crisply square as when first cut into cubes, but so transparent that one could actually read print through them, and with a flavor so delicate as to baffle imitation.

With the strawberries and watermelon pickles, Elizabeth decided this year to serve some of her Damson plum jam. That would complete the patriotic colors to be placed at intervals down the middle of the long tables. She had a pair of glass clover-leaf dishes and doubtless could borrow others. If the number still fell short, she could put the red, white and blue preserves in small individual dishes and group these. Elizabeth felt rather pleased with herself for having thought of this: it was an idea which she had not before used, and one particularly appropriate this year, with patriotism so much in evidence.

Now for the body of the breakfast. There would be platters of fried chicken, of ham and eggs, with golden-brown mashed potato cakes, and the kernel-corn pancakes which her mother and grandmother had made famous in their generations, and which were no less appreciatively received by Elizabeth's contemporaries. In grandmother Phelps' day, the corn had come from her own garden, had been dried by herself. Elizabeth's mother had bought her corn, cut it carefully from the cob, and put it up in glass jars. Elizabeth purchased hers in cans. But the recipe for the pancakes remained the same, although Elizabeth served maple syrup with hers, as had her mother before her, while grandmother Phelps had concocted a delicious substitute which could scarcely be told from the genuine article, by boiling the corn-cobs for several hours in enough water to barely cover, then boiling again with an equal amount of sugar until the proper consistency for syrup was reached.

For hot breads there must be both muffins and pop-overs; and for the older members of the congregation who still retained the tastes of their

New England ancestry, dozens of crullers must be fried and apple pies baked. And from the beginning to the end of the meal, coffee would be served from Elizabeth's great copper-bottomed wash-boiler, coffee made from the blend which Elizabeth herself had perfected by long experimentation.

"You ought to run a boarding house or a tea room, Mrs. Bradley," Elizabeth's neighbors often said. "With your gift for cooking, you'd soon be rich."

They could not understand that painful flush that invariably rose to Elizabeth's thin face at their words. Elizabeth Bradley would no more have commercialized her cooking than she could [have] bartered anything else precious to her. She considered it a gift—a legacy from a long line of homemakers who had excelled in their chosen life work.

Days passed swiftly, with spring cleaning and the renovation of wardrobes occupying every minute of her time at home. For herself, Elizabeth decided upon a new dress—blue silk—which would make its first appearance at May Breakfast and would therefore be her customary church garb until warm weather. This dress would be the most important garment of her year's wardrobe, and next spring would be her second-best, worn on Sunday afternoons at home, and to the few Ladies' Aid meetings and Parent-Teacher gatherings which time permitted her.

On Sundays, acting on the theory that she was doing the Lords' work and therefore committed no sin by pursuing it on the Sabbath, Elizabeth managed to see one neighbor after another when church was over, soliciting the loan of dishes, canaries, flowering plants. From the best cooks among them she secured promises of aid in the actual preparation of the breakfast. An invitation to help Mrs. Bradley with the May Breakfast was regarded as a compliment, and eagerly accepted.

By the third week in April, Elizabeth felt she had everything well in hand. The housecleaning and sewing were finished; the garden lay ready for seeding; the May Breakfast was planned to the last detail. And Elizabeth was tired. She felt that this would be the last year she could manage it. She said as much to Mrs. Cartwright one day.

"But Emmanuel couldn't have a May Breakfast without you to run it," protested Mrs. Cartwright. "The Phelps women have always taken charge, as far back as anyone can remember. I recollected hearing my Aunt Lucy tell—"

"As far as the Phelps family is concerned, the May Breakfast would end with me anyway," interrupted Elizabeth. "Bernice can't learn to boil water without scouring the pan. And I don't have the time, really. I shouldn't have undertaken it this year."

On the following Sunday, Elizabeth was sure everyone in church had been told of her decision. She could actually feel the weight of reproachful glances upon her, even when her eyes were piously lowered.

"I don't care," she thought resentfully. "It's easy for them to talk. Their husbands make money enough so they don't have to slave in a factory all day, and then stay up most of the night to wash and iron and clean."

On the way home, she very nearly made up her mind to leave Emmanuel after the summer vacation and worship at the big church in town where she would be a stranger.

The first Sunday in May fell on the sixth, and by the third, Elizabeth had ordered all supplies needed. As always, she had reserved the lion's share of the labor for herself. On Saturday she would make her crullers and pies, and take these with her preserves and wash-boiler to the church kitchen before dark. Then she would be up again at four Sunday morning, and off to church to fry the chickens and prepare the rest of the food so that the breakfast might be in readiness at the precise moment when, the sunrise service over, the rest of the congregation came trooping down to the dining room in the church basement.

"I've got my time figured out to a split second," Elizabeth confided to Ben Thursday night. "It's going to keep me on the jump, but I shan't mind if only everything goes off smoothly. I'd like my last May Breakfast to stand out as my best."

"You really mean to give it up, don't you?" Ben said. "At first I thought you were just talking, Bessie."

"I meant every word I said," Elizabeth snapped. "I'm sick of carrying the world on my shoulders."

She stayed up late Thursday night to do the wash, usually reserved for Saturday morning; and waked to the harsh call of the alarm clock on Friday feeling stiff and tired, and very irritable. The day dragged endlessly, and she was thankful when closing time came. And then, just as she was preparing to clean up her bench, the forewoman came over, a troubled expression on her face.

"I hate to ask this, Mrs. Bradley, but will you put in a full day tomorrow? We've just had a rush order come in, for fifteen-hundred coils of off-standard size. A very important order. I couldn't trust anyone else to turn them out—"

For just a moment, Elizabeth was stunned into silence. To be asked to work tomorrow, of all days—. Yet there was no one else in the room capable of turning out the required number of coils in a day. The shrill, sudden blast of the factory whistle drowned out Elizabeth's involuntary sigh.

"I'll be here in the morning," she said evenly.

She didn't go to bed at all Saturday night. After Ben and the children were asleep she fried crullers, made apple pipes, packed up preserves, dishes, linen and silver. Sometime after midnight she heard the sound of rain on the roof; rain of the steady, drizzling kind that usually lasts for hours. Rain! Sunrise service and a May Breakfast in the rain!

"Well, I'm doing my part," she thought. "It isn't my fault if everything is working at cross-purposes. I've done my best."

At four o'clock she made strong coffee and drank two cups as hot as she could bear it, took a quick bath, donned clean clothes and combed anew the thick brown hair threaded with grey. Then she put on a fresh house apron, and folded the blue silk dress carefully into a hat box. At the last moment, when the breakfast was ready to serve, she would make a lightning change from apron to silk dress, authentically changing her role from cook to hostess.

She took an umbrella from the hall stand and went out into the pitch dark carrying the hat box. The clothes-basket heaped with crullers, the carton containing jars of preserves, the ten carefully wrapped apple pies, the wash-boiler filled with linen and silver, were left conspicuously displayed upon the kitchen table, where Jed Martin could find them quickly. Trudging along the familiar road that was now strange in the darkness and the rain, she felt numb with weariness and lack of sleep.

Arriving at the church, she opened the basement door, and stepped into the kitchen. How still and unreal everything seemed, here alone in the dark. She snapped on a light and set briskly to work. Half an hour later, when Jed and Hattie Martin, Mrs. Cartwright, Alice Hopkins and Mrs. Doctor Longworth arrived in a body, wedged into the Martins' car, Elizabeth had things well underway.

Jed turned the car about and went for the articles in Elizabeth's kitchen, while the four women began taking off their wraps. They were quiet and subdued, their spirits dampened by the drizzling rain.

"Our last May Breakfast, too," sniffed Alice Hopkins.

Alice was such a sentimental fool, Elizabeth thought irritably, and wished she had asked someone else in her place.

Aloud, she said sharply, "Nonsense Alice. Emmanuel will probably be having May Breakfasts long after you and I are dead and gone. Come now, let's get to work. You'll find linen and silver in those boxes to the right, and Jed will be back with more soon. You help her, Hattie, will you? And Mrs. Cartwright, if you and Mrs. Doctor Longworth will just give me a hand with these chickens. . . ."

The four women worked swiftly, efficiently, for they had teamed together before and knew each other's ways. A clock on the wall ticked away the time, but there came no perceptible lifting of the darkness outside. After a while there came the sound of many feet overhead, and then the swell of organ music. The five women accelerated their speed, racing against time.

"Look!" Hattie Martin cried suddenly, excitedly. "Look, everybody, the sun!"

Sure enough, the dark clouds had parted and were scurrying off toward the west; while the sun, a brilliant crescent above the green hills, shone brightly upon a new, glittering world.

"Reverend Baker will be glad," Elizabeth thought. "Now he'll be able to take the congregation outside for prayer." And sure enough again there was the sound of walking feet above them and a draught from the open door was catching her skirts as she hurried about. Everything was ready now, with just enough time left to enable the five women to slip into their good clothes before receiving their guests. Elizabeth was the last to go into the ladies' room with her hatbox. Almost at once she was out again.

Once more the organ music, and the thump and shuffle of many feet. Now they were coming downstairs. . . . Queer, this sense of excitement that caught at her throat and made her breath come quickly. Had her mother and grandmother felt this way, standing in this very place, waiting for the congregation to come downstairs?

Now they were in view of the tables, with their bouquets of red, white, and blue flowers; and were assailed with the tempting aromas which came from the kitchen. There arose a spontaneous murmur of pleasure and anticipation, which was to Elizabeth what thunderous applause is to an actress. For just a moment she stood very still, savoring it all to the utmost. Then she was hurrying about again, greeting neighbors, meeting their guests, supervising the seating. Reverend Baker, at the head of the table, called out:

"Here, here—where are you ladies going to sit? Nothing of the kind, now. You're going to have your breakfast with us, and we'll all take turns waiting on table. This is your place at the head, Mrs. Bradley."

"Oh, no, Reverend Baker, I'm needed in the kitchen."

Bernice was at her elbow.

"Let us wait on the tables, mother," she said. "I'll round up a crew, and we'll tend to everybody. You super chefs just relax, you've done more than your share."

Elizabeth looked at her daughter in surprise. It was the first time Bernice had ever taken the initiative where work was concerned.

"All right, Bernice," she said. "I know I can leave everything in your hands."

The strange thing was that Elizabeth meant it, for as she looked into her daughter's eyes she realized they were the steady grey eyes of grandfather Phelps. Bernice might have Ben's blond hair and cleft chin, his charming smile and careless manner, but she would not grow up shiftless—Elizabeth felt sure of that now.

"Maybe I've expected too much of her because she's my own. Why, she's only a child. She may be the most capable woman of the line, when she's had time to grow up."

She sat with bowed head while Reverend Baker said the grace, but realized with a sense of guilt that she heard few of his words. From under lowered lids, she stole a glance at Ben, far down the table, and then at Charles, sitting with the small fry. Then again, her gaze rested on Bernice, standing with a group of young girls waiting near the door. How capable the child had been. Marshaling her own crew of assistants without undue flurry or fuss. A born manager, Elizabeth realized with deep satisfaction. The picture was clear now, of Bernice carrying on the long tradition of the Phelps women at the May Breakfasts. Pleasant to feel that when she, Elizabeth, gave up her place, her own daughter would step forward to fill it.

Sunshine flooded the big dining room in the church basement. A canary began to sing lustily. By one and twos other birds joined in, a musical accompaniment to Reverend Baker's grace.

Scarcely had the word "Amen" left his lips, when Bernice and her helpers were serving the breakfast. Platters of steaming ham and eggs, of crisp fried chicken and potato cakes. Crullers and muffins and pop-overs, and the famous Phelps corn pancakes. Hot, fragrant coffee and flaky apple pie. How good everything looked and smelled. Everyone was talking and laughing at once, exclaiming over the food, the decorations, calling compliments to Elizabeth.

"Everything is just perfect!" "Those red, white and blue preserves are an inspiration, Mrs. Bradley." "I haven't tasted anything so wonderful since this time last year." "This is the best May Breakfast of all, Elizabeth."

She drew a deep breath. Now was the time to let them know, she thought. To make them understand she wasn't giving up Emmanuel's May Breakfasts after all—not for years—not until Bernice was ready to take over.

"Thank you so much," she said. "All of us—Mrs. Cartwright, Mrs. Martin, Miss Hopkins, Mrs. Doctor Longworth and I—appreciate your compliments. We only hope you'll be able to say as nice things about our May Breakfast next year."

The Undertaker's Meal
Funeral Ceremonies

Funeral Cry Feast of the Choctaw Indians
from the Oklahoma Office

One of the most ancient customs of the Choctaw Indians and one that is to some extent followed to this day, is the funeral cry. When a member of the family dies, he is quietly buried with some or all of his personal belongings, at which time the stoicism of the Indian is apparent for it is not often that any tears are shed at the burial service.

On the day of the burial the head of the family cuts and trims nicely twenty-eight little sticks which he lays up in the cracks of the log cabin as representing the twenty-eight days of the moon month. Every morning he takes down one of these sticks until there are seven remaining, then he sends out invitations to his kinsmen and friends to come to the funeral cry, which is to be on the day the last stick is taken down. The kinsmen and guests are required to bring with them a specific amount of food or provisions. One is allotted so much meal, another so much flour, and another so much beef, etc. This request is strictly complied with.

The congregation of relatives, friends, and even strangers meet at the grove near the grave of the late deceased, where a circular place has been cleaned of all shrubs and grass, in the midst of which a table is spread for the immediate family. At intervals around this center table are tables arranged for all other kinsmen, and still outside of these are tables for friends and visitors. Before the feast is spread, some relative of the deceased rises and begins an oration, telling of the good qualities of the deceased, of his courage and prowess and as he proceeds he grows more and more eloquent and impassioned. When the cry starts, then begins a copious flow of tears, something of which the Indian is very sparing, accompanied by low wailing and moaning that forces the onlooker to join in the cry.

When the cry has gone on for some time the feast of pashofa, bonahana, and kettle pies (cobblers) is spread, and certain ones of the deceased's relatives are appointed to wait upon the inner table and others are selected to wait on the other tables.

The alternate ceremony of feasting, crying, and wailing, is kept up for two or three days. The intrusion and curiosity of the white people have tended to lessen the frequency and publicity of the funeral cry as well as many other ancient customs and ceremonies of the Choctaw Indians. Many people regard the funeral cry of the Indian as a relic of barbarism but really it is like a ceremony of some of the Christian denominations except that the latter confine themselves to fasting and prayers for the dead, leaving off the feasting and wailing.

If it is not convenient, or if weather conditions are not such that the cry can be held at the grave of the deceased, the relatives and friends go to the church where the feast is spread and candles are lighted around which they assemble in prayer and weeping, dividing their time between the candles and the festive board and local oratory.

★   ★   ★   ★   ★

Martha Ferguson's aunt was tired of taking the medicine for her diabetes. It burned inside her and, besides, her aunt said, she longed to smell something sweet again. So she started eating cantaloupe and sweet late-summer watermelon to flush away the toxins from the medicines inside her. It worked for a while and then it didn't. When a red-feathered bird smashed against the sliding glass doors of the house where her aunt lay, the family knew she was dying.

"My aunt loved red birds. Before the day was gone, she was gone, too."

Later that night, when Martha walked into her aunt's house, it smelled so sweetly.

At the family annual memorial reunion in the mountains near Jackson,
Kentucky, August 1940. (Marion Post Wolcott)

"I know you're here surrounding us," she cried out. As she speaks about this, Martha smiles to remember how full the house seemed of her aunt's spirit.

Martha is the cultural liaison for her tribe. She's usually at the small museum across from the tribe's government building but, today, she sits in the museum's gift shop on the ground floor of the Silver Star Casino on the Pearl River Reservation outside of Meridian, Mississippi. She is a petite, pretty woman with silver strands weaving into the black hair at her temples and, even though she is uncomfortable talking about the funeral cry and her aunt, she is trying mightily to be polite to me. It is hard to hide her edginess because what she is being asked about are private matters, not to be intruded upon. Even though I really want to know, I'm trying not to push. It is much easier for her to talk about what led to her aunt's death—the diabetes that runs lawlessly through the tribe. So, for a little while, as I cover our awkwardness by admiring the handmade baskets the tribe is known for but which, at the casino, are priced way out of my league, we talk about the illness.

Truth is, the Choctaw Indians in Mississippi could easily provide a sharp snapshot of the dangers posed by the adulteration of the American diet after World War II. The tribe was always unique among Indians because, rather than relying on a single method for gathering food, the Choctaw raised crops as well as hunted and fished, providing them with a inimitably rich and varied diet. But as their lands were taken away from them and their hunting grounds were depleted or usurped by white settlers, the tribe came to rely more and more on government-issued, or cheap, food stock, especially dried corn in the form of hominy. Beginning in 1832, the peoples were split apart, with about fifteen thousand accepting a treaty and moving north from their ancestral homes in the south to what is now Oklahoma on what became known as the Trail of Tears. The Mississippi band are the descendants of those who refused to move away. Over the years, the grinding poverty that has long affected everyone who settled in the area further deteriorated the tribe's diet. By the 1960s census, the Mississippi Choctaws were noted to be among the poorest tribes in the country, the government calling the reservation "the worst poverty pocket in the United States." Families lived on less than two thousand dollars a year and they didn't expect to live long—fifty being considered old.

Then along came a new tribal leader, Phillip Martin, and he began to improve conditions on the reservation by initiating innovative industrial partnerships. New housing began to be built, an industrial park was completed, and economic incentives attracted to the reservation such companies as American Greetings cards. Unemployment fell, life expectancy increased by ten years. By 1994, the tribe opened their first casino; by 2000, they were among the top ten employers in the state of Mississippi.

Most members of the tribe now live in middle-class comfort, but they still die relatively young. The oldest person listed in the obituaries in the *Choctaw Community News* is liable to be sixty-four. The rest are in their late forties. Except for the teenagers and people in their twenties who die in car accidents, no causes of death are listed.

What maims and kills the Choctaw Indians the most is diabetes. Despite their flourishing economy, the tribe still has one of the highest rates of adult-onset diabetes and the highest rate of diabetes-related amputation and chronic kidney disease in America. To combat this, they have built a state-of-the-art health facility on the reservation. Probably more beneficial to the ongoing health of its people, in the last several years, the tribe has organized a farmers' market to bring into the community fresh fruits and vegetables. They've also created a program that supports local tribal farmers who contribute to the market.

Yet, in a disheartening sort of way, diabetes seems to be an accepted part of life on the reservation. In the Silver Star gift shop, what is finally said is this: people get tired of the disease and what it does to them, of the restrictions diabetes places on their lives. Martha's aunt was not unique in wanting what she should not have. So she made a choice and went back to old ways.

Let's talk, then, about the funeral feast. Martha smiles.

The funeral cry takes place at least a month after the death, when the heavy mourning for the departed has begun to lift. Now it is time to say good-bye to the spirit and help it move on to the next life, and for those who are left behind to once more take up their own life on earth. The funeral cry for Martha's aunt lasted three days. As is the custom, the women in the family organized the cry, calling the relatives and friends, deciding what the menu would be and who would cook what dishes. Most times, before they die, people request a special song to be sung at their funeral, and so they wove Martha's aunt's requests into the cry, singing the songs she had chosen.

"A Choctaw woman's cry is something you don't forget," Martha says. It is something that is distinct and of her own: a high, long pitch; followed by a shorter, lower pitch; then a quiet moan. They cried for Martha's aunt day and night, never letting up.

"My family was able to afford the feast but if a family doesn't have the money, they can go to the tribe, the social service office, you know, and it will help out. But people bring things, too. In honor of my aunt, people baked lots of cakes and pies. Oh, there were so many of them in the house. They were so good! And there were biscuits and ham, fried chicken and corn bread. And lots of hominy and whatever meat we had to go with it."

Martha's family sat for a long time after they had eaten and then, one by one, they stood and told sweet stories about her aunt. They spoke of the good things she had done, how she was loved, the funny moments and the strong times when she'd cared for others or done a good deed.

Anger or bad thoughts about the departed are never mentioned at the funeral cry: it is a time of remembering, of healing, of praising the person's spirit and wishing him or her well. As the stories about Martha's aunt piled up, her family felt the relief of knowing her life had been touched with happiness and blessings, that she would be missed and her memory cherished. That is the benefit of the funeral cry—to let go and give praise. When the funeral cry ended and Martha's family set off for their homes, their sadness had been leavened with a true celebration of life.

A Pitch-In Dinner After a Funeral Service
from the Indiana Office

They had just buried Uncle John in the little cemetery next to the Methodist church down in the village and now Aunt Mary and the relatives

Mountain men carrying homemade coffin to the family grove, up South Fork of the Kentucky River near Jackson, Kentucky, September 1940. (Marion Post Wolcott)

and friends were back in the farmhouse where Uncle John and Aunt Mary had lived and worked so long. Saturday morning Uncle John had come to the living room before daybreak to shake the fire as usual and a few minutes later Aunt Mary had found him slumped in front of the stove. "I'm glad he could go that way," Aunt Mary said. "John was a good man and it would have been hard to see him suffer like some have to."

Two hired girls from the neighboring farms had come early that morning and when the funeral party returned the house was scrubbed and clean and the table set. Neighbors and relatives had brought table silver, most of it marked with colored thread for identification, and plenty of food. There was a kettle of thick vegetable soup to warm up, baked potatoes, cold roast beef and cold roast pork, two roasted chickens, home canned tomatoes, home canned succotash made with green beans and lima beans and sweet corn; sweet pickles and sour pickles, jellies, strawberry preserves, apple pies and cherry pies and cakes and cakes and cakes—and plenty of coffee.

Everyone urged Aunt Mary to eat and tried to think of something she would like. She wasn't hungry but these were her friends trying to help her so she must try. In spite of the buzz of low-toned conversation and the clatter of silver the room seemed quiet, almost vacant, and her mind kept drifting back across the years to the time John brought her here as a bride. It had taken patience and time to learn to cook many things the way John liked them. Someone mentioned John's family and Aunt Mary said, "Yes, John had a little Dutch blood. He was always thrifty and hardworking and a hearty eater. I had a terrible time learning to make scrapple to suit him, and that mush made with graham flour that he liked as well. But he was always one to praise me, even when things didn't turn out so well. John was a good man."

For years Aunt Mary had been known locally as a master cook and when she talked about that art the younger women not only listened but hoped that she would go on. "What is the secret of that kraut you make, Aunt Mary?" One of them asked. Aunt Mary's mind again flew back to those first years as she said: "Well, I'll tell you. It took me three seasons to learn just how to do it. It's all in getting just the right proportion of salt in it and then I always wash three or four good, tart apples clean and put them in with the cabbage in different places in the keg. I can't tell you just how much salt by weight to use in proportion to the cabbage but come over next fall and I'll show you."

From that the talk went to cabbage relish and how many hot peppers to put in a five-pound crock of it, and then corn relish and the proper function of horseradish in pickling and finally came to a pause when a distant cousin brought up the subject of Uncle John's famous smoked hams. "I never had to bother with anything about curing the meat," Aunt Mary said. "John would hardly let anyone come near the smokehouse when he was smoking hams and shoulders. Always used green hickory and finished them off with sassafras. He was fine at making sausage too. Knew exactly how much sage and salt and pepper to use. I'm afraid I can't help you with that."

"Why don't you sell the place and come and live with Dan and me in Kokomo?" asked a niece. "You know you would be welcome and you could pay your way if you wanted to. It would take your mind off things here. Seems to me you would enjoy town living for a spell after all these years on the farm." Aunt Mary thought for only a moment before answering. "No, I'm not going to sell the place, anyway not for a while. There is some money in the bank and I can let the land out on shares. Of course I'll sell the livestock but I'm going to keep the chickens—they bring in quite a bit you know—and I'm going to have a garden. It wouldn't seem like living not to have sweet corn and green beans and tomatoes and things like that. Somehow vegetables don't ever taste the same when you buy them out of a store. I'll raise some cucumbers for pickles, too. And I'll probably dry some apples and can peaches and cherries just as usual, only not so many. And I expect I'll pickle some pears and put up a few jars of persimmon pudding in case company comes sometimes. That is, if the old persimmon tree down in the back lot has a crop. Some years it is loaded and some years there's hardly a one on it. Persimmons are queer that way."

After a while everyone had finished eating and the bustle of getting dishes and silver together to take home began. One by one the women, and the men too, slipped up to Aunt Mary for good-byes and offers of help, "any time I can do anything, just let me know," and finally they were all gone. Bill Daniels would be coming back later to take care of the stock and "do the chores."

Aunt Mary sat alone and tried to knit the threads of things together. It would be lonesome and for the first time she realized that she was old and tired and alone. Yes, it would be different with John gone.

★   ★   ★   ★   ★

This quietly beautiful *America Eats!* story shows how important a funeral is for passing on traditions. But although death continues to be one of the few remaining aspects of life that shakes us to our core, funerals no longer make the same social demands they once did. Here's why: Relatives no longer live so close together and women are working at jobs away from home just as hard as men are. These two factors, it can be argued, have changed American eating customs more than has anything else in recent years and funerals are particularly affected by this. The American funeral business, however, as has been its wont from its beginnings, has discerned this state of affairs and has very nicely stepped in to fill the void.

At a recent family funeral in Cleveland, for instance, the luncheon took place at a modern funeral facility, in what was called the "Community House," a separate building behind the funeral home's garage where the hearse and limos are stashed. It was a pleasing, light-filled room that could be easily divided into two rooms by track doors. The Italian family who owned the facility cooked the meal—trays of baked ziti, chicken Marsala, sliced roast beef in gravy, cookies and puff pastries. The Irish family that was mourning didn't care that the food was Italian and only winced a few times when the funeral party on the other side of the divide played polka music. Many of the relatives were old, tottering in on the arms of their children who were squeezing in the trip between work schedules. Most came from several states away and even those in town were running behind schedule by lingering over the meal. No one had the time, let alone the stove and the energy, to prepare what was second nature only ten years before at the last big family funeral: home-baked cinnamon rolls; honey-baked ham; a very large dish of tuna-noodle casserole; and mint–Oreo cookie pie—the family's guilty favorite, although made that time by a neighbor. It was, without a doubt, a good meal the funeral home prepared and served. And the fact is, if the home had not done it, the family would probably have gathered at some anonymous restaurant nearby.

But there is no denying that something was lost in the day. While there were plenty of reminiscences of the beloved, plenty of family stories told, and catching up done, little of the comfort was to be gained from tasting a familiar family dish. Nor was there the inevitable conversation that would have accompanied it, the passing on of important information—whose grandmother made it first or best; which aunt always sprinkled too much thyme in it; which daughter inherited the dish it was made in.

Cemetery Cleanings
in a note from the Florida Office

Cemetery Cleaning. The annual cemetery cleaning is a custom practiced in many small towns throughout North Florida. On some set date on the fall of the year, many residents drive out for an all-day picnic at the community cemetery. The purpose is to clean graves, rake paths and plant flowers; but the event of the day is the one o'clock dinner. Food is brought by all families attending and the best cooking of the region is offered.

Annual cemetery cleaning. Person County, North Carolina, July 1939.
(Dorothea Lange)

Chicken fried, baked and stewed, salads of endless variety, pickles, biscuits and sweet milk, coffee and tea, watermelon and orange preserves, pies, chocolate, banana and pineapple cakes—all are spread out at once on long tables underneath the trees.

To eat from one's own basket would show lack of appreciation for a neighbor's cooking. The picnickers wander along the tables selecting at will the dishes, and praising the contributions of friends.

After the meal, work in the cemetery is resumed in a somewhat desultory manner.

It is the procedure to clean one's own family lot, then to help those with larger plots, and finally to work on the graves of those who have no surviving relatives.

Recipes

The following two recipes come directly from the Mississippi band of Choctaw Indians.

Banaha Indian Bread

>2 cups cornmeal
>1 teaspoon baking soda
>1 teaspoon salt
>Corn shucks (boil about 10 minutes before using)
>1½ cups boiling water

Mix the dry ingredients together. Add the water and stir until a fairly stiff dough forms. Take about 2 tablespoons of the dough and pat it into an oblong shape. Wrap it in a corn shuck and tie it closed with a piece of corn shuck string.

Drop the bundles into a deep pot of boiling water. Cover and cook for 40 minutes.

Serve the bundles hot.

Pashofa

> 2 cups uncooked hominy grits
> 3 pounds pork backbones or ribs
> Salt and pepper

Place the hominy in a bowl and pour in enough hot water to completely cover. Skim off the dry husks that rise to the water surface.

When all the husks have been removed, drain the hominy and place in a Dutch oven (tradition calls for it to be cooked over an open flame outdoors but it can also be made on a stove or even a Crock-Pot). Cover with 2 or 3 quarts of fresh water and bring to a simmer. Cook slowly for about 4 hours, or until the hominy is still slightly hard. Add the pork, and salt and pepper to taste, and stir. Return the mixture to a simmer and cook for about 1 to 2 more hours, until the hominy completely thickens and the meat is tender and falling from the bones, adding more water if necessary.

Before serving, pick out any bones that remain and add more seasoning if desired.

Serves about 6.

Eudora Welty's recipe for beaten biscuits from the Mississippi office:

Beaten Biscuits

> ¼ cup milk
> ¼ cup ice water
> 4 cups all-purpose flour, sifted
> ¾ cup lard
> 1 teaspoon salt
> 4 teaspoons sugar

Preheat the oven to 400°F.

Blend the milk and water together in a small bowl. Combine all the other ingredients in a large bowl, cutting in the lard until it is evenly distributed. Make a well in the center of the flour, then pour in the liquid. Knead lightly until a dough forms.

On a lightly floured surface, roll out the dough to about a ¼-inch thickness. Cut circles from the dough using a biscuit cutter or the lip of a juice glass. Place the circles on a lightly greased baking sheet and prick the tops with a fork.

Bake for 6 to 8 minutes, or until the tops are light brown. Turn off the oven and leave the biscuits inside with the oven door open. The biscuits will sink a little as they cool.

Makes about 3 dozen.

From my mom's recipe box:

Chess Pie

> **CRUST:**
> 2 cups all-purpose flour
> ⅛ teaspoon salt
> ¾ cups chilled lard
> About ⅓ cup ice water
>
> **FILLING:**
> 8 tablespoons (1 stick) butter
> 2 cups sugar
> 6 eggs
> 1 teaspoon vanilla extract
> ½ cup chopped pecans
> ¾ cup milk

MAKE THE CRUST:
Mix the flour and salt together in a large mixing bowl. Cut in the lard and work lightly into the flour with your fingertips until the mixture has the texture of cornmeal. Make a well in the center of the flour and, while stirring the flour with a wooden spoon, gradually add the ice water until a dough begins to form. (You may find yourself using less than all the water.)

Form the dough into a ball, wrap in plastic wrap, and refrigerate for at least 30 minutes.

Once chilled, take the dough out and, on a lightly floured surface, roll it out to fit a 9-inch pie plate. Carefully roll up the dough onto your rolling pin, then drape it across the pie plate. Press the dough lightly into the plate, trim and flute the edges.

Refrigerate the piecrust while you make the filling.

MAKE THE FILLING:

Set the oven rack on its lowest level and preheat oven to 350°F.

Cream the butter and sugar together until light and fluffy. Add the eggs, one at a time, beating well after each addition. Add the milk and vanilla. Stir in the pecans.

Pour the mixture into the pie shell and bake for 15 minutes. Lower the oven to 325°F and keep baking for another 50 to 60 minutes.

★　　★　　★　　★　　★　　★　　★　　★　　★　　★

Velorios (Wakes)
from the New Mexico Office

In New Mexico, a wake is next to a dance or a fiesta in social importance. It is a valid excuse for everyone in the village as well as relatives and friends from neighboring farms and settlement to come together, visit, and catch up on news and gossip.

When it is evident that death is impending, preparations for the wake and funeral are begun. As the church bell tolls, doors are flung open and windows raised to hear the announcement from the belfry; but before the echoes die there is much activity already under way in the stricken home. Wood is chopped. Adobe ovens outdoors are fed with burning logs in advance of the baking, and an animal, sheep, calf, or pig is butchered.

Barbarita, wife of Merejildo, who was expected to die, asked a neighbor to kill her pig, which she had been feeding and keeping for Merejildo's wake. After the hog had been scaled and scraped, the neighbor's wife helped Barbarita with the meat which was cut from the bones. The bones were later roasted and hung up on a line in the store room.

All the fat was cut from the meat, fried, and made into chicharones (cracklings). Earthen jars of chili were prepared with oregano and much garlic. Meat was added, making carne adobada (preserved meat), then the jars stored. The hide was cut in strips and hung on a line, to be cooked later with the posole (hominy). Two days after these preparations were completed, Merejildo died.

Barbarita sent her boy to tell the neighbors. They would tell others. Two men came and laid Merejildo out in a mortaja (shroud) instead of his best clothes, and a piece of rope was tied around his waist. He was then laid on the bare floor where he had lain on sheepskins during his illness. He was a Penitente and believed in doing penance until he died, so he had refused to lie on the bed. Wood was cursed since the Death on the Cross, and he would not lie in the wooden bed. The mortaja had been made under his direction a month before when he sent his wife to town for the black cloth. She had made it and put it away.

By evening, the neighbors began to arrive for the wake, some on foot, some in wagons, and others on horseback. The women brought all their children. The men built fires outdoors and stood around talking while the women wailed and consoled Barbarita, who cried aloud as each new arrival entered. The children ran in and out, playing and laughing, but so long as they stayed out of the way, nothing was said to them.

When it was dark, the rezador (lay reader) came. He was the hermano mayor (elder brother or head) of Merejildo's Penitente lodge. He went into the room where Merejildo lay surrounded by lighted candles. Other members of the lodge and one or two women followed.

The rezador led, the others saying the responses. When the prayers were finished, alabados (hymns) were sung by all present. Then the rezador asked all who were not members of the lodge to go into the next room and close the door, because the hermanos (brothers) alone would pray for Merejildo.

During lulls of wailing and lamentation, the pito (rude pipe used by the Penitentes to accompany their singing) could be heard, the voice of the rezador, crying: "Salgan, vivos y difuntos; aquí," were rattled and the throb of a small cow hide drum was heard.

The rezador went over to Barbarita and whispered in her ear. Tearfully, she went and removed the bedding from the bed in the corner and laid it on the floor. The rezador removed the springs from the bedstead and carried his burden into the next room.

Nothing could be seen when the door was opened. All was dark.

The bed spring was taken outside, and Merejildo was laid upon it. Then the brothers picked it up and carried it off. Over the hills, down and up arroyos they went, chanting to the accompaniment of the pito, performing the dispidida del mundo (taking the dead to bid the world good-bye).

While they were on this duty, the men and women at the house were talking and making final preparations. The children were laid on pallets on the floor and went to sleep.

After an hour had passed, the brothers, still singing, returned, went back into the room, laid Merejildo's body on the floor, closed the door and went out.

The rezador opened the door and announced that the brothers had gone and that those in the house were free to do as they pleased. Some of the women went to the kitchen and prepared the media noche cena (midnight supper), while others talked quietly together.

When supper was ready, the men were called first. Pots of chili and posole were placed on the floor and the men helped themselves, using tortillas to carry the food to their mouths. The hominy had been soaked in lye to remove the hulls, then washed in several waters before it was cooked. With pork rind and seasoning, it made a substantial dish. The carne adobada was strong with chili and herbs and spices, but it was a dish to which all ages were accustomed. The emphasis has always been on substantial food, and food served on such occasions was no exception. Coffee was drunk with the meal.

When the men had finished, the women and children were called. They also sat on the floor around the steaming jars of food, talking and discussing the details of the funeral.

After all had finished eating and cigarettes were smoked, the rezador called them into the room where the body lay, and prayers and hymns continued until dawn.

When the sun was up, the bed spring was again taken outdoors and the body laid upon it. Barbarita handed the rezador a bag containing salt, about five pounds of it. Four men picked up a corner of the bed spring and went toward the burial ground, the other men following. The women and children stayed at home.

The rezador, carrying the bag of salt, which was supposed to keep the body from decomposing, led the cortege to a field north of the house where a grave had been dug the day before. Merejildo had chosen this spot himself.

When they arrived at the open grave, the body was laid onto two ropes, and by these was lowered into the grave. A cloth was placed over

Merejildo's face and the bag of salt laid at his feet. Then the earth was shoveled onto the body until the mound was formed. All stood around until the last shovelful was thrown in.

This done, they returned to the house where the women had breakfast ready. Breakfast consisted of the supper remains warmed over, with fresh coffee brewed and more tortillas.

Breakfast over, all left except a few women who stayed behind to help Barbarita. Horses were saddled, teams hitched to wagons, and the children put in. After tearful goodbyes, they drove off.

Now that Barbarita was a widow, she was not to wash her face or comb her hair for eight days. If she did, people would say she was glad Merejildo was dead.

★ 9 ★

Stomping at the Post
SOCIAL CLUB CELEBRATIONS

The Lodge Supper
from the Colorado Office

Lodge suppers and dinners are typical Colorado entertainments whether given in the rural districts, small towns or cities. Sometimes this form of entertainment is given for the purpose of raising funds for carrying on the philanthropies of the lodge, but more often it takes the form of a jovial social get-together.

In my experience of such affairs, one in particular stands out as a long-to-be remembered occasion. It was held in a small central Colorado town—it was a social occasion, in honor of the 45th anniversary of the founding of the lodge.

When we arrived at the lodge hall, a large crowd had already assembled. Some of the children were running back and forth across the long lodge hall, playing hide-and-seek, while a few of the smaller more timid ones were staying close to their mothers, busy in the kitchen preparing coffee, and producing delicious looking food from well-packed hampers. The men were gathered in groups about the hall, discussing base ball, the foreign war situation, or the fluctuations of the stock market.

The lodge hall was tastefully decorated with green and pink (the lodge colors) bunting, gracefully festooned about the sides of the long hall. An American flag stood at the right of the chief officer's chair on an elevated platform, and the lodge standard was placed on the left. Autumn vines and flowers were draped and festooned about the posts at the end of the hall.

The long tables were covered with snowy white cloths, and the lodge silverware and china was in place. Beautiful bouquets of dahlias and chrysanthemums were placed at intervals along the tables, adding an attractive color note to the occasion. Pink and white napkins were placed beside the plates.

There were attractive dishes of sweet pickles, bright red beet pickles and piccalilli placed at intervals on the table, as well as glistening molds of bright cranberry jelly. There was also plum and grape jelly in shining round glass dishes. Dishes of sparkling tomato preserves contrasted brightly with the snowy whiteness of the cloth. Long flat glass dishes contained crisp looking celery.

When all had been seated at the long tables, the ladies on the committee to serve passed heaping platters of fried chicken and cold sliced pink ham. The delicious odor of freshly made coffee permeated the room, as the ladies passed steaming cups of it, as well as glasses of lemonade, to those who desired it. The men guests invariably wanted their coffee with cream, the women preferred the black coffee.

Delicious looking bowls of potato salad, covered with slices of hard-boiled eggs were passed. Casseroles containing hot macaroni and cheese were a favorite with most of the crowd. The tempting bowls of glorified rice pleased every one, as well as the scalloped potatoes, and Waldorf salad. Nearly every one wanted a second helping of the cole slaw, brightened with bits of red pimento, and served in attractive round salad bowls. The cottage cheese served with pineapple proved to be a favorite with the men guests. Small white buns and butter were served with vegetables and meat.

When the group had done full justice to these delicious viands the ladies brought on pumpkin and mince pie, as well as delicious looking platters of light and dark cake. Everyone wanted a piece of Mrs. Mitchell's cake, a delicious concoction, that only she, of those present, knew the recipe for. She was the proud possessor of at least ten prizes won at county fairs. She had obtained this recipe from her aunt of Owensboro, Kentucky, famous in half a dozen counties for her culinary skill. Mr. Mitchell was jokingly asked by those around him at the table, how he rated such an exceptional cook as his wife. He laughingly explained that they often ate cornbread and beans at home, but on certain occasions his wife brightened their dull menu by something especially pleasing. (No one believed this—he is the town's banker.) With the cake tempting bars of pink and white ice cream were served.

When even the children present could eat no more of the cake and ice cream, Mr. Mulloy (Noble Grand) presided as toast master and master of ceremonies. Appropriate toasts relative to the lodge's anniversary were given, and lodge songs were sung by the group. Then all joined in singing "God Bless America" and "My Country 'Tis of Thee."

Mary and Harry Fields (twins) did a tap-dance number, with their proud parents the most appreciative of the large audience. Miss Mehitabel Smith then sang "When You and I Were Young Maggie," in her own inimitable way.

At about 8:30 o'clock a five piece orchestra from Denver appeared with their instruments, and an air of expectancy settled over the crowd. No lodge or grange affair was ever appropriately ended without a dance in this community, and on one occasion a Methodist church party had scandalized the town by winding up with a dance.

A fish fry held by the American Legion, Post 39, Louisville, Kentucky, August 1940.
(Marion Post Wolcott)

The heavy green velvet carpet had previously been rolled from the Lodge floor in expectancy of the dance. Soon the whole assembly were dancing to the strains of "The Missouri Waltz," the "Beer Barrel Polka" and "It Makes a Difference Now."

At intermission, Mr. John McIntosh produced his bagpipe and entertained the crowd with Scotch tunes and airs. He is a native of Scotland. His "Annie Laurie" and "I'll Take You Home Again, Kathleen," made an instant hit with the crowd. A Highland Fling was given by a young couple of the teen age. These numbers were all received with loud applause, and it was only when the orchestra again started playing that the crowd's clapping and shouting was ended by the music.

At about midnight, the crowd broke up, with many cheers and hearty good-nights. Everyone hoped the occasion would be repeated next year, when another anniversary of the Lodge had rolled around.

★   ★   ★   ★   ★

How lonely it is to come into a town—let alone an enormous country—and not know a single soul! How can a home begin to be made in such a place? How can one truly thrive without the presence of family and friends?

This is where social clubs, brotherhoods, and ethnic cultural centers come in. These were the places to which a newcomer to a town or the country could gravitate and know he or she might hopefully find kindred spirits or, failing that, convivial company for an hour or two. Friendships were forged, spouses sometimes found. Here, people learned who was hiring or where there might be rooms to rent. They learned the local customs and mores, and gathered the fortitude to muddle through another day.

Just as important, in these grand or modest establishments, the dishes and recipes from other countries were kept alive and handed down into the surrounding community. Unlike the same dishes made in restaurants, where their flavors were too often watered down for the general public, at gatherings in ethnic social clubs traditional methods and ingredients were more likely to be used because their members would know the difference. Think of the trays of lasagna served at the Knights of Columbus; the pierogies and hunter stews ladled out at the Polish Falcon; the pots upon pots of arroz con pollo dished at the local Puerto Rican Social Club.

More important, for the whole of American cooking, subtle cross-breeding of cooking styles began to occur, just as it did when a federal writer noted at one Colorado tavern that a "possum dinner, especially cooked by old German women, found great favor," seasoned as it was with more than the usual sweet potatoes.

Consider, then, the Basque of Boise, Idaho. You can't possibly imagine a lonelier, more out-of-place people trying to settle in as different a country from the one they were born in! Spend an afternoon (it'd have to start around three) at their social club and it will be quickly understood how important these establishments were to the making of America—if only by providing a little sanity to its newer citizens.

Basques of the Boise Valley
from the Idaho Office

Just as the Swedes hold forth with their Smorgasbord and other banquets in north Idaho, so the annual Sheepherders Ball of the Basque in south Idaho has attracted much attention.

Following the first World War, many Basques came to this country. The usual practice was for a brother to send for his nearest male kin, until the whole clan followed.

"Bosco" a colloquial name for themselves and their tongue, is spoken universally. Yet most of them also speak Spanish and English fluently.

They play cards but rarely gamble, drink but do not become boisterous or vulgar.

At the annual Sheepherders Ball, where dress clothes are prohibited and denim overalls quite the thing, the feasting is attended with dancing their own folk numbers, as well as American and Spanish dances. The men wear bright sashes.

★   ★   ★   ★   ★

This doesn't at all do justice to what the Basque went through as they made their way in America and it certainly doesn't begin to relate the joy of the Sheepherders' Ball that still takes place in Boise every year.

But, before the ball, a short history of the Basque in America: Many came to this country between 1900 and 1920 and worked, as most immigrants before and after them have done, at a hard job that no one else wanted to do. In the case of the Basque, that was herding sheep up in the high desert mountains of the west. The precise nature of being an immigrant is to be estranged, but the Basque were separated further by the very job they signed up to do—for much of the year living by themselves in nomadic isolation in the mountains. To make matters worse, they were shepherding in cattle country and often found themselves and their flocks in violent, even deadly conflict with cowboys who didn't much appreciate sheep, let alone foreigners, crowding the increasingly shrinking public range space. Cattle companies hired gunmen at fifty dollars a month to keep shepherds off what were considered cattle ranges. The federal government seemed, at times, against the shepherds, too: some of the legislation that hemmed in the public lands and created national parks and forests limited grazing access to only American citizens who owned private ranches—a measure that was widely praised in the local press as a victory over "Basque tramp sheepmen."

The early Basque settlers were primarily young men used to a lush countryside and a strong family life. They held a deep love for their homeland, where dancing and music were important and where sitting down together over a long meal was integral to their well-being. Now, in this new country, they found themselves, in their late teens and early twenties, living in arid mountains furred with sagebrush, windy, cold, and desolate, with just a horse or a mule, a dog, and up to a thousand sheep for company. In their loneliness and boredom, the men populated the barren landscape with women—their faces and full bodies—whittled in the bark of the surrounding aspen trees. While their flocks grazed out on the rugged open pastures, the shepherds passed their time by piling rocks on top of one another, sometimes as high as six feet tall. Known as *harrimutilaks*, or stone boys, the stones marked shepherd routes and kept them company, their silent compatriots, through the long nights.

The only human contact they had were the camp-tenders who checked in on them every now and again, delivering supplies and fresh bread baked in small stone ovens constructed in the hills. Because they owed money to ranchers for their passage over, many Basque men lived like this for years on end. Somewhere in the mountains above Boise, a shepherd carved these words into a tree: "I would rather be dead than live like this."

And then autumn arrived, the swift descent of early snow in the high pastures, and the Basque shepherds drove the sheep down from the mountains to breed and graze in lowland pastures. They would come into town and find a room in one of the boarding houses run by Basque families. Returning to these houses felt like returning home. They could speak their own language, hear their own music, and find waiting for them mail from family overseas. Most of all, there were Basque women who had come over to work in the boarding houses. Sundays, the one day of complete rest, were especially festive, the dining tables laden with plates of chorizo and stews thick with chilies and broad beans. Over glasses of good red wine, the men played jai alai and cards and, at night, joined the women in dancing and playing music.

By the time Christmas drew near, the hardships of the mountains, if not completely forgotten, seemed sufferable and still far enough away to put out of mind until the new year began. For now, there were the holidays to celebrate and, best of all, the annual Sheepherders' Ball to attend.

Colonel Lilly auctioning off a piece of cake at a pie supper, Muskogee County, Florida, February 1940. (Russell Lee)

There are several Sheepherders' Balls held across the west in towns where a Basque community formed. Rumor has it that the ball in Caldwell, Idaho, was a particularly wild one, with bars set up in the four corners of the hall and all the drinks anyone would ever want. But the ball in Boise that is held each year at the Basque Center has the distinction of being the oldest and the biggest.

The center caps Grove Street, the official seat of all things Basque in downtown Boise. The block contains a marketplace; two old boarding houses—one, the oldest brick building in Boise and the other, a fronton, or Basque handball court; the Basque Museum and Cultural Center (which houses a terrific exhibit on the history of the Basque, as well as a library, archive, and classrooms where the Basque language is taught two times a week); and Gernika, a pretty good Basque bar where the Saturday special is a spicy beef tongue platter and you can always find chorizo, the slightly hard, spicy pork sausage that is as big as knockwurst at this establishment.

The Basque national colors fly over the center, a two-story white stucco building with clay roof tiles that would not be out of place in Spain or the south of France. The front doors, hung with handsome wooden plaques showing Basque crests composed of lions, the sacred Gernikako Arbola tree, and fleurs-de-lis, open into a room where men are either playing at a game that looks a lot like skee ball, or sitting at the bar drinking coffee. A lone woman walking into the place is not greeted as a welcoming sight, but no one openly complains. Instead, the men turn back to their game and coffee cups, to the episode of *X-Files* playing on the TV screen. The young college student tending the bar continues to carefully unwrap a thin cigar for an elderly gentleman and, as he lights it and then pours more coffee into the big cup on the bar, rib him about who he might take to the ball.

"I'm not dancing anymore," the man says, his English cushioned in a thick accent. "Too much, too much," he adds, waving his hand and looking a little askance as I take the seat beside him at the bar.

Julian Lete, the manager of the Basque Center, is very busy setting up for the ball that will take place in the big hall next to the bar. A dinner will be served downstairs before the music and dancing begin. The kitchen is already busy preparing lamb stew, garlic mashed potatoes, baked fish (fresh from local waters), and chocolate pudding—all for twenty dollars, which includes all the wine and coffee you can drink and entry to the ball.

When Lete comes upstairs from the dining room with a box of wine for the bar, I introduce myself and ask if I can buy a ticket for the dinner and the ball.

"Mostly families come to the dinner," Lete says, which seems to be his polite way of saying outsiders do not usually sit down for the dinner—not that they're not welcome but, as he quickly adds, "It's usually our families that come and only two hundred and fifty people can fit in the dining room.

"You come at eight and see the dancing, and stay for the ball," he adds. "It's special this year. Our new dancers will perform."

I'm not about to move from the bar without a ticket, not with the prospect of lamb stew before me. So, eventually, a ticket is offered, if only so the men can get back to not having a woman in their midst.

"I've been waiting all year for the ball," says the young woman tending the gift shop at the museum. She's not Basque but many of her friends are and she says a lot of her friends in Boise eagerly attend the ball each year. When I tell her I also have a ticket for the dinner, she raises her eyebrows and gives me some advice: "It's a long night so you have to pace yourself but, really, everyone goes to the ball. You just have to see for yourself."

The doors open promptly the next night at five thirty for the dinner and, by six, the small room downstairs fills to near capacity, indeed with families, all of whom seem to know each other intimately. There's no one to greet me, no one hailing me to their table when I enter, and so I quickly stick out like the stranger I am among these happy people. One family graciously offers up a corner of their table for me to sit and I take it as if I have found a safe port. Thank God the food begins to arrive—and a lot of it, too: the thick, dark, flavorful stew poured over mashed potatoes, chocolate pudding, and especially the wine, help a lot to ease my discomfort of being the odd shoe in the mix.

I'm not so alone upstairs in the hall. By seven thirty, the hall and the bar are already crowded. Families and friends have used bottles of wine and coats to claim parts of the long tables that are arranged around the dance floor before the hall's stage. Flags from the Basque regions flutter from the high ceiling and there's an excited whirr of children running between the tables while the adults lounge back in their metal folding chairs, sip their drinks, and chat. If anyone is a shepherd just down from the mountains, they don't stand out at all. It seems to be a typical Saturday night crowd in a western city, all casually dressed with a few of the women in rhinestone-decorated jeans and a couple of the men sporting impressive cowboy hats. A bar set up in back is tended by two very friendly men who, along with drinks, are cooking and serving chorizo sandwiches. In the center's main room, the bar is three deep and the young guy from the previous day is muttering to himself that he's been left stranded and can't handle the crush.

"I don't know what I'm doing here," he says to no one in particular, but still manages to fill five shouted orders at once.

Through the ceiling overhead comes the sound of pounding feet—the dancers rehearsing; outside the open front door, a couple is spied on the corner in native garb (the man in billowing white pants and shirt cinched by a crimson sash at his waist, the woman in an aproned black skirt, her hair pinned up under a ribbon wreath). Practicing some intricate steps, they whirl up the street, then around the stop sign, around the corner and out of sight.

Back in the hall, anyone who stands too long in the vicinity of the bar is adopted by the two bartenders. Between filling drink and food orders, they begin to share stories with me about their families, along with some jokes. (What does a Basque man give his wife on their wedding day that is long and hard? His name.)

Dave Aspitarte's grandfather left the town of San Sebastián when he was nineteen; Don Totorica's grandfather arrived in 1916 with his sons—including Don's father who was five at the time. They were all shepherds up in the Juniper Mountains and eventually owned a ranch with five thousand sheep. The ranch is now owned by Don's brother.

A man comes up and shouts "*zazbi zazbi*," at Dave.

He translates, "That's a seven-and-seven. That's about the extent most people here know of the old language." He shrugs and moves away to make the drink.

One of the dancers is Dave's daughter, Daniela, a pretty, dark-haired seventeen-year-old who comes downstairs to ask her dad where her mom is: she needs her to hold her cell phone while she's dancing. Since she was three, her Sundays have been devoted to dance lessons at the center. Lately she's added Tuesday nights to take accordion lessons.

"None of my friends at school do this but I don't care," she says, adjusting the ribbon wreath in her hair. "It makes me unique. It's who I am."

Her father comes over to tell another joke that goes like this: A Basque man comes to America during Franco's time. The man lands in Manhattan and goes straight to a Basque boarding house. He is poor and used to eating nothing but beans, but at the boarding house he's given a great meal of everything he loves. He eats and eats. At night, he shares a room with a sick man whom the boarding house owners are looking after. At some point in the middle of the night, the wife comes in to give the sick man an enema but, in the darkness, she gets mixed up and gives it to the newcomer, instead. The next morning, when a new guy shows up at the boarding house, the man says to him, "It's a great country but don't eat too much or they'll take it away from you."

"Oh, Dad," Daniela sighs and drifts off to join the dancers who are marching into the room behind drummers and flag holders.

On the stage, musicians are warming up an accordion and pipes. The drummers join them and, after a short introduction, the dancing begins. Everyone in the room presses forward around the dance floor as the first dancer—a slightly embarrassed-looking teenage boy—begins a very strenuous series of high leaps, twirls, and kicks. The dances continue one after another and as they become more fiery and complicated, the audience claps and hollers louder and louder. By the last dance, young men in the audience in their everyday jeans and T-shirts have joined the festively garbed troupe. The floor vibrates with all the foot stomping. The lamb that is to be auctioned after the dancing, and which has suddenly appeared in a black cage near the bar, baaaaaaaaaaaaaaaaaaahs plaintively in alarm.

"It's all right, darling," a man says to the lamb as he leans with his beer bottle against the cage. This is one cute lamb—velvety black face and legs, creamy wooly coat, a pert bow around its neck.

A little girl pushes the last of her chorizo sandwich through the bars for the lamb to nibble but it turns its head and bahs once more.

As soon as the dancers march out of the hall, the lamb's cage is wheeled up front. Some people begin to leave but others crowd even tighter around the dance floor. The center has engaged a professional auctioneer and the money that will be raised will benefit the Basque Foundation, which extends help to members in need of emergency or medical assistance. This year, the money will help a member of the community fly back from Seattle to be near his family for cancer treatments.

The auction starts at a thousand dollars, then quickly jumps to four thousand. The lamb in its little black cage gilded with a gold ribbon doesn't look a bit happy about the proceedings and is letting go a stream

Drinking beer at the square dance, Pie Town, New Mexico,
June 1940. (Russell Lee)

of nervous pee every time the auctioneer struts near the cage. Here's an important tip to remember at a livestock auction: if you're not looking to buy, do not move any part of your body. Not knowing this fine point and having brushed my hair back from my face several times, I slowly come to the realization that I am the proud owner of one very expensive lamb. This starts me fretting about whether the center accepts credit cards, and how does one get a lamb through airport security, or how to explain its sudden presence in my backyard to the myriad other animals and humans already living in the house. Not to mention, would the lamb be happy living in Brooklyn? The closest patch of grass is in a park two blocks away. My brain is freezing around a vision of leading the lamb through traffic to pasture.

Thankfully, after a few long minutes, someone steps up to raise the bid. The auction proceeds swiftly over several rounds with the lamb won and given back at least four times. Eventually, about twenty thousand dollars is raised and the lamb, instead of flying to Brooklyn, is wheeled off to a local butcher to be made into a feast that will take place at the center later in the month.

It's almost ten o'clock and most of the remaining families are leaving. But that doesn't mean the ball is over. On the contrary, a new band is setting up on the stage and every person in downtown Boise who is between the ages of nineteen and thirty seems to be crowding through the hall. The dancers are still in their native dress but now many of them circulate the room holding beer bottles, mingling with their friends in low-riding jeans, tightly cropped shirts (for the women) and baggy sport jerseys. In years past, when the ball was held in the pavilion at the fairground, there would be almost fifteen hundred people in attendance, many of them teenagers drawn by the certainty that they would be able to sneak some beers and glasses of wine.

"Oh, it was out of control there for a while," the center's manager, Julian Lete, says. Not that it isn't a little chaotic now as he helps out behind the bar. Over the heads of those crowding in front of him demanding his attention, he explains how the center wanted to return the ball to how it used to be—just for the Basque community and their guests. Those requirements are still on the books for the ball but no one is checking the membership list at the door and, while the distinct dark features of the Basque people are predominant, a good amount of lighter hair is mingling in. Soon the great hall is bursting to capacity—a good five to six hundred people if you count the folks jammed around the main bar. The band is jumping into gear with an eclectic mix of traditional, rock, and alternative music. It's all pretty boisterous and, as a girl gets giddily swung high into the air by her partner, it's easy to imagine why the ball is something eagerly looked forward to each year.

Another Kind of Social Gathering Recorded by *America Eats!*

One of the most joyful aspects of reading through the federal writers' papers is in catching a glimpse of how life was once lived in America. In the files of Midwest and Western states, I came across a handful of stories about social events whose sole purpose was to offer something to do at night that was cheap and fun, where people could get together and share a meal and a laugh.

Take, for instance, the gatherings that were called "fun feeds":

A Fun Feed
from the Nebraska Office

Old Man Depression scored a major victory when in power. He taught Nebraska farm and city folks a great deal about living. He developed a real community spirit throughout the state. When the old maestro "Prosperity" previously forgot practically all local rural areas and home life, a rejuvenated interest in knowing each other's neighbors has developed in Nebraska, and these neighbors, after all, aren't such a bad lot.

With this change has come the increase in home talent affairs such as the Family Fun Feeds. They have been the rage in many rural Nebraska areas this past year. New "finds" have been made. Some local farmwife, it has been found, can make people laugh as loud, if not louder, than some skilled magician in a distant city.

Probably you are wondering just what "fun feeds" are and what they accomplish. They are merely events of hilarity for local people who bring a covered dish or two into a local meeting place and listen to take-offs and stunts. There is very little seriousness injected into the program. The affairs give farm and town people an opportunity to relax and get acquainted once again.

Everywhere in Thayer county people speak highly of the events. Ex-bankers, farmers, local women of prominence, editors and educators alike pass on the good word. It gives them recreation with no cash outlay of expenditure.

It's a covered dish affair. Every family is invited to attend. A menu is set beforehand. Each family brings in bread and butter sandwiches, enough for the family, and two other covered dishes. The menu, fit for any city high-powered banquet, usually consists of something like the following: scalloped potatoes, meat or chicken pie, baked beans, corn, pickles, jelly, salads of all kinds and descriptions. Coffee is usually furnished by a committee of town people.

Starting in the early evening, these events run off according to schedule. Into the towns the country people come. They bring their food. The "covered dish" is plentiful. No one goes home hungry. There is community singing. Every one joins in on popular and old-fashioned tunes. Some local individual usually serves as toastmaster. Local talent puts on skits. It may be a German band number or the local women's club putting on a musical number. There are short speeches, playlets and other stunts.

★   ★   ★   ★   ★

I scoured Thayer County, Nebraska, and pretty much every other county in the state, and there wasn't a fun feed to be found. That doesn't mean these nights of entertainment don't exist. Some form of them continues on among groups of people who generally have a common link to one another—say, as part of a wide circle of friends or as a co-op, or if they have a shared interest. They put together a costume party, a slide show of art work or travel, possibly a karaoke night, then spread out a collective banquet of dishes whose repertory now includes all kinds of recipes our ancestors wouldn't know anything about—things like Far Eastern noodle and rice dishes or vegan tofu concoctions—and have themselves a really merry night.

These evenings, though, are different from the spirit of the fun feed. The feed was an event where all kinds of people in a community, people who wouldn't in general have much social interaction with one another, got together to amuse themselves for the simple reason that there was nothing else to do. That, and they were all in the same boat, in regard to a situation such as the Depression, and thus the corollary need for a few laughs to muddle through.

It was that sense of citizens pulling together and making the best of a situation that I was looking for in a modern-day fun feed equivalent. The closest I personally came were memories of the 2003 blackout on the East Coast, when many folks banded together spontaneously as the hot night lengthened. It was in no way an organized fun feed, but the situation at hand did create a need for people to find among themselves some amusement to make the ordeal a little better. Front doors opened, stoops became bleachers; plastic chairs and card tables were arranged on sidewalks. With no air-conditioning or fans, everyone was trying to catch a breeze and find some solace in complaining to one another. A great feast of food soon materialized from fast-warming refrigerators. All kinds of ingredients from different households went into making interesting dishes, with lots of thawing meat thrown on communal grills and arranged on plates in sometimes preposterous combinations—a bowl full of goat, chicken, and mackerel with a side bowl of butter-pecan ice cream being a personal favorite. With no electricity for televisions or radios, people began to talk to neighbors they never knew they had. They organized games for the kids and played untold rounds of poker, gin rummy, and dominoes while the talk went round and joke after joke was told.

But when the electricity returned, the hubbub of social noise that filled the streets disappeared seemingly in a breath. Televisions were back on; radios were turned up loud. Cheap amusement moved back into our own homes, once all our electronic gadgets were finally working and demanding our attention. Although we all did know something more about our neighbors and developed a kinship we didn't have before, there's been no need since to meet them outside for a laugh.

This is a real tragedy for American social life in general, and for our food in particular. When times of social trouble or upheaval, such as the Great Depression, are visited upon communities, gathering strangers and friends together is a uniting factor. It allows us to suffer together and protect one another. Because we are a country without a common ancestry, the strengths of our communities rely on those moments when we can find equal ground and create a joint experience. No one can argue with the fact that you are inclined to think of your neighbors a little better once you have sat down with them and shared a few laughs.

At the same time, what was at the heart of the fun feed gatherings was a quiet understanding that resources were being spread around from those who had to those who may not have had. As noted in the last *America Eats!* article, "No one goes hungry." Families that were doing without through that hard period got a good meal—no questions asked and no shame needed to be felt when sitting across the table from you was the local banker and his family sharing the same meal. There have been times in our recent past when this type of social gathering would have come in handy: For longer than any one wants to think about, whole neighborhoods in New Orleans after Hurricane Katrina

A fish fry at the American Legion, Post 39, Louisville, Kentucky,
August 1940. (Marion Post Wolcott)

could have benefited from a communal smile and a meal. Probably many still can.

I know this comes down to bigger issues—the force of media in our lives, to name the biggest challenge—but we stand to lose so much of our cohesiveness as a country if we don't find more ways to gather together. The fun feed is an especially hard loss because it cloaked the necessity to survive in the best possible way. Giving us a reason to share with one another our talents, our covered dishes, our family jokes and idiosyncracies, is something we should cherish and make room for again.

Recipes

The fried chicken and macaroni and cheese recipes here come from my kitchen through many different influences, cookbooks, and trials. The Basque lamb stew recipe—the closest I could find in flavor to the Basque Center's stew—is a mutt of different versions.

Fried Chicken

> 1 frying chicken, cut into pieces
> Buttermilk
> All-purpose flour (depending on the amount of chicken to be
>   fried, about ½ cup)
> Yellow cornmeal (same quantity as flour)
> Salt and pepper
> Bacon fat and lard for frying (olive oil is a healthy alternative)

Place the chicken pieces in a bowl and pour enough buttermilk over them to cover. Let sit for at least an hour.

Mix together the flour, cornmeal, and salt and pepper in a medium-size soup bowl. Take the chicken out of the buttermilk. Pat dry. Roll the chicken pieces in the flour mixture until they are completely covered. Set on a plate while the fat heats.

Combine the fats in a heavy cast-iron skillet and heat over a medium-high flame—the melted fats should be at least halfway up the skillet. Test that the temperature is right for frying by putting a piece of onion or scallion into the oil. If the oil bubbles and then quickly turns the onion golden brown, the oil is ready.

Slip each piece of chicken carefully into the oil and fry until golden brown—20 to 25 minutes, turning every now and then to make sure the crust is golden on all sides. As each piece is done, remove from the oil and drain on a brown paper bag or newspaper.

Serves 4.

Macaroni and Cheese Casserole

> 1 pound elbow macaroni
> 4 tablespoons butter
> ¼ cup all-purpose flour
> 2 cups warm milk
> 2 cups freshly grated Cheddar cheese (the sharper the better)
> Salt and pepper
> ½ cup dry bread crumbs

Preheat the oven to 350°F and lightly grease a medium-size casserole dish. Set aside.

Fill a large saucepan with water. Bring to a boil and stir in the macaroni. Cook the macaroni until it's almost done (not too soft—it will cook more later in the oven), then drain. Place back in the pan and set aside.

In a smaller saucepan, melt the butter, then stir in the flour. Cook, stirring over medium-low heat until the paste is a little brown. Gradually stir in the warm milk, stirring to smooth any lumps, then cook the sauce until it thickens—about 7 minutes. Remove the sauce from the heat and stir in the grated cheese. Stir until the cheese melts and the sauce is smooth.

Pour the sauce over the macaroni and stir to make sure the macaroni is completely covered. Season to taste, then turn the macaroni into the prepared casserole dish. Sprinkle the bread crumbs over the top of the casserole.

Bake for 35 or 40 minutes, or until the crumbs are brown and bubbly.

Serves 4 to 6.

Basque Lamb Stew

⅔ cup olive oil
4 garlic cloves, peeled
3 pounds lamb, cut into pieces
6 ounces lamb liver, in one piece
2 dried red bell peppers
2 bay leaves
1 tablespoon flavorful paprika
2 cups red wine
8 black peppercorns
4 whole cloves
Salt and pepper

Heat the oil in a Dutch oven and sauté the garlic until lightly browned, then remove from the pan and reserve.

Add the lamb pieces and the liver to the oil. Stir to evenly cook the meat on all sides. When the liver turns brown, remove and set aside. Add the bell pepper, bay leaves, and paprika to the lamb pieces and stir to blend, then add the wine. It should cover the meat—if it doesn't, add more. Bring to a simmer, cover, and cook for about 45 minutes.

As the meat cooks, crush the peppercorns and cloves, cooked garlic, and liver in a mortar and pestle (you can also use a food processor. Pulse a few times—you want the ingredients to be rough). Stir the mixture into the stew. Check the seasoning and add salt and pepper if needed. Continue to cook until the meat is tender—about another 30 minutes or so.

Serves about 4.

★　　★　　★　　★　　★　　★　　★　　★　　★　　★

'Possum Party
by Luther Clark, Alabama Office

"And don't forget the marshmallows," I was cautioned as the planning group broke up. The ingredients for the "trail snack" had been apportioned to the various boys of the party, on a more or less equitable cooperative basis. Two fellows were to bring two pounds each of weiners, two others were to bring two dozen rolls apiece, one was to get pickle and mustard, and my contribution had been set as three pounds of marshmallow. We were to meet at the home of Mary Gordon at seven o'clock—just about dark.

Willis Jenks had the best 'possum dogs in the community, and Willis himself was a 'possum hunter of renown, so we had each "chipped in" two bits to hire Willis and his dogs. In addition, he would have the hides of any 'possums caught.

I was about three minutes late at the meeting-place and was accused of having stopped to collect a token from Nan on the way. Both of us had to explain that the delay was caused by Nan's father who didn't want to lend her his bed overalls.

We piled into two cars and made a bee line over the field road to Thatcher's woods, where Willis assured us the fattest 'possums lived. Down at the end of the corn rows we parked the cars and loaded the eats onto Willis' boy, Dodge Jim. (They call him "Dodge" because of his uncanny ability to evade field work.) Willis himself carried his ax and a flashlight. He had already set Rip and Snorter, the dogs on the ground with an urgent order to "Go gittum," which sent them circling already. (He told us he gave them names because the first 'possum they ever treed "sho' was a rip-snorter.")

"Boy, dem dogs done smell 'Old Man Sam' a'ready," Willis told us enthusiastically.

"That's all right, Willis," called Bill Treadwell, "they don't need to rush. We got all night."

A round of giggles and guffaws showed that most of the crowd had heard the "smack" of Bill taking a token from Sue Wells as he helped her over a log. None of us were using our flashlights as we could see well enough to follow Willis and Dodge Jim.

Far to our right, one of the dogs and then the other gave a succession of short, sharp, excited "trail barks." Everyone stood perfectly still while we "coursed" the dogs. In two minutes Willis started on. "Trail gittin' wahm," he announced, "Old Man Sam ain't so fur ahaid."

Dodge Jim followed his father on silent feet, and we "white folks" trailed them as softly as hail on a loose tin roof. An occasional louder crash, followed by "oomph, ouch," or some such remark, hinted delicately that some one—or two—had found a vine or dead limb in the way.

In all the falling and threshing around, Nan and I were missing our share. Somebody made a remark about "old surefoot," meaning me, and Nan called back, "Four feet are surer than two, you know." She didn't have to say that. I like to follow that old adjuration about never letting your left hand know what my right one is doing, and when she said that some smarty flashed his light on us before I could move that right arm. But all the laugh was not on us at that. Bill Treadwell and Sue jumped out of line to see what sort of hold I was using, And Bill fell over a high log with Sue on top of him. For a few seconds their feet were almost straight up, and Nan called, "But even four feet are not good off the ground!"

Every hundred yards or so we stopped to "course" the dogs again. They were still yapping the quick, trail bark, and seemed to be going the other way gradually on a shuttling trail. Old Man Sam had probably crossed his own trail several times to confuse and slow them.

We had blundered ahead for thirty minutes or more when we came to a branch that was pretty full from recent rains. Willis began walking up and down the bank, looking for a way to get us across dry. Some of the more ambitious tried to follow him but Nan and I chose to sit down and wait. In a few minutes Dodge Jim yelled back, "heah un lawg us kin coon."

We laggards made a rush in that direction, and that brought calamity. Somebody must have put that rattan vine where Nan and I found it—with our shins. The splash must have been tremendous but my ears were too full of water to know. As we scrambled and sputtered back to a dripping verticality that doggoned Bill Treadwell shouted: "We don't need any log, Jim. Old Sure-Four-Foot has knocked out all the water!"

Well, the crowd was entitled to that. We had had our laugh. But that water was cold. Since we were already wet, we waded on across and began walking rapidly so our teeth wouldn't shag too much. Willis was already across and holding his big light for the crowd to see how to slide—"coon"—across the slick sapling. Jack Burton was going along very cautiously when his hands slipped and he swung under the log. He finished the crossing monkey style instead of cooning.

Just about the time we were ready to go on, there came the long, solemn "tree bark" of Rip, followed a moment later by the shriller echo of Snorter. Above his light, I could see the gleam of Willis' teeth. "Dey done got Old Man Sam up a tree," he said proudly.

My fun was all wet. And so was Nan's, but we tore out through the underbrush with the rest of the crowd, in a mad race to be first at the tree. No use. Willis, as might have been expected, was there when we arrived, dancing around the trunk of the sweetgum tree at which the dogs were clawing, and weaving the beam of his powerful light over all the limbs as he tried to "shine the eyes" of Old Man Sam, the 'possum. If a treed 'possum were smart enough to close his eyes, the hunters would seldom find him.

"Dah he, dah he!" yelled Dodge Jim, pointing excitedly, and sure enough there were two flashes on the limb he indicated—the light reflected from the 'possum's eyes.

Willis unshouldered his ax. "Jim, you hold dem dogs outen de way," he ordered. "Dis tree too big to clam, so uh'll hafta cut it."

While he chopped methodically away, I collected a stack of fat pine "lightard knots" and built a fire. Dodge Jim had handed Bill the sack of food, and some of the more impatient were soon holding weiners over the blaze on pointed sticks cut from nearby bushes.

Nan and I were standing close to the fire, trying to dry out our clammy clothes when the tree came down with a jarring "whoo-am!" Jim loosed the dogs and they made a mad rush for the treetop. All of the crowd followed them. The way was light in front of me as I ran, but sud-

denly my feet hit something and I did a broadside flop. There was an excited squeak behind me, followed by much chattering. As soon as I could
get my breath back I looked to see what the new excitement was and
found I had tripped over the escaping 'possum and Clay Weldon had
picked him up before the dogs ever figured out where he went.

Instead of "playing 'possum" or "sulling"—feigning death or
unconsciousness—this particular Old Man Sam was trying to climb his
own heavy, whip-like tail to reach the hand by which Clay held him aloft.
With his teeth bared in the frightful "'possum grin," and his body bent
double while his front feet clasped his tail, he showed plainly that he had
his fighting clothes on. Usually Old Man Sam is quiet enough unless a
careless hand gets too near his mouth. Then it is always "look out, finger."

Willis quickly cut a "'possum stick"—a pole about seven feet long and
three inches in diameter—and split it about a foot. Old Man Sam's tail
was stuck through the split, and the ax pulled out so he would be held
firmly by his caudal appendage. He promptly wrapped all four feet around
the pole, and Willis leaned the simple trap against a tree. The dogs, at first
frantic to set their teeth in their quarry, had finally been shooed away to
seek another trail.

With Old Man Sam disposed of for the moment, we really began the
serious business of eating. The past hours of exercise in the clean, nippy
air had our appetites razor keen. After five hot dogs and eleven toasted
marshmallows, I got to thinking about my delicate stomach and would
not eat any more. The others were too busy to notice what a sissy eater
I was.

The gusto of the eaters gradually diminished, and finally the last one
leaned back with a long sigh. It wouldn't be fair to mention her name.
Several minutes before then, some bright boy had begun telling a ghost
story, and when he completed it, another was ready to start.

The fire burned low and was rebuilt, burnt low and was rebuilt again.
Couples huddled closer and closer as the stories became more eerie.
Dodge Jim slept soundly—and what a sound!—with his head on a log.
Between arm loads of wood Willis nodded beside the 'possum pole, and
sometimes snored.

Finally somebody shook him and he jumped up. "Willis, don't these
ghost stories make you scared?"

Willis scratched around his ear. "What say, Misto Jack?" "Don't these
ghost stories make you scared?" "Law me, no suh, dey don't bother me

none a-tall." "Don't you believe in ghosts?" "Yassuh, yassuh, ah b'lieves in 'em all right," and he rushed off to get more wood—and change the subject. I wouldn't tell on poor Willis to that thoughtless crowd, for a pretty [*sic*] but when he scratched his ear as he was being questioned, I saw him pull a wad of cotton out of his ear which he stuck back in place as he went after the wood. Willis was making sure that the ghost stories did not "bother him none a-tall."

Several heads began to nod. Sue was frankly sleeping with her head on Bill's shoulder. "Let's go home," Josie Mason suggested sleepily.

We blundered up on drowsy feet and looked around. Nobody knew which way we should go. Even Willis, mighty hunter, could find no bearings.

Sue flopped back down. "Siddown, Bill," she mumbled sleepily, "I'm going back to sleep." And she did.

Gradually others dozed off. Once a huge owl nearby became curious and shouted at us. The effect of the ghost stories showed in the terrifying shrieks that followed. I didn't say anything but I did have to pull my hat down.

Bright daylight came and we weaved a foggy trail back to the Fords. Then back to Mary's home.

"Be over at seven for 'possum and 'taters," she reminded us as we left.

There was a strong answering chorus: "We will!"

Nan and I were not late that time. She was all spruced up in her own toggery so she hadn't wasted any time arguing with her father about his clothes. To tell you the honest truth, we reached Mary's home about half-past six, because we wanted to see that 'possum properly cooked.

The cook was just taking the big boiler off the stove when we went into the kitchen. Old Man Sam was fat as a butterball, and the water in which he had been boiled, with salt and red pepper tossed in for seasoning, was already a rich gray gravy.

The long roaster was waiting, and into it the cook carefully set the 'possum. In a pan nearby were some large, golden-red Porto Rico sweet potatoes. Already peeled. These the cook placed carefully around the meat, only leaving space in a couple of places to dip the basting ladle down.

After all this placing was done, she poured the boiling-gravy over the meat and potatoes, put the lid on the roaster, and slipped it into the oven. She really had that stove roaring hot, too. The oven thermometer showed

450 degrees. We stood around for about five minutes, and she pulled out the roaster, dipped up the gravy from the bottom of the roaster, and poured it over the meat, very methodically covering every part of it.

"You chilluns go shoo, now," she ordered us after that. "You done see how dis is done, and you is cluttering up mah way, 'caze I'se got plenty wu'k to do."

Knowing how much depended on the cook, we promptly shooed.

The crowd was popping into the living room when we went back out there, and somebody suggested that we [do] some stunts. I had one I liked to do, so, as soon as I could, I showed it to them.

It is a quite simple trick of balance. I stick one leg out in front of me and sit down on the other heel. Then I stand up again, still holding that leg out in front and clear the floor. It looks so very easy that all the girls usually want to try it. They did then, with the usual result.

The heavier ones started lowering themselves—and went right on over on their backs with their feet up. The thinner ones mostly sat down all right. But when they started to get back up they found more ways of sprawling than could be imagined by the uninitiate. Several of them were still trying to regain their composure when the cook hammered on the big bell for us to go and eat. We were making so much noise we couldn't hear the little bell.

Now, brethren, that table was something. The 'possum and 'taters was on a big, long dish in the middle. There were two or three dishes of slaw around, and several stacks of fluffy, hot biscuit.

And at every place there was a cup of strong black coffee boiled in a pot.

We ate, and ate, and ate. As the cook came in with more coffee I caught a glimpse of two-inch meringue on a kitchen table, and slowed down. I received my just reward for that. I was able to eat two slices of lemon pie, while hardly any of the others could manage more than one.

Bill Treadwell got up from the table and looked down at himself in mock woe. "I'm afraid I've ruined my girlish figure," he moaned.

"Why, Sue!" exclaimed Clay Weldon, dropping his fork.

★ 10 ★

The Frontier

Mexicans, Indians, and Cowboys

Introduction to the Southwest
from the Arizona Office

With an appetite as big as all-out-doors, the southwest eats with gusto. Its taste was early shaped by the spareness of scrub country, the "isolateness" of mountain and desert. The lack of formality that has long characterized its table manners is of pioneer stock, induced by hard living. Of the countless hardships borne in the settlement of this vast region, lack of human companionship was alone insufferable. Eating without formality, then, could satisfy this craving for company better. Fingers in lieu of forks bespoke no impoverishment of living, but more gusto—the appeasement of hidden hunger by the most simple fare, with the variety of all kinds of human companions—stalwart, rogue and charlatan—to supplement the bare diet afforded. And today the southwest sets its table with the hospitality of the south; for, indeed, many southerners live there. But this is a hospitality of a gregarious nature—a cordiality that gets in exchange for the giving: the adventurer's yearnings for companionship now deep-rooted in the folkways of its tables.

★   ★   ★   ★   ★

Ofelia Sandoval rolling out tortillas near Taos, New Mexico,
September 1939. (Russell Lee)

Arthur Brooks, the editor in the Phoenix office who composed this introduction, had a heck of a time wrestling with the notes of writers
who were spread out across five different states. They were sending
him stories that did not fit into the outline the editors in Washington
had sent him for this section, which read in part: "Spanish, Indian, and
range influence in arid region—spices and condiments, tomato sauces,
sheep and cattle." Instead, the writers composed stories about the
mythical presence of American cowboys and hardy pioneer settlers,
with just a smattering of notes on what Indians ate and how Mexicans
lived.

A handful of pages from the final southwest manuscript remain in the
Library of Congress. A fuller manuscript may yet turn up in the basement of a state archives. Or, perhaps Brooks simply petered out with his
struggle, running out of time to complete his task before Congress denied the project further funding. I'm inclined to think he would have

struggled no matter what. The individual stories he had to work with and that have survived are very colorful, redolent of the spirit of the great American West. But there's hardly a clear-eyed view among them, certainly nothing that would have helped Brooks find his way to a firm understanding of the Southwest's cuisine.

The stories are driven instead by the iconic nature of the region. They are framed in a landscape imbued with legends and romance, with tall tales that forgo the historical reality. Life in this part of the country is dictated by the area's demanding physical nature and its cultural development, which makes it as different from the rest of the United States as it can be. Nowhere is this more apparent than in Southwestern cooking. Not only are the dishes influenced from a heritage other than Anglo or French, but they incorporate ingredients that, in the 1930s, were generally not available—let alone familiar—to the rest of the country. To explain all this in the short space *America Eats!* would allot to the region was a formidable challenge, indeed.

Happily for me, there exists now a firm appreciation of Southwestern cooking. Salsa, after all, has outstripped ketchup to become our number one condiment on the table. Tacos, tortillas, the Mexican/Texan barbecue style of using seasoned spice rubs instead of the sauce-drenched method of the American South, are now ubiquitous, even in the nation's most isolated communities.

So what is there left for me to explore? I thought I'd look for traces of the cuisine's beginnings, and this—as the original Washington outline suggested—leads straight to Spain.

Of all the great European powers that once laid claim to this land, Spain continues to exert a powerful influence through the culture that took root under its domination. Its long occupation of the territory and the continuing presence so close to our borders of Mexico—its principal outpost—has ensured that the Southwest maintains customs and flavors that are distinct from the British and French traditions that predominate elsewhere. This region suited the Spanish because it was so similar to their homeland. They knew what to do with the arid conditions. They understood how to cope with the heat and sunlight. The dishes they made at home could be readily translated to what they found here, and the Spanish were responsible for bringing to these shores many of the fruits and vegetables that continue to grow here today. If you are dining outdoors, eating a thick spicy stew or meat that has been cooked over smoldering wood, you are essentially eating the way the conquistadors once did.

One of the results of the interaction of the Spanish-Mexican descendants is the style of cooking we think of as Tex-Mex or Southwestern. It's been in development now for a few hundred years, maybe the oldest to be flourishing in our collective recipe box.

But when the federal writers took up the subject of the local cuisine, they saw it in romantic terms, as it is in this piece:

The Municipal Market in San Antonio
from the Texas Office

One follows his nose past the Municipal Market in search of the source of an aroma which, once sniffed, is never forgotten—the fragrance of burning mesquite wood. He turns a corner and runs squarely into old Mexico, as abruptly as walking onto a Hollywood movie set. Tables are spread outdoors along the whole block and behind them women and girls tend fires and charcoal braziers above which Mexican foods are stacked. Three Mexican minstrels, brave in embroidered costumes and high-peaked hats, pluck their guitars tentatively, ready to serenade.

A Mexican family, plainly in modest circumstances, sits at the first long table, giving itself a night out. He wears his Sunday best and his wife her best reboza (shawl), one end of it thrown gracefully across her shoulder. There are patches on the clothes of the three small children, but the general effect is one of being scrubbed and starched. The waitress comes to take the order and finally takes it, but only after a long conversation that covers the balminess of the air, neighborhood news, the high cost of living, and remedies for colds. Everything here moves slowly and with graceful ease.

The children have tacos, tasty favorite of shine boy and banker alike—a tortilla folded and fried crisp and stuffed with seasoned meat and chopped greens. After much deliberation the parents fix on enchiladas—tortillas dipped in chili sauce, covered with chopped onion and grated cheese and done up jelly-roll style. And now the husband—this obviously is an occasion for special celebration—glances significantly at the expectant musicians. They come to stand close behind the family. Plaintive tenors blend with plaintive guitars in a song about a little princess who, from all accounts, was deeply in love. The children munch their tacos. The man and his wife smile at each other across the heads of their brood.

★　　★　　★　　★　　★

The Municipal Market that survives in San Antonio is hardly Little Mexico. It remains festive, though, but festive for tourists. It's too expensive for anyone else to dine there. The girls who once tended the charcoal braziers where food was cooked were known as chili queens, but they are long gone, too. The foods now offered in the restaurants around the market are Mexican in spirit, but they are tame and lack the natural vitality of authenticity. Which is not to say San Antonio, in all its beauty, does not have great Mexican food; it's just not at the market and not served in the casual, lively way that it was back when the chili queens ruled the plazas.

There are, to be sure, unbelievable establishments throughout the West serving authentic Mexican—and for that matter, Tex-Mex—cooking. A lot has been written about them and they're pretty easy to find. But for something closer to the scene witnessed by the federal writers, the roach coaches parked along South Sixth Avenue in Tucson must be explored because, in their straightforward simplicity and by offering what is, in essence, everyday fare, they are providing the dishes that allow survival in a new world. Most of them are owned and operated by Mexicans—either outright immigrants or people who travel back and forth across the border. And what they offer is anything but the usual run-of-the-mill Mexican food.

When I pull into the dirt parking lot where a coach is moored for the day (some are more permanent structures but most are trucks on wheels that may have their usual corners and sites but can be moved when need be), I'm greeted with unveiled amusement as I scan the posted offerings, most of which seem strange even though I have a good working knowledge of Mexican food. Or at least Mexican food offered in Northeast cities, which—while standing in the hot parking lot on the side of a busy road in Tucson—I begin to realize may not mean much of anything in the Southwest. This is because the Mexican food available in these states is always evolving with new ideas and trends from across the border.

It takes a while for these influences to filter into the rest of the country through immigration and travel, so I'm definitely behind the eight ball as I look over the truck menus.

Plus, I'm Anglo and, as the lunch hour approaches, I'm a decided minority. Everyone else in line knows what he or she wants and the patrons soon succeed in nudging me away from the counter. Some trucks are known for particular dishes and it's not unheard-of to drive down the street, gathering up a substantial multicourse meal along the way. All the food can be described as homemade. This means that tortillas are not just handy vehicles for stuffing. Instead, they're hand formed with a pleasing rough texture. They are tiny but enormously tasty, and come accompanied by a whole line of interesting condiments (grilled scallions and jalapeño peppers; cold sliced radishes and cucumbers, and at least three wildly different, freshly made sauces). Slightly familiar is *menudo*—tripe soup that's guaranteed to settle the stomach and head after a night of drinking. But then there's *estilo Sonora* (a big soft bun stuffed with a meaty beef hot dog piled high with beans, cheese, and onions); *coctel de elote* (corn cocktail—a cup of fresh corn kernels in the broth they were simmered in and topped with a scoop of Mexican cheese and a lime wedge); and *pico de gallo* (slices of fresh fruit with a fiery red chili sprinkled on top). Some of the coaches offer ceviche, generally accompanied by a little note that reads: "To consume raw or rare seafood can increase the risk of disease. Thank you for your comprehension—Health Department." Not that this indicates that the coaches are particularly lax in hygiene, but eating raw fish on the side of a busy, dirt-swirling, generally broiling road just truly seems to be toying with one's mortality and the existence of a benevolent God.

In any case, no matter of its curative powers, the *menudo* is terrific. The *estilo Sonora* is interesting. The *coctel* is a decidedly acquired taste. More addictive is *pico de gallo*, made from in-season ripe fruit such as papaya, watermelon, cantaloupe, and coconut. Although it may be a hot day and the fruit looks so refreshing, do not rush to bite into it. Rather, suck the flesh slowly to dilute the power of the crushed red pepper sprinkled over the fruit: it is, to say the least, a bracing, although surprisingly rejuvenating, experience. The near relative to *pico de gallo* is *raspadas*, a cup full of shaved ice doused with a syrup of a fruit that is in season, then topped with cheap but flavorful vanilla ice cream and, finally, with the fresh fruit of the syrup, diced into bite-size pieces. The whole is simply lovely on a broiling day.

When the Spanish missionaries pushed into the area above the Rio Grande, they found a people with a rich diet. It's estimated that Native Americans in this region used to harvest over two thousand different plants and animals. That was before 1860, when the Navajos were imprisoned at Fort Summer, New Mexico, and the Apaches were driven from much of their lands. Tribal livestock was confiscated; their orchards and crops destroyed. Year after year—and well into the twentieth century because of the mammoth sprawl of cities such as Phoenix and Albuquerque—Native Americans lost more farmland and their hunting practices were severely restricted. By the time the federal writers were gathering material for *America Eats!*, the tribes in the Southwest, as was true of their counterparts through the rest of the country, had been reduced to relying on government food programs to survive.

This may be why the writers concentrated so deeply on writing about what Native Americans used to eat. At the very least it was more interesting to read about:

General Camp Life Among the Kiowa, Comanche, and Apache Tribes
*from the Oklahoma Office**

The Cheyenne and Arapaho Indians are very fond of dog: they have a dainty dish when they can get a fat puppy and boil it and drink the soup. They take a young dog, tie a string around his neck and hang him until he choked to death, then they hold the body over a blaze until the hair is all singed off. The body is then placed on the hot ground, and covered with dirt and a fire is built over it and it is roasted until done. Roasted dog is served at all special occasions.

They roast the common land terrapin alive, keeping a watch around the camp fire to prevent the terrapin from escaping. Previous to the feast

---

* Collected for another project, *Indians & Pioneer*, but to be included in *America Eats!*

the Indian men go out and round up the terrapins and the women come and carry them to the camp ground. In cooking fresh water (snapping) turtles they puncture the shell just above each hind leg; the turtle is then cast into the fire to roast. They remove the lower part of the shell from both terrapins and turtles and eat the cooked meat from the upper half.

[The Creeks'] *soc-quo-nir-kee* was made of meat and corn. Flint corn grits were boiled about three hours, grease and salt were added, then either duck or squirrel was put in and the whole cooked until the meat was tender.

The vast region we now call Idaho did not produce maize or native grains. But in many sections, such as the famous Camas Prairie, it did grow small white vapid onion, highly praised by the natives as food.

The wapato was another native bulbous root with nourishing qualities. Among native fruits were crabapples, grape, blackberry, huckleberry, gooseberry, raspberry, salmon berry, strawberry, thimble berry, currant, alder berry, mountain cherry, and service berry. For meat, buffalo figured strongest, especially in south Idaho. They ate bison, deer, salmon, sturgeons, beaver (practically unmolested by the Indians, until the whites put a price on their pelts), and porcupine, among others.

The principal food of the Sioux was meat. In the winter they ate muskrats, badgers, otters and raccoons, in the spring they ate fish and the roots of certain wild plants, in the summer they had wild pigeons and cranes as well as fish and certain roots, and in the autumn they killed wild ducks, geese and muskrats.

★   ★   ★   ★   ★

Once established on reservations, the tribes' diets began to crumble and their health suffered. The government provided them with processed cheese, poor quality (often canned) meat, and refined sugar and flour. The government even tried to regulate how the food they gave to the tribes was prepared:

> On issue day when beef was given to the Indians the women would take the entrails to the river and wash them and then take them to their camp and string them around on their meat poles or rack until they were ready to use. They ate them raw and also dumped them into their cooking pots and made soup out of them.

When government agents, shocked by this practice, began to butcher beef before issuing the meat, certain new digestive troubles resulted which the Indians said were due to the fact that they were not permitted to eat all parts of the animal: this rounded meat diet was necessary to keep them healthy.

—Oklahoma Office

Under such restrictions, traditional recipes were gradually translated to make use of the foodstuff that was available. People got used to how their food tasted even though it was far less good for them.

Indians and spectators at annual fair on the Crow Reservation, Montana, September 1941. (Marion Post Wolcott)

This is what happened to flatbread. Anywhere you go on the many reservations covering the southwest, you are liable to come across some version of it. There is a historical Apache and Navajo recipe, but the grains used for the dough were gathered from wild grasses such as pigweed and dropseed, and the resulting bread was highly nutritious and flavorful. On the reservations, the tribes were given processed wheat flour and the women did the best they could by mixing it with lard. The resulting bread was, at the very least, filling, and provided some bulk to compensate for meager food allotments.

Many tribal members today continue to receive help from government food programs. It's the same that many other low-income people in the country receive. But what is really unnerving, or just plain galling, is how the federal government tries to put a good spin on what they're providing, by handing out cookbooks to teach people how to use this stuff. One such cookbook, *A River of Recipes: Native American Recipes Using Commodity Food*, is compiled by the Food Division and the Food and Nutrition Services of the USDA and described on the USDA Web site as providing "many recipes of interest to Native Americans incorporating foods that are distributed through Commodity Foods Programs." It's hard to imagine anyone having any interest in many of the recipes in the pamphlet, which includes a drink called—honestly—Orange Geronimo (orange juice, instant nonfat dry milk, and corn syrup), baked spaghetti (filled with diced lunch meat), Commodity Cheese Pizza (canned spaghetti sauce and American cheese), loads of recipes for ground beef, and only five for any kind of vegetables, most of them from a can. The pamphlet—still in circulation—was last revised in July 2003 but doesn't take into consideration any recent developments from the last twenty years in nutrition or health. To top it off, the recipes aren't even appetizing, to say the least.

I really wanted to find traditional flatbread made from wild grasses but it was unavailable on any of the reservations I visited in New Mexico and Arizona. In Tucson, I picked up a suggestion from a local food expert to visit the Tohono O'odham reservation, where I was told I could find some incredible things to eat, including variations on flatbread. My directions were: look for the church and follow my nose.

The church turns out to be San Xavier Mission del Bac, the glorious mission built on the tribe's land in 1783 under the direction of the Spanish Franciscans. The mission was considered the end of the civilized world and the church, rising bone white from the desert floor, still appears to be the final outpost of beauty and order in the midst of its wild scrub landscape. Inside the church, perfumed with the smell of wax from candles burning before all the saints, gawping tourists mix with praying parishioners: the tourists arrange themselves before the altars and take over pews to snap pictures of themselves, while the faithful bow their heads, quietly reciting the rosary or kneeling with their hands folded, staring up at the figure of Christ above the main altar.

Outside in the cut-glass sun, everything is bleached tan and white. A scraggy dog wanders down from the hill where a large concrete cross looms over the mission. He ambles across the plaza to the semicircle of makeshift arbors roofed in blue plastic tarps before the church. Since this is a weekday in the off-season, only a few of the arbors are occupied, displaying chalkboards or cardboard signs that list the different dishes for sale. All of them feature flatbreads: plain, cinnamon, or cheese-stuffed. The most expensive is filled with "red" meat, which translates into some sort of meat thickly covered in a red chili paste.

My nose leads me to the arbor where the dog has come to rest. A collection of enameled pots simmer on a little camp stove behind a table. As I ask the woman at the booth for flatbread with red meat, the dog moves close beside me and together we watch as the woman takes a disk of dough from an aluminum pan and flattens it out between her palms before easing it into a frying pan full of bubbling oil, where it quickly puffs up into a golden dome. She forks the hot bread onto a paper plate, fills the crevice with a bright crimson mixture from one of the pots, then folds the paper plate in half before handing it to me. The dog looks up as I take a bite. Having lit a candle inside the church and whispered a few prayers, I thankfully have only one thing to say about what I am tasting: God Almighty! Flatbread and red meat is incredibly good. The chili sauce is so powerful, I can't quite figure out what kind of meat is in it, so I ask. I'm especially curious since my source suggested the meat could be anything— including rattlesnake or some other desert native. The woman breaks off a conversation with a friend about a birthday celebration in the park to shyly respond.

"Sometimes beef."

"What about chicken?"

The woman shakes her head and purses her lips. "That's flatbread with chicken."

"Pork?"

The woman shrugs her shoulders a little and goes back to talking to her friend.

So much for the investigation. Truth is, though, with something this delicious in hand, it's hard to finally muster up a hoot about what exactly it is. The realization that occurs to me as I walk back across the plaza under the glaring sun, and with the dog now a devoted friend at my heels, is that flatbread and a stuffing of some sort is not only filling, it is also incredibly scrumptious, a meal in itself. I understand it's not good for me, considering it's just flour, sugar, and some kind of trans-fat dripping through the paper plate. The mystery meat has been tenderized by a long, slow simmer in a pungent, hand-ground, still rough and thick chili sauce. Despite everything I know about what's good and bad for my stomach, I'm hooked.

Leaning against the car to finish the rest of the flatbread, and sharing a little taste every now and then with my new friend who rests his nose companionably against my leg, a thought comes circling through about how hard it would be to change a food habit that's now so thoroughly ingrained into a people's way of life. This thought crystallizes after visits to local markets: the Southwest may be the last region in the nation where tubs—no, buckets—of pure lard are still on sale. There are blocks of it, too, which if you're a pie maker, are tempting to ship back home. Bags of fried pig skin as big as bed pillows are inevitably on display nearby. But near the lard there are signs of hope in the pyramid of fresh produce offered for sale. The miracle of irrigation throughout the region has brought an abundance of fruits and vegetables to all the markets I stop in to. There are also a lot of interesting whole grains and spices; fairly good quality, locally raised meats; fish and shellfish from the nearby Gulf Coast.

Best of all are the slew of good farmers' markets I stumble upon, including a surprising number in small towns and along the remote roads I drive on. Local producers, most of whom claim they raise organic and pesticide-free crops, share space with home gardeners offering their surplus fruits and vegetables—all of them a tiny miracle, considering the drought conditions that have gripped the West and made farming in the area increasingly tougher. What would happen, I wonder, if the government's Commodity Programs helped out local farmers and growers and distributed fresh, well-grown ingredients instead of processed food to low-income people? Wouldn't everyone benefit? Maybe even the nutritional quality of flatbread would return.

The last people to think about the quality of what they ate were cowboys. Mostly, they were just trying to survive and that meant they were happy with whatever was served them. It's worth noting that Arizona and New Mexico did not become states until 1912 and that until then—and for years afterward—much of this area was, and felt like, the frontier. Out on the wide plains were Native Americans and ranchers. There were not too many city people, even in the cities. The kind of food a traveler was apt to find was usually straightforward, nothing more fancy than a steak. Maybe ham and eggs if you were lucky, since both were considered a delicacy, this being beef and sheep, not chicken or pork, country.

In any case, although Mexicans and Native Americans had first claim to taming the land, the cowboys and their partners quickly grabbed all the attention. When they demanded food, they demanded a lot of it, which was why the chuck wagon was invented by the Texas cattle rancher Charles Goodnight (of the Goodnight-Loving trail). He fitted the back of a covered wagon with a neat multicompartment cabinet whose fold-down table provided cooks on cattle drives with a place to prepare food for the cowboys' dinners.

The Chuck Wagon
(Including Son-of-a-Gun Stew)
from the Texas Office

Wherever, throughout the ranching areas of the Southwest, there is a reunion of cattlemen, ex-cowboys, or old trail drivers, a feature of the gathering is almost certain to be a meal that centers around an old-time chuck wagon.

It had no other name, this essential of the cattle industry in range days—a field kitchen that accompanied the cow-waddies on their chores of rounding up, branding, driving, and otherwise conditioning cattle for the market. It went with the men and their herds, even on the epic treks of the trail drives to northern markets. Of roads there were few or none.

Cowboys of the SMS Ranch serving themselves at dinner at a chuck wagon, near Spur, Texas, May 1939. (Russell Lee)

The chuck wagon moved from day to day over every kind of terrain across which a cowboy could ride a horse or drive a steer.

In this modified prairie schooner the cook was a monarch. His domain included a circle around his stronghold, a radius of about sixty feet, but varying with cooks and local customs. At the back of the wagon was a let-down shelf from which the hungry cowboy took his eating tools and such food as the cook saw fit to hand out there. He then went over to the fire and helped himself to whatever else had been concocted or brewed for his sustenance.

Except for rare feasts, generally before round-ups, the meals were plain and monotonous—beans, salt pork (usually "side-meats," modernly called bacon), fresh unfattened beef from the range, and sourdough biscuits. Various criteria were used in judging chuck-wagon cooks, but it is generally agreed that in the evaluation of these always important personages, good sourdough biscuits would cover a multitude of other sins, for sourdough biscuits were the bread of life of the Texas plains.

Into their construction the competent range cook put time and loving care. He started, usually, with a potato, some sugar, and a little flour. These—the potato being grated—were worked together until smooth and set in a warm place to ferment—often, under range conditions, being wrapped in a blanket and placed near the fire. When the dough had risen, more water and flour were kneaded in, together with salt, soda, and sugar if required. The mixture having reached the proper smoothness, pieces were pinched off and molded in the hollow of the hand. Dutch ovens were preferred for baking. Shoved into hot ashes and covered with ashes and coals, they became hot and held their heat, and the bread could be baked in them without danger of burning.

Surrounded as he was by the great open spaces and without much companionship—the men that he served appeared from their range labors only at mealtimes, and he seldom saw anyone else—the genius who reigned at the chuck wagon sometimes felt the urge to let his visions roam beyond the dull routine of his daily vocation, to dream artistically of menu complexities that might be accomplished within the limitations of his normal materials. Such an artist evolved a dish that today, in one of several similar forms, is the main feature of every chuck-wagon banquet.

Precisely how and why it gained its original name has been lost in the mists of antiquity, and that name, in the interest of politeness, has long since been amended. Except by the older cattle set—and by them only on rare and wholly masculine occasions—it is now called son-of-a-gun stew.

The dish—at first a general preparation designed to use appetizingly the best parts of a freshly killed calf—developed specialists with varying recipes. Aging men with slightly bowed legs and handle-bar mustaches still argue, and will until they die, as to the relative merits of what these super-cooks worked out. John Snyder, of Amarillo in the Texas Panhandle, who is nationally famous as a barbecue artist, is also held in high esteem for his son-of-a-gun and this is his recipe:

"You kill and dress the fattest calf that can be found. Then you take parts of the liver, heart, sweetbreads, marrow gut, tongue, and some of the tenderloin, and choice bits of flank steak. You start the cooking by putting some bits of suet in the round-up kettle, to be frying while you cut the ingredients into small pieces. You add the pieces, cover well with warm water, and add hot water from time to time, as needed. Season with salt, pepper, and a little onion. Last of all, you add the brains. Cook until tender, which will take about two hours." He and all the other experts seem to agree that the result can never be satisfactory unless the cooking begins at the earliest possible moment after the killing of the calf.

Many a one-time cowboy will maintain that there positively is no other dish on land or sea with which this can be compared. Driven to it, he may admit that you can get a mild and altogether imperfect idea of how it tastes by thinking of the best chicken giblets and gravy you ever ate. Serious offense could be given in the old days by claiming that any part of the concoction was better than any other, and it was not etiquette to be in the slightest degree choosey. When it was served from beside the chuck wagon the cook was wont to announce:

"Come and get it! Get all you want—but don't pick!"

John Arnot, also of the Texas Panhandle and a former president of the T Anchor cowboy reunion, who ate his first son-of-a-gun at a Cimarron River cow camp in 1884, observed through the years the reaction of womenfolk to the dish, and was quoted on the subject by the *Amarillo Sunday News* in 1938:

"First the ladies act suspicious of it, as if they thought there was something mean and ornery about it—because of the name, I suppose. Then they see everybody eating, and they get a whiff of how it smells, and they say, 'I believe I'll take just a small spoonful, please.' And in a few minutes their plates come back, and they don't say anything about a small spoonful."

★　　★　　★　　★　　★

To eat alongside some cowboys, I figured I had to find a chuck wagon, which is why I found myself at the Festival of the West in Phoenix, Arizona. The theme to the old television show *Rawhide* is pouring mercilessly through loudspeakers as I wait to get in. Scattered among the regular folks dressed in shorts and baseball hats, fanny packs parked below their thick waistlines, are women in long prime calico-printed dresses, lace gloves, parasols, and sunbonnets, who are holding onto the arms of men sporting chaps and clinking spurs. A sign by the wooden gate surrounding the compound where the festival is taking place informs the crowd that no loaded firearms or ammunition, in- cluding black powder, is allowed inside. A young boy who looks to be on the cusp of the surly teen years, growls, "Oh, man!" as his father de- mands he take his bullet belt back to the car. Meanwhile, his slightly older brother, completely duded-up in stiff black jeans, leather vest, and silver spurs, practices twirling his gun around his finger and into his hip-holster. He drops the revolver every time. When he finally suc- ceeds, an older, much-sunburned, cowboy smiles at him and says, "You're supposed to tip your hat like this," and, with a flourish, whips off his sparkling white ten-gallon hat and extends it out with the crown upside down as he takes a gallant bow. "You give 'em a little show. Make the ladies happy."

On that note, the gates open and, with the final "Giddyup!" yelp from the *Rawhide* music, we all tramp through to find some real cow- boys riding into a rodeo arena to rope bulls. Across a dusty yard from the arena, at least a dozen covered wagons are drawn in a loose circle around a patch of lush grass. At each campsite, long, shallow trenches that have been torn through the grass are filled with carefully tended embers, on top of which sit various cast-iron Dutch ovens. Most of the pots have little feet on the bottom to allow air to circulate and heat the entire vessel. This kind of pot is good for baking bread and cobblers. Other pots are suspended above the fire from an iron brace set into the ground: inside these, stews and beans will be cooked. On almost every fire is a cast-iron skillet—the utensil that one *America Eats!* editor in Washington claimed "almost wrecked America," for cooking food too fast. Chops and sides of beef are, indeed, being broiled fairly quickly in all of them.

The folks tending the pots and the fires have all signed up for the chuck wagon cook-off. They're akin to Civil War reenactors and mem- bers of the Society for Creative Anachronism: for the duration of the cook-off, perhaps a day or two, they sleep, and dress, and cook as if they're out there on the Chisholm trail instead of, say, on the back lot of a resort hotel. They are all extremely proud of what they are doing, proud of a heritage almost all of them were raised in the shadows of, if haven't been an actual part of. To enter the competition, participants must have a covered wagon fitted with a genuine chuck box—a nifty cabinet with shelves for supplies and a fold-down work table that is secured to the back end of the wagon. Many of the wagons are authentically old, acquired at western shows in places like Las Vegas or Houston ("I got mine on eBay," a contestant joked).

Cooks on cattle drives were middle-aged to older men, generally described as having a crabby, if not outright unpleasant, disposition. The outfits participating in the cook-offs have a blend of women and men, with two teams being composed entirely of men, and one (the Cowgirls Forever) just of women. The hems of the women's long calico dresses drag precariously close to the hot embers in the cooking pits; the men, in jeans and chaps, are wearing cowboy hats and spurs. All the cooking utensils are decidedly old, too—cast-iron or enameled pots and pans, spatulas, spoons, and forks. It's quite a financial layout on display—as well as time, when you consider how long it takes to haul the wagons and set up a campsite, dig a decent pit and build a fire, and prepare the food.

The menu is the same at each campsite: beans, steak, some kind of potatoes (mashed, generally, although a few roasted), sourdough biscuits, and a variation on fruit cobbler. The differences come by way of a fancy addition—say, fresh rosemary in potatoes, or a lavish pour of Amaretto added to a "spotted pup" (raisin bread pudding). The most welcoming and cheerful wagon in the circle—the one you'd want to come upon out in the nearby Sonoran Desert if you were lost—is the Curly Cue Camp. They serve chicken-fried steak coated in soda-cracker bread crumbs, mashed 'taters, and sourdough biscuits that are tangy and amazingly light.

"Here! Here! Here! Taste a little of this," the cook says, straightening up from the fire with a spoonful of something amber-brown and juicy. Without waiting a second, she scoops it onto a little plate and presents it. "Apple pandowny. What do you think of that?"

The only possible thought is that it's pretty damn good. The cook is Terrie, sister of Clint, the slightly manic collector of the one-hundred-year old wagon and all the utensils on display—a small fortune in antique cookware and furniture. In her yellow gown and sunbonnet, Terrie gracefully maneuvers about the crowded campsite, giving orders to the men to shift pots from one fire to another, stooping to peek under lids, checking on the pounding of crackers for bread crumbs, making sure visitors have a cup of cool water.

"I just love this," she says. "I love the costumes and the cooking. When we first started competing five years ago, I didn't know what I was doing. It's been trial-and-error and asking [for] a lot of advice about how you cook like this."

She must have learned fast because the Curly Cue Camp generally wins prizes at these events. What she has learned to do is to think of the Dutch oven, when embedded in embers, as a moveable oven chamber. The trick to cooking with it is to have a good, hot fire—a pit of charcoal and wood that takes several hours to get to the right ember stage—and a sense for when to shift the pots around to vary the heat inside. (For a good source to learn more about Dutch oven cooking, check out: http://papadutch.home.comcast.net.)

People mill about from campsite to campsite. As noon approaches, the crowd grows steadily hungrier, urged on by the aromas escaping from under the cast-iron lids. Spectators' growling stomachs and their acute sense of anticipation mimic the situation that was faced by chuck wagon cooks in olden times: they have to worry about having enough to feed everyone—and having some left over for the judges.

"We're gonna have to watch our portions, people," shouts a cowboy over in the Biscuit Flats camp.

Looking out over the competing camps in a black cowboy hat and an impeccable white shirt buttoned up to his throat is Tom Perini. He represents Pico Salsa sauce, one of the corporate sponsors for the festival and the competition. He also runs his family's ranch down in Buffalo Gap, Texas, where in 1983 he opened a steakhouse that has a pretty good reputation. Besides being a cook, himself, Tom knows a lot about the old West and to listen to him describe cowboy life is something anyone interested in American history and folklore should do.

"This is what cowboys really ate," he says, lifting the lid off a cast-iron pot suspended over a wood fire. In it bubbles a watery concoction of brown beans with bits of fatty bacon floating greasily on top. "About a pound a day for each cowboy. They had beans, rice, cornmeal—and a lot of sourdough because the starter didn't spoil out on the trail. This stuff here," and Tom waves a big spoon around the area to take in the different camps now in a final tizzy before the judging, "this is all make-believe."

I ask him when was the last time cowboys used a chuck wagon.

"You know there's no more cattle drives, right?"

"Yeah."

"Just checking," he smiles and I feel like his best pupil. "Trails all got fenced in by farmers or ranchers."

With that, Tom is off and running with a good survey-level lecture on the demise of cattle drives and the establishment of modern cowboy traditions. To summarize: These days, ranchers and their hands tend to their herds on large ranches and transport them by rail. By law, the ranchers must provide housing for their employees if none exists close by, and the same is true of food. It's not unusual to see ranchers with a cell phone in their free hand while riding their horses, and when the work requires them to be far from the main house, out come four-wheel-drive trucks packed with coolers. The variety of offerings in the coolers is staggering, compared to what was carried in the old chuck wagon days. Instead of beans and biscuits, the coolers hold sandwiches and various containers from fast-food and take-out places if any are nearby, snack packs of chips and jerky, sodas, bottled water—even, on occasion, espresso.

Here's where I jump into Tom's lecture to tell him about driving through Idaho the week before, where there seemed to be an endless line of tiny drive-through huts even along the most desolate roadsides. Usually inside a hut would be a nice young woman quick to dispense a thick and potent brew, offering a generous number of syrups and additives to tame the robust beans. That was amazing enough to me, but the serving window was the best: it was inevitably a little higher than what I was used to out east, to accommodate the height of pickup truck cabs and the seat of work horses. This meant that after I pulled in to one of these little huts behind a guy on a horse, I had to get out of the car and stand on tiptoes to place my order.

"Coffee is life's blood out here," Tom replies when I'm through.

I ask about son-of-a-bitch stew and he brightens. Tom really warms to the dish—it's a highlight of his cook-off lecture—and relishes every kind of offal that flavors the recipe. He also has great respect for the fact that there are verified historical accounts of people actually eating and liking the dish.

"You got to understand how hungry these people were. The appetite they worked up doing the kind of work they were doing—fifteen-, sixteen-hour days, most in the saddle, surviving all kinds of weather: heat, storms, sudden snow squalls. It weren't nobody's idea of a social. But when those boys came back to camp and saw a fire going and something cooking for them—well, you can just imagine."

I ask him what he thinks is the most overlooked aspect of cowboy cooking and he doesn't even pause to think: the influence of black and Hispanic cowboys.

"The thing about a cattle drive or even working a ranch back then is that it was a mix of cultures. A lot of time, the drives consisted of two whites, two blacks, and two Hispanics. The blacks, they came over from the South because they got a better shake out here—not perfect, but better. And they were good around animals. Like the Hispanics were. They're just not celebrated enough for what they did.

"And as for cooks—well, black cowboys knew how to make something out of nothing. I know of this one ranch in south Texas. Had some black hands working there and one year the river was flooded with crabs up from the Gulf. Well, the ranch had pecan trees on it, so the hands caught a bunch of crabs and coated them with ground pecans and fried them up. That meal's still talked about."

Sharp at noon, all the camps are ready to begin serving. The judges get their tastes and then the hordes of spectators are allowed to buy tickets to load up on the camps' offerings. I have chicken-fried steak and

Mexican Indian before peppers, Isleta, New Mexico, September 1940. (Russell Lee)

apple cobbler at the Curly Cue, beans from the Biscuit Flats, and biscuits at the Brown Dirt Cowboys campsite. Love them all, especially the biscuits, which are everything you would hope for in a biscuit—crisp outer shell, fluffy and tangy soft bread inside. I don't know if I could live for a time on this fare—after this one day, I'm on the lookout for some greens and vegetables. But there's no denying how these dishes would be a welcoming thought to gallop back to after a long day on the range.

Sow-belly
from the Arizona Office

Had it not been for the lowly pinto beans, known locally as frijoles—the Spanish name for them[—]sow-belly, as the cowboys called salt pork, and "Mormon" gravy, Arizona would still be a howling wilderness and a dreary desert. Hence we suggest that somewhere in the broad expanse of this state of magnificent distances a monument be erected to this diet that made pioneering possible.

Beans were seasoned with rinds from salt pork or home cured bacon. Sometimes if visitors came in unexpectedly it turned out to be bean soup, one bean to a quart of water.

Gravy could be made in many ways. The best, of course, was made of milk, and flour in the pan where meat was fried or roasted, but it could be made by browning the flour in any kind of fat and with water instead of milk.

One family who would not use pig meat in any form used beef tallow to make their gravy. If this tallow "stuck to their ribs" like it did to the roof of the mouths, it probably served its purpose.

A tasty gravy could be made by frying onions then adding flour and milk or water. This could be varied by seasoning it with curry powder. This curry gravy was particularly good on cold nights, and was often served in the winter if the supply of milk for the usual supper of bread and milk was limited.

"Lumpy Dick" was a favorite dish in early pioneer families, only milk, flour and salt were needed for it.

Recipe

The following recipe derives from the federal writers' papers with my modern interpretation.

A True Son-of-a-Gun Stew

　　1 (1-pound) beef tongue
　　½ pound beef tripe
　　½ pound beef kidneys
　　1 pound beef heart
　　½ pound beef liver
　　½ pound beef or veal brains
　　½ pound beef or veal sweetbreads
　　¼ pound salt pork
　　3 to 4 medium-size onions, peeled and sliced into thin rings
　　4 cups hot water
　　1 tablespoon salt
　　¼ teaspoon pepper
　　2 teaspoons Worcestershire sauce

¼ teaspoon dried marjoram
¼ teaspoon dried thyme
2 to 3 tablespoons all-purpose flour or cornmeal (optional)
Cold water (optional)

Place the beef tongue and tripe in a kettle and cover with water. Bring to a boil, then lower the heat to a simmer and cook, uncovered, for 30 minutes. Lift the tripe from the water and place on a plate, letting the tongue continue to cook for another 30 minutes or so. Meanwhile, when the tripe is cool enough to handle, cut it into serving-size strips. When the tongue is tender (a fork should pierce it easily), remove it from the water and let it cool enough so that you are able to pull off the skin. Trim the fat and gristly parts from the tongue and cut the flesh into cubes.

While the meat is cooking, soak the kidney in salted water for about 1 hour, then cut into cubes, being careful to remove all white veins and fat. Cube into bite-size pieces the heart and liver. Parboil the brains and sweetbreads together in lightly salted water for about 15 minutes, then remove the brains and cut them into serving pieces, as well. Remove the membrane from the sweetbreads and cut or break them into pieces.

Dice the salt pork and, over a medium-high flame, fry it until crispy brown in a large, heavy Dutch oven or kettle. Add the onions and cook until translucent and beginning to brown, then add all the meats except the brains and sweetbreads. Stir the ingredients with a big wooden spoon while you cook them, for about 10 to 15 minutes. Now add the hot water and all of the seasonings. Cover and simmer for 2 to 2½ hours, or until the meats are tender. Add the brains and sweetbreads, and continue simmering for another 30 minutes or so.

If you would like a thicker broth, blend the flour with the cold water to form a paste and slowly add it to the stew, stirring so you don't get lumps. The stew is good served over rice, mashed potatoes, or buttered noodles. Corn bread is a traditional accompaniment.

Makes 8 to 10 servings.

★　　★　　★　　★　　★　　★　　★　　★　　★　　★

Camp Chuck
by Bessie A. Carlock, Arizona Office

In the early spring of 1941, the writer had occasion to make a trip up the Black Canyon Road, which started on its circuitous route four miles west of Phoenix. Until we crossed the canal, some five miles north, the road was just another Arizona highway. When we reached the canal on our northward journey, as if by magic the valley or what remained of it— between us and the velvet verdure of the foothills, which were shadowed by hazy purple heights in the background—changed. The transformation was startlingly abrupt. The road for perhaps ten miles was a desert symphony of pastel tones, harmonious and beautiful. Ironwood trees wore gay spring dresses of apple blossom texture and similarity; pale verde trees with their eternally youthful contours, smooth lined and satin skinned, were the coquettes of this strange locality. They flaunted evening gowns of rare old gold. Tall saguaros, stationed here and there like stern sentinels, stiffly formal, had, in a moment of amorous weakness, allowed some passing breeze to drop a garland or lei of exotic beauty upon each thorny head. Even their unyielding arms wore bracelets of blossoms, white and wax-like, and as large and as lovely as water-lilies. The great landscape gardener who had designed this desert garden had been thorough and painstakingly careful—no harsh notes for the Spring Festival of flowers. Mesquite, a bit gnarl and grotesque usually, had been draped with soft dusty silver foliage (reminding one of the pussy willows back home in their swaddling garments) and, as if an extra touch was impulsively added by Mother Nature, a pale yellow scarf of chiffon dotted with tiny star flowers concealed the rheumatic limbs. The desert floor was a Persian Carpet of rich blend. Here and there the tapestry brocade stood out vividly in the shape of cacti shrubbery blossoming in gorgeous array defying description. But the road before us beckoned on.

We began a serpentine ascent. No time now to exclaim or marvel over Arizona's desert surprises. The highway ahead held thrills! Up one hill— down another; on one side a steep perpendicular cliff, on the other side— Ugh! No wonder the name Black Canyon was given to this particular trail. A deep shadowy bowl of such immensity, such gigantic proportions attracted ones attention to the left. We gazed across it to the pine-clad Bradshaws that seemed so near, and wondered how such miracles of nature were performed. Scientific answers did not satisfy. We were fascinated. Then suddenly we were at our journeys end. We had passed through Rock Springs, New River, Canyon and Bumble Bee—all picturesque, mountain villages or mining camps. Now a sign post pointed west toward Horse Thief Basin. This was our cue to turn. A short sharp series of jolts and we were there—at Jenny Hayes'. We had reached our destination. The house, a clap board affair of three rooms and a side porch, had been fashioned and built mostly by Jenny herself, and of make-shifts. Its brown outline blended with the background of desert hills like some wayward stone that had lost its balance and rolled into a natural setting. As we drove up the steep incline from which Jenny's gingerbread house was speculatively re-garding us from its cataract-eyed windows, Jenny came out and stood upon the porch. She was a picture any artist might want to draw.

Outlined vividly against the somber brown was a woman of the West. Her smooth gray hair was gathered into a severe knot in the back—all but a few kindly wisps that curled carelessly about the care-worn face. And what a face. Deep-set eyes, suntanned almost leathery skin, and a firm determined chin—these were minor details. Nor was the stooped figure clad in clean old fashioned full gathered skirt that reached the floor and topped by a mannish shirt—important details; or the masculine shoes, worn now to a gentle softness, the white enveloping waist apron, or the gnarled hands clasped loosely and expectantly at her waist.

No, these were superficial details. The real picture towered above these just as the great heights of Bradshaw loomed above Jenny Hayes' valley—the Black Canyon. There was resourcefulness, character, ruggedness—originality in that background.

With true western hospitality, the firm, tortured old hand was extended in greeting. "Get out—dinner's almost ready—the men will be in directly. I board the miners here abouts," she explained. "Specially them that's tired of batchin'—and they're a plenty."

She shoved us ahead of her into a great living room to 'set' until din-ner was announced. We gazed about curiously. The full-sized beds, an enormous clothes press, an antique bureau and a marble-topped table—these were the furnishings. The windows that had stared at us so oddly were explained now. The cataract substance was paste-board inserted to substitute for broken panes. To our right was a bed-room, clean and bare except for a bed and wash-stand on which a great white porcelain pitcher and an enormous wash-bowl were seen. There were no shades at the windows—no coverings on the floors. Somehow they would have seemed out of place. The floors however were immaculately scrubbed and white and the windows were guiltless of the mountain rash "fly-specks."

"Come on an' eat, folks." Jenny stood in the kitchen door smiling invitingly. "Here's places at the end." We sat down to our first real western meal. "This is Don to your right—and Jack—then John and Joe"—and so on around the table—"boys these folks are friends of mine—Mr. D. And Mrs. C—" "Pitch in now and help yourselves" she encouraged. "Ridin' makes folks hungry—time I ride from here to Phoenix I'm plumb starved," she added.

She was right. We were hungry. The crude home-made table was covered with oil-cloth. Thick heavy cups and saucers, almost indestructible, were used and the plates would have probably made good bullet shields. But there was courtesy and welcome in every clatter and thud from those ponderous utensils. And the food—*that* was something to remember! Genuine "Chuck!" "We're mountain people—an minin' people," Jenny apologized. "Our facilities are limited but the boys manage to keep an appetite spite of it," she winked at me jovially.

"They certainly do keep their appetites," I felt like muttering, half in surprise. (I will say to be polite,) those men really did justice to that meal!

This was the menu: Great, round biscuits—one wondered if they could dispose of one, and ended up by eating three; a bowl of fresh sweet homemade butter; green onions arranged like a bouquet in a tall spoon holder; cornbread in squares the size and thickness of a cook sized cake of laundry soap, brown and delicious as any that mother used to make; a great earthen mixing bowl of navy beans, (the best I ever tasted); a dish of cold [*sic*] slaw; and the 'piece de resistance' was a huge platter of beef. Some one in the vicinity had butchered a yearling. The slices, big as a man's palm, had been pounded, rolled in flour and dropped into heavy iron skillets, deep with lard (this I had seen from my place in the living room). The result was an excellent finished product, a platter of thick juicy steaks that would have done justice to a Waldorf-Astoria Chef. Then there was a veritable Pikes Peak of mashed potatoes, seasoned with butter and pure cream. A bath tub tureen full of steak gravy and a yellow bowl of syrupy dried peaches rounded the menu. Coffee was served once—twice—thrice to several of the huskier miners—and it *was* coffee, rich and black with a delicious aroma and an exhilarating flavor. After satisfying their hunger the men pushed back their splint-bottomed chairs with heavy screechings and scrapings from those much abused pieces of household furnishings, rose in a body, reached for their sombreros and strode off down the hill to the "diggings."

Jenny Hayes and I were left alone. "May I help you with the dishes," I asked, noting her pitifully rheumatic warped hands. To this overture of friendliness she remonstrated stoutly, "The spring water is hard—it makes your hands crack open and bleed unless you use strong soap, but," she added as an afterthought, "you can churn the mornin' cream if you want, while I do the dishes, then we'll go for a walk before time for you to go home."

She brought a half gallon mason jar half-filled with deep yellow cream. "There" she smiled unceremoniously, as she thrust the cloth covered jar in my arms. I looked at it foolishly. "Shall I put it in the churn?" I asked timidly, (meaning the cream). "You're holdin' the churn," she laughed. "Just shake it this way—see."

I saw all right and began to wonder if this odd little lady with the whimsical smile was stringing me along. She wasn't. In less time than it took Jenny to do her dishes the butter arrived—firm, golden, nugget weighting 1¼ pounds! It swam in a pool of yellow flecked buttermilk.

"Now you go along and look around," Jenny urged "whilst I put this butter into shape." "Close the screen good dearie," she cautioned as I started toward the door. "Don left it open one night last week and a pesky rattler walked in."

"I'd rather watch you 'pat' your butter than go for a walk, Mrs. Hayes. It's too hot to climb hills anyway."

Jenny's eyes were twinkling, "Now I've scared you with that snake story. But it was a true one—you needn't be afraid. Rattlers are lazy in day-time—they lay an' bakes in the sun. So go on enjoy the view—you'll like it."

Thus reassured I started down the hill toward the spring—Jenny Hayes owned the only springs in that locality—but I wasn't noticing the scenery. My eyes were glued on the path ahead of me in search of rattlers, scorpions, Gila monsters, tarantulas, and lizards (they had all been cussed and discussed at the dinner table). I heard a soft rhythmic thud behind me and felt something cold touch my hand. Slowly I turned—Jenny Hayes' burro was saying "howdy stranger" in his own inimitable way. We became friends. The little fellow slipped politely ahead as if he meant to clear the way. The Spring was sheltered by a great overhanging cottonweed.

The burro reached it first, disappeared beneath the green curtain and I followed.

Then I stood transfixed. The biggest bull I ever expected to see was there with his harem of three cows drinking the cool spring water. I could almost imagine that burro laughed as I flew up that hill. He *did* make a mocking noise all right. Jenny Hayes stood at the kitchen window, her apron held high in her trembling hands and tears streamed down her face. She was laughing that hard.

"That bull wouldn't hurt a mouse," she gasped between paroxysms of laughter. "He belongs to the big ranch join' my claims—he's harmless."

But we didn't go for a walk. I was tired.

Just as the sun slid over the Bradshaw and the long, black shadows began fingering their way across the enclosure, we bade Jenny Hayes goodbye. She stood on the little porch as we drove away. When we reached the road again and were looking far down into the smoky depths of Black Canyon, a white blur stood out in bold relief against the little cabin. It was her apron.

"What a woman," I mused. "And what a country—weird—indescribable."

"What a dinner," my companion retorted prosaically. "Boy that was tops!"

City Life

A Walk between Then and Now

McSorley's Tavern
from the New York City Office

Picturesque McSorley's Irish Ale House, on 7th Street, near Third Avenue has been the subject of two noted paintings: *A Mug of Ale at McSorley's* and *McSorley's Bar on Saturday Night*, by the well-known artist, John Sloan. A faded playbill adorning the west wall shows, too, that it was once the subject of a comedy, *McSorley's Inflation*, staged by the old-time comedians, Harrigan and Hart. Another wall decoration is a special article on McSorley's by B. Hutchins Hapgood which appeared in *Harper's Weekly*, October 25, 1913, illustrated by Sloan's "Mug of Ale" sketch.

The founder of this tavern, back in 1854, was John McSorley, a handsome old patriarch with tremendous sideburns, whose portrait occupies a niche in the east wall. McSorley was a horseman of real note and writers of his era classed his nags with those of his most famous track rival, Commodore Vanderbilt. An array of group photos of the members of McSorley's Pickle Club, Chowder Club, Baseball Club, and McSorley's "Cabinet," made up of noted Irish New Yorkers of his day, show that this host of the old school was a gentleman of diversified activities.

McSorley believed in the right of the male to peace and ease while enjoying his standard delicacies of ale and onions and to this day, women may see only one side of the door, the side facing the street. This policy has been followed so strictly that only two members of the fair sex, so far as is known, have passed through these portals. One, a well-known actress, was allowed to view the portrait of her husband in one of the famous picnic groups; the other, a newspaper woman, paid a short visit. Neither partook of bite or sup, or even sniffed an onion.

An antiquary would be delighted with some of the articles of furniture in this famous old inn. There is an ice-chest, clock, table, and some chairs, all over a hundred years old. In the front room the ancient pot-bellied stove still glows cheerfully on a winter's night and the original wooden beer-pump still rests behind the bar. Another treasured relic is a tattered American flag embroidered by an old lady who sold peanuts in the block.

The walls are lined with illustrations of famous persons and events of the past, among them King Edward VII, Jenny Lind, Parnell and the Irish Parliament in 1886, the United States Senate in 1850, the mourning edition of the *New York Herald*, April 16, 1865, announcing the death of President Lincoln; the attempted assassination of Secretary Seward; New York theatrical stars from 1838 to 1890, and the death of President Garfield.

For many generations McSorley's has been a favored rendezvous for well-known New York artists, writers, politicians, and business and professional men. One of its habitues was Peter Cooper, whose memorial hall (Cooper Union,) and statue are but a few steps from the tavern door. Mr. Cooper's chair at McSorley's was fitted with a rubber cushion of his own invention.

One particularly prized and hoary relic hangs in a frame on the west wall of the inn. It is a copy of the *London Times* dated June 22, 1815, containing a description of the Battle of Waterloo by an eyewitness.

On the death of the pioneer McSorley in 1910, the tavern passed to his son, William, who, before his death sold it to his old friend, Daniel O'Connell, ex-member of New York's Finest and of the old 69th Regiment. O'Connell, who died in 1939 and whose picture and shield now hangs over the bar, willed it to his daughter. She is now Mrs. Harry Kirwan and her husband manages the tavern.

The fame of McSorley's Ale House was due in part to its excellent nut-brown ale, brewed from a secret formula and handed down through the years. The old traditions are still observed including the serving of food dear to Irish hearts, such as Irish stew, pig's knuckles, spare ribs and sauerkraut. The most important is the corned beef and cabbage, served on Saturdays—still a great day at McSorley's.

Chef in Marconi's Restaurant on Mulberry Street, New York, New York, December 1942. (Marjory Collins)

★   ★   ★   ★   ★

McSorley's is a perfect post in which to meditate on the state of eating in the city today. It stands, as it has for more than a hundred and fifty years, at Astor Place on East 7th Street, which is something of a crossroads for the old and the new in New York City.

Before any discussion can get under way, however, it should be understood how *America Eats!* intended to look at urban eating, for the papers—or rather the editors—had a rather jaundiced view of the situation. The introduction to city eating in the Northeast section of the manuscript states: "Regional cooking has been gradually forced out [of cities] by the products of fast freight and of the canning factory and to some extent by the influence of immigrants."

What a peculiar statement to make when many of our cities were—as they continue to be—readily identified by iconic American dishes: What about Baltimore crab cakes? Philadelphia pretzels and pepper pot? There's nothing in the papers so far about San Francisco, even though at the time this city was as big a food haven with unique characteristics as it is today. California, in general, was the victim of some East Coast snobbery among the editors who believed the state—particularly Los Angeles—was little more than an uncultivated, soulless hole, especially ruinous to American cuisine for its proliferation of fast food. Boston would receive a lone nod, but only for its baked beans.

Instead, the American city was to be explored by the federal writers for the "influence of foreign foods and mass cooking on the eating customs of the region," as one memorandum put it. New York City, alone, was chosen to explore these themes because it had both a large foreign population and a concentration of hotels, lunch counters, and banquet halls. Anything else connected to city dining—say, its vibrant street food, or even its famous hot dogs at Coney Island—was not open to discussion.

It's hard these days to talk about American food and *not* say anything about other cities—Californian cities, especially, since they have become so central to many current developments in our cooking. But I wanted to stay true to the papers and decided to stick to New York City, walking to the places the federal writers wrote about and, along the way, try to take a reading of where American urban eating is today.

And so, I begin by tanking up for the journey at McSorley's. Once two mugs of ale arrive, the old creaking chairs seem to impart a comforting hug, especially in the afternoon when the place is blessedly empty of crowds. As in any good saloon, time settles in and becomes not so much a physical state as a metaphysical, psychological, even philosophical concept: it may be noon outside McSorley's doors, but it's just another round inside.

Let's talk first about how things are in McSorley's before we venture outside to discover what's new in the city: the tavern is still a dusty, scarred, tobacco-stained way station. John F. Kennedy—in a bust behind the bar (wearing a marine's hat instead of the navy's), and in pictures on the wall—has joined the other presidents who have been assassinated since the ale house opened. There may be a few other new pictures and trinkets wedged among the junk encrusting the walls and ceiling, but who can tell for sure? Still, Peter Cooper's portrait—God rest his soul—more faded and brown, rules over the back room as he did in real life in the saloon's early days. He remains with his nearby partner, the naked lady with her parrot. The sawdust on the floor is fresh but a thicker accumulation of old bits sculpt the lower portions of the bar where a broom is too lazy to go. The bartender and his waiter are fine curmudgeons: they've seen everything and nothing impresses them. They pull a stingy mug of beer—one-third head. This has gotten them a bad reputation in the blog world because the newer element that comes swinging through the doors thinks this is like every other bar in the city. Well, it isn't, and the bartender and waiter don't care. But when I lean over the bar and whisper to the bartender something my Irish grandmother always said, which is "half souls never get to heaven," he appears to remember his own grandmother saying the exact same thing and retrieves my mug to fill it to the top the way she taught him to. Another thing that's the same as ever is the food—for lunch I have an acceptable hamburger on an acceptable bun with a generous heap of fried potatoes: all that a lunch is really required to be in a saloon. There's nothing too Irish about the other menu offerings except the plate of cheese and onions, and saltine crackers in their waxed paper sleeve, universally recognized by those who grew up around their Irish grandmothers as the proper hors d'oeuvre to serve with beer.

Even in McSorley's, though, changes have occurred. There's a television in the back room and that seems a desecration. But also, there's the crowd. For one thing, women are allowed in now (secured by a Supreme Court ruling in 1970). Not that I'm not personally grateful for this: this afternoon, there happens to be three of us—one lounging quite comfortably by herself at the table by the front window, reading the newspaper with her mug and cheese plate; another standing at the bar laughing with a guy; and me in the back room, sitting with a helpful son to cover my tracks. By and large, though, the chairs that line up against the battered wainscoting in the front room and around the potbellied stove are vacant of what *Harper's Weekly* called the "quiet working class." Except for the staff, no one would register as much of a character, nowhere near eccentric, let alone humble. Through the afternoon, a trickle of men in shirtsleeves meander in and talk about things men in the past wouldn't dream of airing in public, such as the two at a nearby table who are puzzling over women ("If my girlfriends were that easy, I never would have gotten married"), while another table mourns the state of Google stocks, which apparently took a small dive, requiring another round to forget. Along the bar lean a few curiosity-seekers: a fraternity of student hipsters from Cooper Union and a coterie with guidebooks in their back pockets. The bartender and waiter get noticeably more grouchy around them, except when they're having some fun needling them, which happens when one of the students requests a rum and Coke. The bartender folds his arms tighter around the black plastic apron that spans his front and, for a long beat, regards the young man with an unkind gaze. The regulars look up, anticipating the response, which is a tiny bottle of Coke skidded across the bar at the poor dope. Point taken; nothing else but beer is drunk at McSorley's, and the young man quietly changes his order.

What's true most of all is that the clock in the back room that once lent the gentle heartbeat of the womb is fainter, barely heard anymore.

"Times have changed," Bill McSorley, the son of the founder, was recorded as saying once by Joseph Mitchell in his famous piece, "McSorley's Wonderful Saloon."

"You said it, Bill," his companion replied.

But let's not get sentimental. Not about McSorley's, anyway, which in reality is doing just fine even if the class of clientele is not the same and it feels a little like a museum exhibit, with its once great usefulness to a community in measured decline. This is because the city outside its doors has changed and, the more it has, the more beloved McSorley's becomes because its oddity—its layers and layers of grime, its surliness, its very survival when thousands of other bars encrusted with their owners' idiosyncrasies have faded away—makes it that much more visible in a world that is fast becoming more uniform.

Further uptown in the old meat-packing district, near enough to the Hudson River that it is always a presence, there was a modern-day McSorley's, a bar called Passerby, run by a guy named Toby Cecchini. Passerby looked like a working-class bar: it was nestled among factories and garages on a pockmarked run-down street, and was tiny tiny *tiny*, its walls plywood, its bar what looked like a hunk of wood, and its floor strange lighted cubes that could have been salvaged from a defunct disco joint. Everything in it, though, was a verifiable work of art, and the duality of the place—its high and low fashion that mirrored its owner's character—made the bar a comfortable place to settle into and nurse a drink, especially in the few quiet hours early in the evening or sometime before dawn. The deception was due to Cecchini's own peculiar sensibilities—his love of the working-class bars his dad used to take him to in his midwestern hometown, as well as the artistic romance of a fabled New York City—and as much a peculiar character (he's a grouchy literate handsome touchy funny artistic endearing down-to-earth snob) as John McSorley ever was. Despite the fact that his bar was phenomenally successful, an important hub of that neighborhood's hip gallery/auction house scene, and that Cecchini is famous for reinventing the modern-day Cosmopolitan cocktail and has a loyal following of people who are addicted to his inventive drinks (many made with fresh fruits and unusual liquors), Passerby was being forced to close. Why? Because the landlord wanted to turn the space into something more lucrative and upmarket: condos. This is how things are progressively going in our cities. All you have to do is step outside McSorley's door to see that the old working-class, immigrant neighborhood the saloon once served is completely gone.

The nearby Bowery is so smoothly glittery with the construction of new expensive apartment buildings, with a Whole Foods market and countless drop-dead restaurants already in place to serve the incoming well-heeled hordes, that it's hard to imagine that not so long ago it was the grand boulevard of craggy flophouses and gin bars, outlaw rock clubs, funky theaters, and a couple of brothels. The city is in danger of losing its jittery distinction, the element of surprise, of discovering something bizarre or fascinating, gritty, or lovely around every corner, this tumultuous variation the fountainhead of a city's exuberance.

One of the offshoots of a more homogenized city is that the culture of food—arguably among a city's most distinct traits—becomes decidedly less dynamic because the economics are now so forbidding to anyone but the upper class and corporations. (You can take Portland, Oregon, as a current example—as it continues to swell with new residents, it's beginning to tilt away from what has made it so unique and liveable.) When this happens, the interesting nooks and crannies that make city life so interesting begin to disappear. These days, it's harder and harder to find a comfortable mom-and-pop eatery or bar in Manhattan. They're surviving in the outer boroughs, along with another important establishment—restaurants or bars owned and operated by immigrants trying to gain a foothold in the American dream. But as these places succeed—and many times spur a revival of a fading neighborhood—they attract the attention of developers who subsequently come in and begin to jeopardize the very elements that allowed small establishments to flourish. The distinct nature of a community is threatened and soon lost.

For the eating life of the city, the people who have been most affected by the rising cost of doing business in Manhattan are the immigrant restaurant owners and grocers. When the federal writers working on the project went out looking for foreign food in New York City, they found it on almost every corner:

Celebrating in a restaurant on Mulberry Street, New York, New York, December 1942. (Marjory Collins)

"Dining Abroad" in New York
from the New York City Office

Since New York's population represents almost every civilized race and nationality in the world, one of its most interesting features is the opportunity afforded for "dining abroad"—in almost any language. The oldest and probably strongest influence is French, which is basic in the cuisine of the great hotels and many of the expensive restaurants, although a number of modest establishments are devoted to hors d'oeuvres and stews cooked with wine. Even more numerous are the places offering forms of spaghetti, macaroni and ravioli, tomato sauce and cheese, with a minor emphasis on veal, chicken, mushrooms and peppers. The Jewish influence presents itself in the form of delicatessens with their arrays of pastrami, corn beef, salami, and herring; stores selling nothing but pickles and relishes; and dairy restaurants whose mainstay is sour cream. Chinese restaurants, while their basic items can be obtained even in drugstores and dance palaces, also offer subtle combinations of lobster, pork and chicken with exotic vegetables and sauces.

★　　★　　★　　★　　★

The story then goes on to list (and very uninterestingly at that) the offerings in restaurants representing eleven different countries grouped somewhat oddly together: Russia with Scandinavia; Turkey and Armenia with India. The other countries covered are Austria (Viennese), Poland, Hungary, Romania, Spain, and Mexico. Without stepping outside McSorley's door to do an actual scientific census, I can tell you for certain that the city today—and many others across the country—contains representation from nearly every cuisine on the face of the earth.

At the moment, though, it's more important to point out that it's close to five, and hunger calls: it's high time to leave McSorley's and start thinking about dinner. In a zigzag sort of way, I head north. Almost all the restaurants I pass are packed, the sidewalks crowded with tables, baby strollers, a jumble of noise. One ready observation: the city is populated with fewer enclaves catering to a particular nationality of cooking. The Indian restaurants concentrated on East 6th Street or Lexington

Avenue in the twenties and the Korean places up on 32nd Street are among the few left. You can no longer say that the Lower East Side is Jewish or Eastern European; or that Spanish Harlem is especially Latino; or Harlem proper totally African American. Not even Chinatown is exclusively Chinese anymore. What happens is that, as all Manhattan real estate escalates, ethnic identities lessen in neighborhoods and the restaurants and food offerings become more varied. This is one of the few upsides—if you want to call it that—to the city's business economics: extremely trendy, pricy restaurants are to be found nestled beside old neighborhood joints. I'm a little ambivalent about this development if only because I like the identity and sense of community that comes with ethnic neighborhoods. I understand, though, that there are clear-cut benefits. But on my current trek, it means I can ignore the banners advertising luxury apartments inside some of the old dumbbell tenement buildings I pass, walk around the hordes cooling their jets in front of the latest "must" eatery on the avenues, and head instead to the old lunch counter a few blocks over.

I'm scouring the streets for a good simple meal, maybe at what *America Eats!* considered one of the city's quintessential dining experiences—the drugstore counter where the pièce de résistance is:

> the toasted "three decker" enclosing 'tween decks unusual and sometimes insidious food combinations. These may include cold meats, fish mixtures called "salads," hamburger, bacon, cheese, jelly, peanut butter, bananas, tomatoes, relish, pickles, and chopped eggs, all garnished with condiments or dressings. The popular cheeseburger is a doughty bit combining grilled hamburger and melted American cheese served on a soft bun and tasty enough to ensnare even the one-cylinder appetite.
>
> —NEW YORK CITY OFFICE

Drugstore lunch counters were a dime a dozen in our grandparents' days but other counters existed, too—remember the ones in Woolworth's? Remember how good the tuna salad was, or how a grilled cheese and a cherry Coke, in the days before everyone was on Prozac, just made life spin a little better?

When I find a counter, I'm going to order something from the following list:

Restaurant sign, Key West, Florida, January 1938. (Arthur Rothstein)

Soda-Luncheonette Slang and Jargon
from the New York City Office

A.C.	American cheese sandwich
All black	Chocolate soda with chocolate ice cream
Angel's delight	Cake with vanilla ice cream
Arkansas chicken	Salt pork
Arm waiter	Waiter who piles stacks of dishes on his arms
Axle grease	Butter
A yard of	Dish of spaghetti
Baby	Glass of milk
Bay State bum	Customer who demands much service and leaves no tip
Bellywash	Soup
Berries	Eggs
Black and white	Chocolate soda with vanilla ice cream
Black cow	Root beer with ice cream
Blimp	Woman
Blind 'em	Two eggs fried on both sides
Blond	Coffee with cream
Blue heaven	Bromo seltzer
B.M.T.	Bacon and tomato sandwich with mayonnaise
Boiled leaves	Tea
Bool	Soup listed on a table d'hote menu
Bottle o'red	Ketchup
Bottle washer	Assistant cook
Break it and shake it	Malted milk with egg
Brunette	Black coffee
Bull's eyes	Two fried eggs
Burn 'er black	Chocolate malted milk
Burn one	An order of toast
Burn one up	See "burn 'er black"
Burn the British	Order for toasted English muffins
Burn with a cackle	See "break it and shake it"
Buss	To carry dirty dishes

Chewed fine	
with a breath	Order for a hamburger with onion
Cherries	Prunes
C.J. on	Cream cheese and jelly on toast
C.O. cocktail	Castor oil in soda
Codfish	See "Bay State bum"
Coke	Coca Cola
Cow	Milk
Cow juice	See "cow"; also, cream
Cup of mud	Cup of coffee
Deep down	
bleeding	Root beer with cherries
Deep one through	
Georgia	A glass of Coca Cola with chocolate
Draw one	Order for coffee; also, water
Draw one in	
the dark	See "brunette"
Draw one on	
the side	Coffee with cream served separately
Dress one pig	Ham sandwich
Dynamite	Baking powder
84	Four glasses of water
81	A customer
86	Supply is exhausted
82	Two glasses of hot chocolate
Emerson	
high ball	See "blue heaven"
51	Hot chocolate
Foul ball	Mistake
Fountaineer	Soda fountain attendant
49	Look at that beautiful girl
14	See "49"
14½	A beautiful girl, a little on the plump side
Freezit	Pepsicola
Fry 'em blind	Order to baste frying eggs
G.I.	Garbage can (General issue)
Gee	Man
Gob	See "fountaineer"

Graveyard stew	Milk toast
Greaser	A cook
Grit	Dishwashing powder
Guinea footballs	Jelly donuts
Bang one	Order to mix a malted milk
Hebrew enemies	Pork chop
Hold	Cancel the order
Holstein highball	See "baby"
Houseboat	Banana split
Hug one	Orange juice
Ice the rice	Rice pudding with ice-cream
I.R.T.	Lettuce and tomato sandwich
Jack Benny	
in the red	Strawberry jello
Jeep	Sandwich cutter and salad man
Jersey cocktail	See "baby"
Jiggs	Corned beef and cabbage
Juggle dishes	To wait on tables
Lake Whitney	See "draw one" (second definition)
Lovers' delight	Chocolate eclair
Make two	
look at me	See "bull's eyes"
Mary Garden	Citrate of magnesia
Money bowl	See "bellywash"
Monkey	Caramelized sugar (used in verbal directions for making gravy)
Murphies	Potatoes
Nervous pudding	Gelatine dessert
95	An expression describing a customer who leaves without paying
Noah's boy with Murphy carrying a wreath	See "Jiggs"
On a raft	Toast
One and a half	Ham and American cheese sandwich
One lump	A camel cigarette
One on a pillow	Hamburger on a bun

One with dynamite	Coca Cola with ammonia
One without the thumb	See "bellywash"
Paint it red	Cherry Coca Cola
Paint it yellow	Lemon Coca Cola
Pie book	Meal ticket
Pop one	See "coke"
Pot walloper	See "greaser"
Put a stretch on it	Sandwich to go out
Red lead	See "bottle o' red"
Repeaters	Beans
Salve	See "axle grease"
Sand	Sugar
Scandal soup	See "boiled leaves"
Shake a white	A plain milk shake
Sheet one	See "coke"
Sinkers	Doughnuts
66	See "49"
Skin taker	See "grit"
Smear one, burn it	Order for toasted cheese sandwich
Sop	Dish rag
Southern Swine	Virginia ham
Stack o'berry	Strawberry ice cream
Stack o'white	Vanilla ice cream
Starved	An expression meaning a bad day for sales
Stretch one	A large "coke" (q.v.)
Stretch sweet Alice	A large "baby" (q.v.)
Sweet Alice	See "baby"
Taxi one	Orangeade
Taxi straight	See "hug one"
Team of greys	Sugared crullers
The works	Banana split
Thin man	Dime tipper
Toastwich	Toasted sandwich

Tonic	Soda
Turn on the radio	Light the gas stove
Twist it, choke it, and make it cackle	Chocolate malted milk with egg
Two-and-a-half	Ham and Swiss cheese sandwich
Two flopped	See "blind 'em"
Two in the dark	Two pieces of rye toast
Uncle Ezra	Alka-Seltzer
Vanilla	Nice-looking girl
Vermont	Maple syrup
Watson, the needle	See "coke"
Whistleberries	See "repeaters"
Wrecks	Broken dishes
Yesterday, today and forever	Hash

★　　★　　★　　★　　★

But the one lunch counter I stumble into is way too hip and suave and I can't even order a plain old Two-and-a-half! Even the tuna salad comes all niçoised and wasabied and I'm seated within earshot of a few pending movie deals and more cell phone mini-plays than I care to be. Also, there's the sweet thing on the next stool who looks me over with a 'you are *not* sitting next to me wearing *that*' attitude. Honestly, it's anything but a Prozac-substitute moment. That's nothing, though, compared to what some may consider the biggest sin of all: my grilled cheese is made with every other cheese but the genuine article—a good sharp Cheddar if not bright orange American. What happened to just simple ingredients in American food? Why does it have to be made glamourous? Okay, it tastes better. Probably better for me, too. But what's that got to do with a grilled cheese sandwich when you really want one?

Maybe the quiet hours spent in McSorley's have affected me, but I retreat after two bites and cross the street to the greenmarket at Union Square.

Since it's close to six, the vendors are beginning to shut down, folding up their white tents and packing their unsold crates of produce back into their trucks. Farmers' markets are one of the great blessings across the country. Their growth over the last few decades has brought new life to our cities while offering fresh, well-grown, and cheap fruits and vegetables to their citizens. The markets also supports the "localism" movement of encouraging sustainable agriculture near populated areas. For most people walking around the market, though, it's just a great hoot to purchase a rich variety of fruits and vegetables for about fifty cents a pound.

Everyone involved with urban greenmarkets should be canonized for improving the American table. What I miss, though—and I suppose it can't be helped—is the sound of the old food peddlers pushing carts or driving trucks slowly up and down city streets, crying out their seductive, fetching chants. The last food peddler I can personally vouch for was heard in the early 1990s in Sunset Park, Brooklyn—a man and his son hanging out the cab of their old truck bellowing: "Waaaaaaaaater-melllllllllllonnnnnnnnns! Get your ruby juicy waaaaaaaaatermelllllllllll-onnnnnnnns!"

As memorable as that was, they had nothing on the chants recorded for *America Eats!*, perhaps by Ralph Ellison when he worked for the writers' project in Harlem:

Peddler Chants
from the New York City Office

THE SORREL WOMAN

Sorrel! Oh, sorrel!
'e tehste lok Granny's wine,
Sorrel! Oh, sorrel!
'e sweet an' 'e too fine!

Sorrel! Oh, sorrel!
'e sure a 'trengh'nin' t'ing,
Sorrel! Oh sorrel!
'e med to suit de king!

THE AH-GOT-UM MAN

Ah got pompanos!
Ah got catfish!
Ah got buffalees!
Ah got um!
Ah got um!

Ah got stringbeans!
Ah got cabbage!
Ah got collard greens!
Ah got um!
Ah got um!

Ah got honeydews!
Ah got can'lopes!
Ah got watermelons!
Ah got um!
Ah got um!

Ah got fish,
Ah got fruits,
Ah got veg, yes 'ndeed!
Ah got any kind o' vittles,
Ah got anything yo' need!

Ah'm de Ah-Got-Um Man!

THE STREET CHEF

Ah'm a natu'al bo'n chef
An' dat aint't no lie,
Ah can fry po'k chops
An' bake a low-down pie
So step right up
An' he'p yo'se'f
Fum de vittles on
Mah Kitchen sh'f!

DE SWEET PERTATER MAN

See dese gread big sweet pertaters
Right chere by dis chicken's side,
Ah'm de one what bakes dese taters
Makes dem fit to suit yo' pride

Dere is taters an' mo' taters,
But de ones ah sells is fine
Yo' kin go fum hyeah to yondah
But yo' won't git none lak mine
'Cause Ah'm de tater man!
(Ah mean!)
De sweet pertater man!

★   ★   ★   ★   ★

The lack of such chants—while a lamented absence from the city's street music—does not make the greenmarket any less miraculous than it is, or negate how essential it has become to urban life. By the time I've walked through it, my arms are as full of sacks of good things to eat as are other people's who are rushing from stall to stall gathering what they need before the farmers leave for the weekend.

Before there were greenmarkets, there were municipal markets, usually constructed on the city outskirts, sometimes near the rail terminals. Long before the entire whole/local-food nation thing took off, these inner-city markets encouraged local farmers and small producers, and made available to city residents quality fruits, vegetables, cheeses, meat, and fish at low costs. Most of the markets were in increasingly decrepit city-owned buildings and to shop in them was not always a pleasant experience, what with the jogging and hustling, the dirt clinging to roots and leaves, and the unmasked scent of real food with a very short shelf life. Good city cooks and eaters knew these were the places where the plumpest, most interesting sausages were made, the freshest trout would be available, the sharpest, creamiest, most exquisite cheeses could be procured.

People eating at Pete's Bar in Washington Street Market, New York,
New York, 1950. (Al Aumuller)

It's nice to report that on my travels this past year, I've discovered that
quite a few municipal markets, many in low-income neighborhoods, have
been spruced up to become a valued centerpiece of an urban/downtown renewal program. As part of their rehabilitation, the markets almost always
include first-rate restaurants or counters whose proximity to the food stalls
offering prime farm produce and meats pretty much ensures a savory experience. This is why, if you're in Philadelphia, you really should head over to
the Reading Terminal on Market Street; if you're in Baltimore, you want
to stop at the Lexington Market near the university medical center; and, of
course, in Richmond, Virginia, the 17th Street Market is a must, even if the
Brunswick Stew Festival isn't taking place. The floors may be mottled with
old bubblegum, slippery with fallen and squashed produce, or slick with
bleached water. The din and bustle of shoppers and merchants that sur-
round you as you tuck into a stool at a serving counter are generally a challenge for intimate conversation. But where else are you going to find fresher

boiled crabs (Baltimore), or Pennsylvania Dutch scrapple sandwiches (Philadelphia), or pulled pork sandwiches and ribs (Kansas City)?

I may be nibbling my way uptown with what I've purchased at the greenmarket, but the memories of the dishes I tasted at markets in other cities fix my mind on a destination and a final meal that will honor one of the city dishes *America Eats!* was going to celebrate. In New York, until the greenmarket revolution occurred in 1976, the city used to run several public market buildings, of which the Lower East Side's Essex Street Market is the lone survivor. When Grand Central Station was restored, a new public market opened in its lower concourse. Okay, it's not exactly like any other public market: nothing grimy about it and no farmers in sight—and it ain't exactly cheap. But by now I'm in midtown. And, in Manhattan, a certain glamour is required. At the very least, this far up-town, produce is expected to be washed.

What's more, the Grand Central Station marketplace is the site of a legend: the Oyster Bar, which is where I'll find my *America Eats!* city dish:

Oyster Stew Supreme
from the New York City Office

To judge by the figures New York is the ostreaphillic capital of the world. Over 10,000,000 pounds of shell oysters and 1,000,000 pounds of shucked ones pass through Fulton Fish Market each year. The greater part remains within the city to be consumed in various forms.

Of the many distinctly American methods, none is more satisfactory to the average man's taste than the Oyster Stew. Indeed, many who cannot abide the sight of a raw oyster admit a passionate fondness for the creamy goodness of a well-made oyster stew. Oyster-lovers who can take their favorite bivalve in any form, also consider the stew the most acceptable method of cooking.

There is one place in New York where this stew is a supreme delight. The Oyster Bar of the Grand Central Terminal, known as a landmark on the American epicure's map. Well-traveled gourmets have been heard to say: "Prunier's of Paris for Lobster Thermidor; Scott's of Piccadilly for Deviled Crab; the Grand Central Oyster Bar for Oyster Stew."

In 1913 when the Terminal was opened the Oyster Bar was a small counter with 3 or 4 seats, set off in a corner of the restaurant. The Oyster Stew served there soon, like the proverbial mouse-trap, brought the world in a well-beaten track to this counter. It was extended and extended again. The number of seats and specially contrived cooking bowls were both augmented. Today there are 42 seats which never seem sufficient to accommodate the hungry crowds that in rush hours sometimes stand three deep. Commuters, snatching a hasty snack to tide them over until dinner at home, form a large portion of its regular customers.

★   ★   ★   ★   ★

The terminal, in general, is crazy with trains coming and going, lots of tourists and folks coming into the city from Westchester and other points for the evening. Just like at McSorley's, outside the Oyster Bar's doors the old has given way to the new—swanky new shops and expensive restaurants. The Oyster Bar, itself, is pretty much the same as it was, except much much bigger—amusement park bigger. Its forty-three seats have been increased by more than four hundred and nearly all of them are taken all the time. But it's glamourous in an Old New York sort of way and, ah! there's one lone chair open at the bar! What luck, especially for a single girl! It is doubly nice to grab a chair at the bar where one's back is to the door: I can settle down with my bags spilling greenmarket produce at my feet and pretend there's no one else but me who needs to be fed, and yet still feel surrounded (though not too close, now!) by the rest of humanity. The bar is tended by a very efficient, taciturn man who succeeds in placing an icy cold martini and hot freshly made oyster stew before me within eight minutes after I order. I take a careful, appreciative sip of one, then the other. At either elbow, fellow city-dwellers tuck into their respective meals. The room is jammed, noisy as Times Square. Another sip of our drinks (a beer and white wine for the others): we don't care. The three of us—as all the others down the bar and along the counters—are in our own little world, minding our own business, as it were. But then we sigh together, sighing over the deliciousness of this simple, well-prepared food. Startled a bit, we cast a glance about, acknowledging with a sly smile our accidental conversation. Then we quickly settle back into the singleness of our drinks, our stews.

Now, that is urbane dining!

Waiter at John's Restaurant on East 12th Street, New York, New York, January 1943. (Marjory Collins)

A Word About New Orleans

It's true *America Eats!* did not have too much to say about New Orleans, one of the major food cities in the world, and the founding seat of some of our country's most glorious dishes:

> In New Orleans—in all southern Louisiana—cooking differs somewhat radically from anywhere else in the South, due of course to the Creole, who has founded a superb school of cuisine.
> —LOUISIANA OFFICE

That's about it before a discussion gets under way about the city's renowned oyster bars. New Orleans's complex cooking is, of course, a bigger story than its oysters and the federal writers could have written a whole book on the subject.

But let's reflect for a moment on the role food is playing in helping New Orleans come back from Hurricane Katrina. Each and every restaurant that reopens gives folks reason to hope that the spirit of their city will flicker back and that the life they so cherish will return.

Demetrius Porche, the dean of the school of nursing at Louisiana State University, observed, "In the weeks after we got back, people were asking about when restaurants would open up again because they were such a part of how we considered ourselves and they were such an important part of our livelihood."

Emotions were running high on the day Rocky & Carlo's, an old and much beloved little roadside eatery out on St. Bernard Highway, reopened in 2007 after being heavily damaged in the storm. The waitress said in her usual manner, "What can I get ya, darlin'?" and nearly everyone standing on the other side of the steam tables seemed to be ready to break down and cry, so happy to have her and the place back serving them the good food they grew up with.

"That was an important one," Porche says about the opening. "Chalmette was one of the worst hit by the storm, so when Rocky & Carlo's came back, it made people think, 'well, things might be getting better.'"

Porche is Creole and his hometown is in Houma, about seventy miles away from New Orleans. He says things like, "When I was growing up, our main meat was seafood," thinking of all the gumbos and crawfish stews he ate in his parents' kitchen. While his house in the French Quarter was damaged, it's his ruined cookbooks that seemed most priceless to him because they contained many family recipes he's having a hard time re-creating.

"There was a killer chocolate cake we used to make that I have to write down before I forget."

Helping New Orleans not to forget its family recipes is the city's newspaper, the *Times-Picayune*. It kept printing during the flood and has been thriving ever since. The newspaper has been one of the main supports for the residents as they've tried to get their lives back together again. The first Thanksgiving after the flood, the paper was swamped with calls asking for recipes. Readers had lost their cookbooks and recipe file boxes and turned to the local paper's archives for help in cooking the dishes that were a part of their traditional holiday dinner.

"When people came back, they replaced their cookbooks first," Judy Walker, the paper's food editor, said. "If they couldn't come back to the city, they called us or e-mailed us for recipes."

With this request: "HELP OTHERS COOK AGAIN: Please help others rebuild their recipe collections! Send in a favorite traditional recipe that you think is important to the city's culinary soul at this time," the paper is now regularly posting recipes on its Web site under the heading, "Rebuilding your recipes with the *Times-Picayune*" (www.nola.com/food). Included in the growing mix are not only personal favorites but recipes of beloved dishes from restaurants that have, so far, not come back.

Recipes

Grand Central Oyster Stew

[Individual portion, as related to Allan Ross Macdougall by the Oyster Bar's chef in 1941 for the New York City Office]

Melt ½ ounce of butter in double boiler; add ⅓ teaspoon of salt, ⅓ teaspoon celery salt, ⅓ teaspoon paprika, one shake of white pepper, 8 drops of Worcestershire sauce, 2 large tablespoons of oyster (or clam) liquor.

Boil briskly for a few minutes with constant stirring. As mixture bubbles high add 8 oysters and cook 3 minutes more, all the while turning the oysters gently. Add ½ pint of rich milk and continue to stir. When mixture begins to boil, pour out into a bowl, add a pat of butter and a shake of paprika. Serve with small round oyster crackers.

Crawfish Bisque

[As related by the Louisiana Office]

Crawfish bisque is a thick rich soup requiring hours of preparation and infinite patience. But when the Cajun housewife informs the family, "I'm gonna make me a crawfish bisque today," she approaches her task almost with reverence. Her husband having brought home a sack of what has been called "the poor man's lobsters," she chooses about forty nice ones, boils them alive, then begins the task of cleaning them. Each must be scrubbed with a brush, washed and re-washed, for the crawfish is a particularly unclean creature. Now heads must be severed, each head cleaned and thirty empty shells set aside. The other ten are set to boil. Meat is removed from the tails and chopped fine, then a paste is made of this, to which is added soaked bread, chopped onions and garlic, parsley, salt and pepper. This paste is carefully stuffed into the heads, and they are again set aside. Green and white onions, parsley, thyme, and bay leaves, and some flour are all fried in butter in a deep iron pot until brown, then the bouillon made of the boiling heads is poured in, and all is seasoned with salt and red pepper. This must boil about a half hour. At serving time, the thirty stuffed heads are taken, rolled in flour and fried in butter until crisp, then thrown into the soup. As with gumbo this is served over boiled rice.

★　　★　　★　　★　　★　　★　　★　　★　　★　　★

Literary Tea
by Jerry Felsheim, New York City Office

As a social institution, the Literary Tea has undergone profound changes in recent years. Originally identified with women's social clubs, it has been taken over by the smart world and transformed into a cocktail party with incidental literary trimmings. Its hours are from five to seven but, as with the cocktail party, no one ever appears before six fifteen and the host is fortunate if his last guests depart by nine. More than anything else, it has become an informal gathering place for intellectual sophisticates on their way to dinner.

Since the publishing world is concentrated in New York, literary teas reach their apex in that city. Their sponsors are usually connected with the business: a publisher trying to put over a new author; an editor celebrating the start of a magazine; or again, just a head hunter hunting another celebrity. In Manhattan, literary teas are given upon the slightest provocation.

The locale of these parties varies from private apartments to special rooms at the smart night clubs and hotels. One condition is paramount, however, the place must always be jammed. Seemingly no literary tea is successful unless it is crowded enough to make an exchange of intellectual ideas an impossibility. The talk is usually limited to the latest publishing blurbs and reviews, Broadway gossip, and inside tips on how much this or that author is making. "Heavy" conversation is invariably frowned upon and *chichi* wit is at a premium.

Tea is a rarity at these gatherings. The conventional beverages are dry martini and Manhattan cocktails, with scotch for those who insist. In this respect, literary teas may be considered slightly more virile than their sister art shows, where tepid sherry is most often the only drink available. Food receives little attention. Usually it consists of a few uninteresting canapes passed haphazardly about, with few takers.

Literary teas are constantly in a state of flux. The uninitiate gravitates toward the author, the author toward the editor or publisher, the publisher toward the reviewer, and the reviewer, in desperation, toward another drink. Since the general rule of conduct is to seek out those who can do the most good, magazine editors and big-name reviewers enjoy much popularity.

If the party happens to be given in honor of a new author, he is almost always completely ignored. In fact, there is a tradition among veteran literary tea-goers to put the young author in his place as soon as possible. They accomplish this by pretending vociferously not to know for whom the party is being given. The young author usually stands awkwardly in a corner, surrounded by a few dull old ladies, with his publisher frantically trying to circulate him among the "right" people.

Ephemeral as all this may be, however, the modern literary tea has its points. It enables its devotees to renew old friendships and make new ones; it gives the publisher an opportunity to tip off the trade as to which writer he is going to push; it allows the ambitious young author to make contacts with editors; and it gives a great many people entertainment, not to mention free drinks, in the hours before dinner.

★ 12 ★

America Eats! Now
HOME FROM THE ROAD,
MULLING THINGS OVER

Outline Indicating Approach to Subject [excerpt]
from the Washington Office

Social gatherings that centered round a meal were early products of the settlement period when houses were scattered and newcomers were eager for news and company. With food abundant, even the poorest household expected friends to stop in for dinner when coming to town to attend market, court, or church. Community enterprises were numerous and, with farms scattered and transportation poor, the householders benefitting by the gathering always expected to provide a dinner after their barn had been raised or quilt completed. Cemetery and church cleanings always brought people together for a noon meal. Hog-killings and stock-roundups, also communal enterprises, were responsible for development of the popular barbecue. Out of community enterprises came the communal meals of various kinds to which each household contributed a share.

The custom of gathering in groups to eat became fixed and was continued when the conditions giving rise to the gatherings was also so firmly fixed that women reverted to traditional cooking methods when preparing their contributions even though they were beginning to feed their families on canned food and factory bread at home. Even today baked beans are cooked for 24 hours before the annual baked bean church supper, and only fish fresh from the water are used at the August fish fry.

★   ★   ★   ★   ★

We are no longer a sparsely populated country. The majority of us don't have to depend on our neighbors to pitch in at hog-killing time or to build a barn. And, yet, because new citizens continue to arrive and because we persist in roaming—moving from one place to another far from our roots—we remain a country of strangers with an abiding need to figure out a way to blend in and get along. The tradition of community meals in which we create a shared experience neatly accomplishes this and, because these kinds of meals have been going on for so long, they remain woven within the fabric of how we live, the custom passed down from one generation to the next.

Arranging food on table at buffet supper of the Jaycees at Eufaula, Oklahoma, February 1940. (Russell Lee)

This is what I discovered in a year of traveling around the country looking for good things to eat. Through July and August—the high season for community get-togethers—it was easy for me to poke my head into several events a week, no matter where I was. In the cities, I happened upon celebrations centered around a block or neighborhood, an organization, or a cause. But more was to be found in small towns and outer boroughs, where there was also a greater sense that the whole community was involved: tiny country fairs, church suppers, founder's days, the Fourth of July were all more eagerly awaited centerpieces to daily life in these places than in the bustle of cities. I discovered plenty of private occasions, too: families reuniting for a day or weekend in state and local parks; picnics for generations of a single ethnic group—sometimes transposing from their old homelands ancestral observances (from Hindu religious festivals to Caribbean feasts), or fashioning fresh customs in their new country. The common factor to all these festivities was the prominence of food. Out of cars and coolers came casseroles and salads, assorted pies, and often a cake or two. Watermelon was cut, grills fired up. Secret homemade barbecue sauces were mixed, then dabbed and slathered across all kinds of meats.

Let me be clear about this: I'm talking about home-cooked food, food we take time with, that we linger over, that makes up the bulk of our family recipes handed down over the generations. They are our regional dishes that we may not eat all the time but, by God, we'll fight for bragging rights and miss them fiercely when we're away from them, even in other parts of the state. They are what make up our notion of comfort food—the dishes that engender a sense of our place in the world: our apple pies, our meat loaves, our ham and eggs with a warm tortilla on the side. For better or worse, our national identity is tied up in such meals, in the plain cooking (which, upon consideration of its historical context, is never as plain as we think it is) we take for granted but cannot get enough of.

And therein lies the rub, American food's tender spot. As summer lengthened into fall, and I skipped about from state to state, I gradually came to observe something that runs quietly through the *America Eats!* papers: while food was always a potent draw to community events, it held secondary importance to the actual proceedings. When I first read through the papers, I often found myself wondering whether, had they been written by cooks and food writers, they would have contained more actual description of the food itself. The editor of the project, Katharine

Kellock, demanded a historical and regional celebration of American food: she forbade any sense of a cookbook invading the final manuscript. And yet, if she and the other editors had left the writers to their own devices, would they have come back with more in-depth reporting that revealed how our food tasted, how dishes evolved over the years?

Somewhere in my travels, I came to realize how accurately Kellock had gauged our cooking. By talking about our food within the context of social engagements, the federal writers were able to reveal something very important about American cooking: It's not actually the taste of our food, but the use of it, that has been important to our cuisine's development. Even at the most food-centric gatherings, emphasis was less on the dishes than on how they supported the reason for people to meet. Almost seventy years later, this is what I observed, as well. Consider all the fine cooks at the Salzburg Gathering down in Savannah: These proud, accomplished cooks, who knew very well the role food played in their heritage, spread their dishes before their friends not so much to allay hunger but to cement their community closer together. Sure, they complimented each other's raisin breads and pies, the varieties of congealed salads and the savory, home-cured ham, but no one would point out the excellence of

Part of Pomp Hall's family eating supper by lamplight, Creek County, Oklahoma, February 1940. (Russell Lee)

the cooking as being more important than the need to actually share the meal. Fact is, if the food was lousy, they still would have enjoyed the gathering—and do it again, year after year.

And that is an important distinction bearing on how Americans think about eating and one of the reasons why we have not evolved a true food-driven culture. We may think about food and we sure eat enough of it. But we don't *cherish* it—and our cooking—the way other cuisines do, because our history as a young country developing fast over a wide frontier meant too often using meals not as a pleasurable occasion but as a means of simply surviving. Other cuisines, developing over many more years, with more periods of settlement under their belt, have had the opportunity to grow beyond subsistence needs. If you think about it, it's only been in the years after the *America Eats!* papers were written and filed away that the majority of Americans have had the means and leisure to experience the more refined enjoyments of the table.

And yet, our cooking will never observe many of the principles in other cuisines. Cooks in other countries adhere more closely than we do to a master recipe and this makes their classic dishes more uniform. Because of the continuing influx of different cultural and ethnic influences, our recipes vary greatly, at times, from one region to the next—even to one cook from another, which is why you can go to a Brunswick stew festival and never taste the same Brunswick stew twice. We may make fun of each other's versions, but ultimately it's not of great concern. Some may see this as a weakness in our cuisine but we accept the variation as par for the course, falling as it does in line with our democratic principles.

> Contributions of national groups to the American table will be given attention, though these are relatively few. Pennsylvania Dutch cookery is quite as much American as it is German, and Mexican cookery, while retaining the Spanish spicing once necessary to disguise toughness and the beginning of decay, is essentially American in its use of tomatoes, corn, and other ingredients. In the Middle West, which was settled fairly late and received large numbers of Northern Europeans with fully developed cookery traditions, some dishes of European origin have been locally adopted.
>
> —WASHINGTON OFFICE

Even after all this time on the road, I haven't quite discerned—or settled in my own mind—exactly when an immigrant group's dishes become sufficiently Americanized to be included in our country's repertory. *America Eats!* didn't, either, and it was one of the major dividing lines between the editors and the writers, with the editors being very strict—and somewhat persnickety—in their decisions to exclude certain dishes (or even talk about a group's influence), while the writers were inclined to include everything, erring on the generous side as they grappled with regional food cultures closely tied to the predominant immigrant heritage.

What I learned on the road was that we are now far more accepting of—in fact we delight in—foreign flavors being added to our dishes. Our worldview is broader than it was in the 1930s and our sensibilities have embraced multicultural attitudes. The widening of our appreciation for other cuisines, as well as the proliferation of influential television food shows, celebrity chefs, and tastemakers have all contributed to our acceptance of lacing alien ingredients into our traditional cooking. Which is why that classic American Sunday dinner—roast chicken—may be found to include lemongrass or cumin; be glazed in soy sauce or rubbed with garlic butter, its underskin packed with tarragon. Our ancestors would not recognize the chicken's different flavorings. But we have grown to welcome these changes and understand how this roast chicken dinner remains as American as they come.

> Lack of the limited traditional foodstuffs and abundance of new ones stirred the inventive faculties of the settlers. Introduction of molasses through the slave trade soon made another ingredient available, especially important in New England where it was even tried in combination with seemingly incompatible foods: A result was baked pork and beans. Other new dishes were crab-cakes, chowder, squash and pumpkin pies, johnny-cake, cornmeal mush, and jam-cake. Plantation owners in the South, who soon became wealthy, imported renaissance recipes from Europe and the Negro cook used them with rich imagination. They were especially interested in cakes and sweets and also invented the endless variety of hot breads and biscuits still found on tables of the region.
> —WASHINGTON OFFICE

The thing that intrigued me most about immigrant cooking was how it reflected back to the original settlers' urgent need to make a sensible meal out of the foodstuff they found on these shores. Truth is, except for Native American dishes, *all* American food is immigrant cooking one way or another. Newer immigrant groups must suffer through much the same process as what old immigrants did: namely, figuring out how to cook their familiar native dishes with what they find locally in American markets. Inevitably, there is cross-pollination, with old recipes freshened by the arrival of new influences.

Our cuisine is always being transformed by this process and, to me, this is the signature glory of American cooking. The federal writers recognized the same whenever they mentioned a new way of doing a native dish: the German woman out west and her renowned 'possum stew, or the Caribbean-born fisherman on the Gulf Coast who made his gumbo from fresh conch.

The writers also traced the role that immigrant influences played in delineating regional food. For instance, Southwestern food is heavily beholden to Spanish sensibilities, whereas many of the forthright dishes of the Midwest can trace a lineage back to Germany, to name just two. Span-

Lunch wagon for bean pickers, Belle Glade, Florida, January 1937.
(Arthur Rothstein)

ish and German ancestral dishes have become enveloped in their particular region's identity and have been accepted and taken as a point of pride by the wider population. So, too, crops were introduced by immigrants to help re-create the food of their native lands. Eventually, these new foods were assimilated into the native culture so completely that no one could remember a time without them.

The notion of regional food leads to another subject: the idea of comfort food. Even in a society that freely moves about as much as we do, the food of our birthplace is intimately tied into our own personal identity. I can't really separate comfort dishes from the rest of American food. After eating scrapple for breakfast, lunch, and dinner throughout my childhood, all I have to do is think of that spicy Pennsylvania Dutch block of meat whose ingredients are better left undissected and I grow homesick—and starving. A friend from the Southwest, in the midst of a long visit to the Northeast, scoured markets looking for the ingredients to make guacamole and tamales from the recipes her family used in their restaurant in Tucson. All of these dishes, in one way or another, are both immigrant and regional dishes, and because we have a childhood identity with them, they are what we turn to for solace when life becomes the least bit hard.

> The traditional element in the cooking and ingredients of the dishes for the group meals will be emphasized in the various sections of the book and stress will be placed on the role of the cook, since preparation of fine food remains a creative activity that cannot be duplicated by factory methods.
>
> The traditional group meals also preserve long-established community attitudes. In spite of the new equality in drinking, men at a hog-killing still go behind the barn to drink their corn liquor and women who now take a Tom Collins at home do not think of sharing this masculine prerogative. Women who contribute to the family income by working in a cotton-mill do not expect men to share in the preparation of the group meal or in the washing of the dishes, even if they do so at home. These and other mores will receive attention in the descriptions.
>
> —WASHINGTON OFFICE

As many food events as I found, though, there were fewer than what the federal writers discovered. In particular, there was less variety in them, and a sharp drop-off once the winter months set in. The federal writers wrote about scores of clubs, ceremonies, and practices that no longer occur anywhere, especially those that provided some entertainment during the bleak snowy months when there wasn't anything—not even work— to fill up the hours. We have lost not only the Nebraska fun feasts I bemoaned the absence of earlier in the book; I'm also sorry to report that the Polk County Possum Club in Mena, Arkansas, no longer exists, especially sad since it appeared to be a hilarious affair—if not for the local possums, then for the club members who drank whiskey, sang outlandish songs, and performed side-splitting skits. Harvest festivals for sauerkraut are few and far between in comparison to yesteryear, and when was the last time you heard about a pie social? Do any ladies in Alabama still meet for tea? And the Mexican ranch hands out in Arizona no longer pause in the middle of their day for a big lunch and siesta under the cottonwood trees.

Back in the 1930s and early '40s, community events were diversions from daily chores, something that provided some form of amusement outside the routine of everyday life. Nowadays, we have so many distractions, so many ways to fill up our time, that the fairs and festivals we attend, the gatherings we commit to, are only peripheral entertainment.

It's not just the competition for our time from modern diversions that has decreased the occasions when we come together. It is also because the traditional roles as stated by the *America Eats!* editors are surprisingly intact. To be fair, men are helping out on many tasks once relegated solely to women, but I was really surprised to observe how firmly the customary functions of women at community events have remained fixed. Peeking into church and social club kitchens, behind food tents, over where the cakes and pies were being cut, I almost always found a gang of women and girls working like demons. Women may be drinking with the men, and men may be wiping down the tables after all the food is gone, but the division of labor at social events remains firmly planted on women's shoulders.

So it goes that, with a far increase in careers, jobs, and family demands, women no longer have the time—maybe even the strength—to commit their free time (if they have any) to all the extra work involved in feeding a roomful of people. Except for the barbecue pits and the Brunswick and booya festivals dominated by men, the women I saw were the guiding hands behind organizing the harvest suppers, church fairs, funeral lunch-cons, and social club banquets—and then they did the cooking! Still, many of the women I spoke to during the year lamented the fact that they no longer had the free time to be as involved in their communities as their mothers and grandmothers had been, and they certainly no longer had the time to cook on a regular basis half the dishes they did for a single event. Even if time was available to them, these women didn't need to make from scratch such time-honored and labor-intensive recipes as egg noodles, beaten biscuits, cakes, preserves, and pickles. Those among us who have memories of how good these homemade dishes are understand, as well, that the skills necessary to set up a sheet of biscuits for supper or an angel food cake for Sunday dessert or persimmon jam for a holiday breakfast are slowly vanishing from the majority of our lives. Cooking knowledge that was once part of our common education is no longer central to the welfare of our everyday life and so we no longer feel the need to pass these skills and recipes on to our children.

It is heartening, then, to see how many children and young people have turned to cooking in recent years. A young friend told me that part of the reason for this trend is the reaction to having mothers out working in the 1980s and never home for dinner. Others tell me that cooking is

Women at a Sunday school picnic, Jere, West Virginia, September 1938.
(Marion Post Wolcott)

now seen more fully for the creative endeavor that it is. It's considered very cool to be a chef, to throw a dinner party, to arrive at friends' with odd dishes mixed together with the contents of a twenty-six-year-old's refrigerator, which explains the chicken burritos baked over garlic mashed potatoes with a crust of Swiss cheese that arrived in my kitchen a few days ago.

The revolution over the last forty years that has engendered in us a reverence for fresh ingredients and purer food is a magnificently hopeful sign that we are on our way to having a vital food culture, one that rises from the best of our cooking through a growing appreciation and care for ingredients and procedures. But what remains frustrating is how slowly this revolution has filtered down to those who could benefit from it most, namely low-income and poverty-stricken households. The rise of diabetes and other diet-related illnesses demands that all of us need to have access to fresh fruits and vegetables, to better meats and more grains. How difficult would it be for good organic markets to open up in inner-city neighborhoods, or for the government to stop peddling inferior food-stuff in its commodity and welfare programs? The year on the road has shown me that, when it comes to what food we sit down to at night, class divides us more than regions do, and that's not a good thing—for our health or our cooking future.

I sat in the car for a while after I finally pulled to a stop behind my house. The interior was a mess of coffee cups, maps, and trinkets: paper fans labeled with politicians' names from the Neshoba County Fair; several wine bottles from North Carolina vineyards; a case of Kansas City barbecue sauce; souvenirs from the Alamo and the Choctaw Reservation Pearl River Casino outside Meridian, Mississippi, to name just a few. I was ten pounds heavier than when I left the year before and had contracted a waterborne parasite from drinking well water in rural Oklahoma.

But I have to tell you, despite missing all the people in my house, I was ready to pull out again and see what else I could find to eat. The best of the food I encountered lived up to my expectations, and the flavors were all the more vivid and delicious when served within the context of fairs and community get-togethers. Yes, I hit some bad patches along the road but, generally, they were in places where the only meal of note was at an Outback Steakhouse—and I'm not knocking them at all, because at least I found there a good fresh salad, hunk of meat, and glass of wine. What bothered me more was when I got stuck trying to find a modern equivalent for what the federal writers wrote about or I was trying my best to follow the Washington editors' directives, and came up empty with both.

So there I sat: glad to be back home but knowing I had had the best year because I got to see an America that is not very often represented in the glossy food magazines. I thought of all the people I had spent time with and how they would listen to my story of how the federal writers once visited their town. It always took them aback, how someone— anyone—would have paid enough attention to what they were doing, what they ate, how they lived, to have written it all down. I considered their surprise to go hand in glove with how we think of our food as being unimportant, not much to think about.

But then they would look at me straight and say, "Make sure you get it right." Almost all the people I met and talked to, whose stories I scribbled in notebooks as I peered into their pots, or walked quickly by their side: almost all of them said to me, "Make sure you tell it right, then."

Pay attention. That's what they meant. Write about what it means to us. How important these rituals are. These traditions we hold lightly but dear, because we've always done them this way and know how important they are.

Reverend Jarman at the August Quarterly in Wilmington, Delaware, said it best: "People think we don't care anymore. But we do and that's important to us. To the country, I mean. It's our link to the past, this food, this ceremony we have every August. Look how far back we go! What we've lived through! And we're still here."

He meant it for the Quarterly specifically, but for all such gatherings, too. And that sense of fellowship that I found—no matter how much a stranger I was (and yes, even at the Sheepherders' Ball)—was something I longed to feel and be a part of once more.

I hope I've honored my promise to the many good folks out there who shared their time and history, their recipes and reminiscences. When the Federal Writers' Program was shut down, the thousands of writers who participated in the project felt they were leaving some of their best work behind, locked up in government file boxes and cabinets, never to be read again. What stayed with many of them was the excitement of discovering new stories about America, of capturing how we live together as a nation.

Some of the writers went on to greatness. Others returned to their libraries and teaching jobs; their desks in a newsroom or behind a corporate window. But all of them cherished their days spent roaming the countryside, looking to explain our country to ourselves, to capture it in its natural splendor, at work and play, as it stood at the stove, sitting down at the table, enjoying its feasts. As I finally climbed from the car, I thought I knew how the federal writers felt when they left behind their work for the last time. But I was glad at least to have had the privilege of pulling one file drawer open and bringing their stories to light.

After the gathering, Eufaula, Oklahoma, February 1940. (Russell Lee)

Acknowledgments

I am deeply grateful to Anne Depue for her long support of the book and her help in the initial shaping of its form. For their encouragement, generosity, and faith thanks to the two women who have my back: my editor, Kathy Belden, and my agent, Laura Nolan. Bloomsbury's wonderful managing editor Michael O'Connor and proofreader Brian Boucher deserve my undying gratitude for their assistance with the English language. Special thanks to the librarians in the Library of Congress Manuscript Division: Lia Apodaca, Fred Augustyn, Jennifer Brathovde, Jeffrey Flannery, Joe Jackson, Patrick Kerwin, and Bruce Kirby; as well as the librarians and researchers in the Prints and Photographs Division. They made the long hours of work pleasurable.

I could not have written this book without the kindness and patience of the many people I met and talked to in my travels. I hope that what I have written about them in these pages does them justice.

Thanks to my courageous traveling companions: my main girl, Michelle Arrington, Stephen Garone, Janna and Moira Gregonis, Mele Martinez, Rita Grace Willard and her brother, Eamon, my sister Sue and brother Joe. Harriet Lowenthal and Lita Gottesman of Rich Travels got me as close as possible to the places I needed to go and always made sure—like the watchful hens they are—that I had a safe place to roost at night.

A big hug is also owed to Rob Gizis for his artistic and culinary skills, his belief and humor.

Most especially, I am blessed to have the enormous love and support of my husband, Chris Finan. Thanks for pushing me out the door, embracing me when I floundered, and being there when I finally came home to you.

Photo Credits

Most of the photographs reprinted herein are courtesy of the Library of Congress Prints & Photographs Division of the Farm Security Administration holdings. Two photos, "Eating Oysters at a Political Rally" on page 105 and "F. M. Gay's Annual Barbecue" on page 141 were taken as part of the original *America Eats!* manuscript. The following are the reproduction call numbers for the individual photographs.

List of Recipes

Index

Page numbers in italics indicate illustrations.

A Note on the Author

PAT WILLARD is the author of *Pie Every Day*, *A Soothing Broth*, and *Secrets of Saffron*, which was nominated for an IACP award for the Best Literary Cookbook. She lives in Brooklyn.